Out of Antarctica

reflections on the origin of peoples

Whence comes the strange allure of those polar regions,
so strong, so tenacious, that even on returning home one forgets
all the moral and physical fatigues, and dreams only of going back to them?
Whence comes the unprecedented charm of those lands, so deserted and terrifying though they be?
Is it the pleasure of the unknown,
the intoxication of the struggle to reach them and live there,
the pride of attempting and succeeding where others have failed,
the sweet pleasure of being far from pettiness and meanness?
Something of all that, but something else, too.

I have long thought that I experienced more vividly,
in this desolation and this death,
the voluptuousness of my own existence and my own life.
But I sense today that these regions at the end of the world
strike us, somehow, with a pervasive religious intensity…
The man who has managed to reach this far feels his soul soaring…

Commandant Charcot

© 2004, Richmond Editions, Periplus Publishing London Ltd,
98 Church Rd, London SW13 0DQ, UK

ISBN: 1-902699-45-9

First published by Richmond Editions in 2003 under the title *L'Antarctide des origines*

Publisher: Danièle Juncqua Naveau

Managing Editor: Nick Easterbrook

Assistant Editor: Jenny Finch

Production Manager: Sophie Chéry

Production Assistants: Arvind Shah, Ludovic Pellé

Picture research: Jane Lowry, Muriel Moity

Translation: Andrew Brown

Reprographics: Periplus Publishing London Ltd

Printed and bound in Italy by Graphicom

Out of Antarctica

reflections on the origin of peoples

ROBERT ARGOD

 Richmond Editions

I would like to express my deepest thanks to Franck Goddio,
without whom this book would never have appeared.

Particular thanks to Jean-Marie de Campredon,
the grandson of Robert Argod, for having patiently and skilfully assembled and
arranged the documents that allowed the manuscript
of this book to be put together.

Mme Elisabeth Argod, 2003

CONTENTS

G rand theories sometimes arise from simple questions or the elementary observation of natural phenomena perceptible to all. History is filled with examples to prove this; not least that, from the examination of a falling body, universal rules were established that for centuries explained the mechanics of the skies.

Where do the Polynesians come from?

The vexed question of the origins of a people, now isolated on the islands of the Pacific Ocean, has attracted the attention of scholars and given rise to many theories. Daring maritime adventures have been launched to test these theories, such as those of Thor Heyerdahl on the *Kon-Tiki* and Éric de Bisschop aboard the *Tahiti-Nui*.

The desire to answer this question was, for Robert Argod, the starting point of an astonishing quest with fascinating ramifications. Polynesian mythology gave him the first leads. In these myths the original land is described in poetic terms: the coming of a long night and an endless cold forced the Polynesians' ancestors to venture on great expeditions across the ocean, in search of more hospitable lands. The legends are filled with strikingly realistic details.

Robert Argod combined an encyclopaedic knowledge of the myths and legends of different races with a quality that is certainly essential to anyone trying to understand maritime migrations – he was a master mariner. What amazing nautical paradoxes have lain in wait for certain scholars who, ignorant of navigation, have never ventured on board a ship and have nonetheless tried to study these problems!

For various reasons, neither America nor Asia seemed to correspond, in his view, to the cradle of the Polynesian people.

When fed by the accumulation of knowledge and experience, intuition often generates fertile discoveries. A name emerged from Argod's research, logical from a maritime perspective but nonetheless hard to believe: Antarctica.

Making sense from a maritime perspective, every other factor seemed initially to militate against such a hypothesis. But this trail had to be explored further before it could be abandoned. Curiously, the more he explored the different domains of cartography, climatology, the theory of continental drift and plate tectonics, new elements, far from invalidating his hypothesis, often reinforced it. Convergent bundles of clues piled up, which gradually gave the answers to his multidisciplinary questions.

A deep friendship united Robert Argod and myself, and I felt great esteem for him. I thus had the privilege to be able to follow, step by step, the long and patient path his thinking followed. He explored in minute detail every field that might bear on his subject. Does not the quest for the original paradise of one people lead to questions about the origin of others?

Pandora's box was open, the paths of further study led in many different directions. He enthusiastically kept me abreast of his results, across the years, in the course of fervent conversations that I will never forget. His was a slow, meticulous, and magnificent investigation, whose implications greatly excited me.

The outcome of this research presents the public with an alluring hypothesis whose novel aspect appears at first glance quite daring. On reading this summa, one's initial spontaneous objections start to fade. The arguments set forth are surprising, but they are also engrossing and convincing.

It is a fine and majestic idea that this ice-covered continent could be the homeland of past civilisations.

After he has immersed himself in this work, the reader will be haunted by one question: what if all this were true?

For my part, I hope with all my heart that, in the future, an archaeologist, faced with mysterious relics exhumed from the icy wastes of these now desolate regions, will feel the same amazement that I did when, one day, diving far out to sea off the coast of Egypt, I was able to gaze on an extraordinary stele of black granite. This astonishing message from the past bore, in hieroglyphs, the name of the submerged town that I had discovered and that was, long ago, according to Herodotus, visited by Helen on her way back to Troy.

Truth is probably accessible only to mathematicians or poets, but destiny sometimes gives attentive observers a chance to perceive, from afar, curious signs that allow them to see beyond the distant horizons.

Franck Goddio
Archaeologist
China Sea, February 2003

How many centuries had to elapse before Europeans discovered that unimaginably vast ocean, the Pacific? It was not until the 16th century that this entire new universe rose on the horizon of the inhabitants of the old world. On each of the continents surrounding this gigantic stretch of water there had arisen, over the course of millennia, highly developed civilisations: on its eastern boundaries, Mexico and Peru; on its western fringe, China, Japan and Indonesia.

The discovery of the Pacific revealed that Europe and the Mediterranean were not perhaps the centre and hearth – both geographical and cultural – of the world. Almost two centuries after the shock of this revelation, the southern seas were finally explored.

At that point, it was discovered that there were human beings living on all sorts of islands forming archipelagos, which comprised perhaps four times the surface area of Europe. The Polynesians alone occupied a territory contained within a vast triangle: in the north, the Hawaii archipelago, with summits rising to over 3,000m and three active volcanoes; to the south-west, New Zealand, with two large islands that stretch between 34° and 47° south and some 1,200km of high summits or glaciers flowing down into the sea; finally, to the south-east, tiny Easter Island.

Within this triangle was the ocean, and a scattering of small islands, high and low, extinct volcanoes and atolls, forming archipelagos: the Society Islands, Marquesas, Tuamotu, Australes, Tonga, Samoa, Fiji… They were all soon to excite the avarice of the great powers: the United States, Great Britain, Germany and France.

The Polynesians were handsome, strong, cheerful, generous and disinterested – they were thus wonderfully suited to fulfilling a role in line with our own complacency, which was immediately and generously ascribed to them, that of the noble savage.

Little by little, it was realised, with surprise, that they far exceeded the limits of this anthropological framework that was restrictive to say the least: the Polynesians were excellent sailors; they could sail through the rollers formed by reefs, despite troughs of 5m or more, even on heavily-laden whalers. They practised agriculture with skill, were fine artists, spending

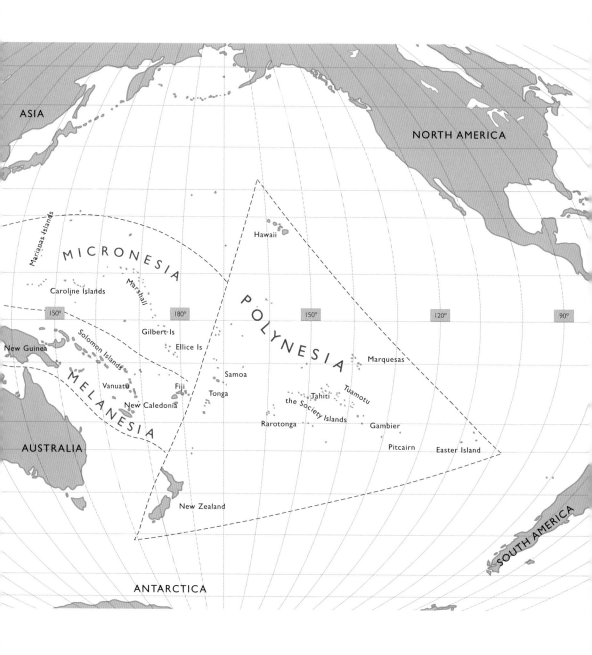

Figure 1. *Map of the Pacific showing the Polynesian triangle.*

days sculpting in wood and stone, and constructing megaliths. They liked to tell stories, act out plays, sing part songs, chants, hymns and other couplets in rhythm, sometimes violent and warlike in nature.

Polynesia arouses a powerful fascination, easily explainable by the beauty and variety of its landscapes, but also thanks to the mystery surrounding the origins of its inhabitants.

The vestiges of their culture, isolated as they are in the midst of an oceanic immensity, do indeed present several shared features with other civilisations. It is thus tempting to seek their origin in one of those centres of culture. We shall discover that it is not as simple as it may appear at first glance.

The Polynesians have been described as belated Neolithics, and it is true that they were unacquainted with metal, which was being worked in such wonderful ways on the Pacific rim. On the other hand, they excelled in stone-working. Maori jade pendants, called *hei-tiki*, were so finely worked that similar perfection can be found only in pre-dynastic Egypt. Likewise, at the foot of Mount Duff, in the Gambier Islands, a gigantic stoup sculpted in an oval shape from a volcanic bomb demonstrates that the hardest stones were worked with care and precision, even without metallic instruments. The Menehunes' aqueduct at Oahu, on Hawaii, the Mehetia wall, on the east of Tahiti, or the Vinapu wall on Easter Island, constitute a series of stone constructions comprising several layers fitted together with care and precision, without the use of any mortar whatsoever. They all recall the buildings of the Incas that can be admired on the sites of Cuzco, Machu Picchu or Sacsahuamán.

One example is the portico-shaped trilithon at Tongatapu, which has a volcanic stone lintel whose weight must be of the order of 30 to 40 tonnes. Evidently, it was brought a great distance by canoe, before reaching its current site.

In other places, lines of menhirs, with circular or square bases, also recall those of Peru. There are massive statues on the Marquesas and Austral Ridge Islands; those on Easter Island, gigantic in size and known throughout the world, reach a height of 18m. The pupils of their eyes were in obsidian, and

3

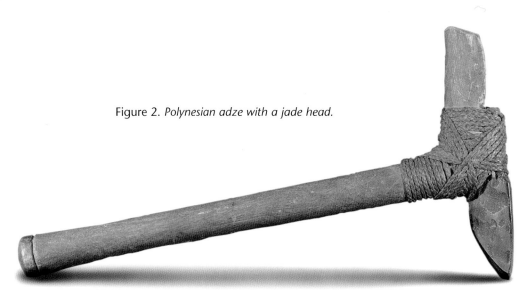

Figure 2. *Polynesian adze with a jade head.*

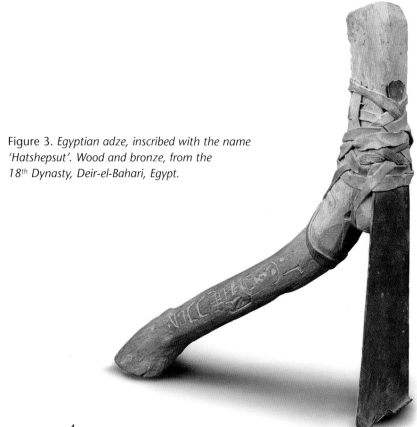

Figure 3. *Egyptian adze, inscribed with the name 'Hatshepsut'. Wood and bronze, from the 18th Dynasty, Deir-el-Bahari, Egypt.*

the irises in coral. They bring to mind Peruvian statues or certain Peruvian steles. Huge cut stones were fashioned, for example, into towing blocks to haul big boats on to land, *pae-pae* (platforms) or *marae*, sacred enclosures in stone or coral, which contain a rectangular altar in the shape of a truncated stepped pyramid serving as a sacrificial altar. Impluvium constructions recall those of Mesopotamia or Mycenae.

One astonishing characteristic is the fact that the wheel was quite unknown to Polynesian civilisation, as was the arch.

The weapons that have been discovered are also extremely interesting. The clubs, javelins, shields and helmets, as well as the near total absence of bows and arrows, make one think of Mexico. The basic tool was the adze, coming in a wide variety of shapes, with a head of polished stone set and tied into a wooden haft. This enabled Polynesians to cut and shape the wood for construction tasks and canoe building. But how does it come about that the model for this object can be found in Egypt, on the wall of Deir-el-Bahari, designed for the building of ships for Queen Hatshepsut? And how are we to explain the fact that before being replaced by the axe, these neolithic adzes existed three million years ago in China?[1]

All kinds of objects, such as the beaters designed to shape the bark of trees, hooks, fishing nets, fibre clothes, stilts, canopies and fly swatters, but also various musical instruments, in particular nose flutes, pan pipes, and drums, enabled Professor Rivet, in *Les origines de l'Homme américain*, and Thor Heyerdahl, in *American Indians in the Pacific*, to establish some 50 or so extremely close similarities between Polynesia and America.

Bone, wood, and mother-of-pearl were minutely worked for even the slightest object, from the prows and sterns of canoes, to bailers, the handles of the fly swats, the rods of authority, and various receptacles. In them, you find wavy and spiral lines, and stylised patterns of a Greek kind, the representations of faces, with wide flat eyes like the Mesopotamian or Cretan 'bespectacled' figurines, but also with mouths and noses stylised in a fashion comparable to that of the representations on Shang bronzes, or to

1   See R. C. Suggs, *The Island Civilizations of Polynesia*, New American Library, New York, 1960.

Aegean frescoes and pots, characterised by their design: a stuck-out tongue, an eye closed, two heads fixed together, complex figures placed around an axis of symmetry.

Agriculture was practised using terraced irrigation. Maize, which had been known in America since the earliest epochs, was unknown, as was rice, even though the latter was being grown, and was indeed an essential crop, in Asia. Coconut trees existed in America, but seem not to have appeared in western Asia until the beginning of our era. Polynesians did not make alcohol from coconuts, unlike the Asians. The sweet potato, called *kumara* by the Polynesians, exists in Peru under almost the same name, *kumar*. American cotton, wild or cultivated, possesses 13 small chromosomes, the Asian variety 13 large chromosomes, while the Polynesian version possesses 13 small and 13 large chromosomes, which presupposes a common origin.

Polynesian society was patriarchal in type, unlike Melanesia, where matriarchy was the rule. It was structured into hereditary castes with fixed boundaries.

The chiefs-priests-teachers, the *tahua*, came first. Their power was based on interdicts that were respected by all; to transgress these laws led automatically to leprosy or death. They lived in isolation, and possessed powers to which they gained access by fasting (they used a belt pulled tight to enable them to tolerate hunger), vigils, solitude, and abstinence. Then a force could overwhelm them and reveal the god who possessed them: this was the *mana* that enabled them to launch an expedition, scale dizzy peaks, or construct a canoe or a temple. An entire small populace helped them, once they had verified the reality of the *mana*.

The *tahua* taught mythology, genealogy, medicine, the art of navigation, cosmography, geography, agriculture, music, sculpture, and the art of tattooing. In particular they taught the basics of worship, including baptism, circumcision (for all, or else reserved to an elite), the religious ceremonies of the *marae*, with costumes, varied rites, prayers, offerings, sacrifices of plants, animals (usually dogs) or humans. For the latter, they fattened and then sacrificed men who had lost their souls, those who had been beaten in war and refused the chance they were offered to take flight on a makeshift raft.

Cannibalism was natural, reserved for great feasts, but it sometimes degenerated into massacres that had been organised in a spirit of vendetta, or even for no particular reason at all.

The *tahuas* organised marriages and funerals – long and complicated ceremonies. The bodies of the dead were dried out on platforms, or in caves, or else emptied of their viscera and brains, treated with plant preparations, and embalmed with such skill that a king could keep his living appearance for more than a year, despite the humid tropical climate. For the Polynesians, there was a form of survival after death.

The sick were given confession, which often cured them. If not, they were treated with plants; certain herbal baths enabled them to save a child who had fallen and broken bones. Trepanning was frequent to cure a blow from a club: the cranium was opened, the scalp being wetted with the sap of an unripe coconut to stanch the flow of blood, and shark teeth were used to clean the fracture. Bone splinters that slipped under the skull were extracted with the nail of the little finger, a piece of coconut or calabash was applied to cover the hole, small holes were pierced with bones to sew the prosthesis, and the scalp was set back in place. The warrior was then fit and ready to face new combats.

The kings, as well as the nobles, were called *arii*. They had no fortune, no guard, but were respected because they had the power of life and death over humans and plants. It is related that when a royal line died out in the Gambier Islands, several plant species also perished.

The kings were carried on sedan chairs, and did not touch the ground of the lands they went to visit – otherwise those lands became their property. A small group of attendants followed them, with a parasol. One small island could have several kings.

There do not seem to have been any attempts to establish hegemony over great territories, i.e., over several islands. The royal family worked at sculpting tools, jewels, spades to dig out canoes, headgear and necklaces. These constituted potential gifts, in principle freely given. However, anyone who accepted a gift without being able to repay it within a reasonable time, was thereby performing an act of submission. Everything concerning the *arii* was hedged about by prohibitions, even their name became *tapu*, a word that comes to us from Polynesia and from which we have formed the word 'taboo'.

The warriors and the lesser chieftains were the *raatira*. A substantial part of Polynesian life was based on preparing for war. Spying, cunning, boldness, temerity, and the skills of war, were all prized attributes for inter-tribal warfare.

Weapons were made of wood and bone: clubs, lances, spears, armour made from fibres with shields of hide, and helmets; there were small forts on elevated spots, with ditches concealing traps and stakes. A hut contained a whole arsenal to which the men could rush to arm themselves rapidly. Bows and arrows were disdained, since they allowed you to kill at a distance without any personal danger.

A certain chivalric sentiment existed. When the British were fighting one of numerous campaigns in New Zealand, their advance came to a sudden halt. The Maori chief sent a messenger to ask the reason for this, and the English admitted that they were waiting for a boat laden with munitions. The Maori called a cessation of hostilities and invited their adversaries to several feasts. Once the boat had arrived, the fighting resumed, until the outgunned Maori were forced to capitulate.

The ordinary people, the *manahune*, were composed of free men, cultivators, and artisans. The Polynesian tradition sometimes describes them with contempt: small, dirty, black, idle, fearful, false. Peter Buck[2] demonstrates that these caste prejudices were absolutely wrong.

The Polynesian had several rare traits: a predilection for cleanliness (daily baths and washing were a necessity for them, something they shared with the Japanese), discretion towards their neighbours, restraint that held them back from getting angry or insulting each other, good temper, a taste for jokes and irony, rapid glances to observe one another closely or make fun of each other.

Money was unknown, as was trade. As for writing, some 25 tablets covered with a precise pictographic script have been collected, including around 300 different signs, engraved in boustrophedon, without punctuation or gaps, following on in parallel lines.

2   P. Buck, *Vikings of the Sunrise*, Frederick A. Stokes, New York, 1938.

One of the few remaining inhabitants of Easter Island with knowledge of the traditional ways was invited to read these 'talking boards', called *kahau rongo rongo*. He chanted each line, reading from right to left, and turning the tablet over once he had reached the end of the line so as to continue on the next side. Was this Easter Islander reading? Or interpreting? The texts were transcribed. But the same man, when asked to read it again several years later, seemed to chant a completely different text.

Dr Thomas Barthel, of the University of Tübingen, studied these tablets for many years. He saw in them an ideographic script comparable to several so-called primitive scripts, and found around 130 signs of the Easter Island language, signs that were quite closely akin to those found in the Indus Valley, from a civilisation which disappeared at the end of the second millennium BC. Several pictograms were also noted, with similarities to signs discovered in Peruvian examples.

The Polynesians also used mnemonic methods: bundles of small notched sticks, bamboo, and in particular knotted cords very similar to those used in ancient China, which Confucius recommended his countrymen return to, in spite of the use of writing, to rediscover ancient wisdom.

Cords knotted in vicuna wool were widely used in Peru, to record the numbers of human beings and the maize harvests. Polynesian knotted cords enabled long-distance messages to be sent, via birds trained as carrier pigeons.

The Polynesian languages are described as agglutinative, with prefixes, suffixes, and infixes. They differ from the monosyllabic tonal languages of South-East Asia, Chinese, Malay, or Munda, as well as from Indo-European languages. Numerous words stem from a common source to those in South America, as Thor Heyerdahl endeavours to demonstrate, in *American Indians in the Pacific*. There is no trace of any Indian Sanskrit word.

Professor Rivet[3] finds a number of similar fundamental roots between these two languages. He concludes: "A more extensive investigation into Sumerian and Oceanian has revealed such clear and numerous similarities that I am now convinced that there are close links between these two

3   P. Rivet, *Sumérien et Océanien*, Collection linguistique, la Société de linguistique de Paris, 1929.

languages, and that Sumerian should be classified in the Oceanian group." For him, the most widespread language in the world is the Oceanian group, covering South-East Asia, Melanesia, Polynesia, the whole of South America, and the western half of North America.

After this rapid survey of Polynesian culture we can now study the different possibilities that have been explored to explain the origins of this people. To do this, we need to take into account the unique wind patterns in the region.

If you look at a map of the Pacific Ocean, you are struck by the fact that a good half of its surface is swept by the trade winds. The high pressure zones between the tropics continually force enormous masses of air out towards latitudes above 30° where pressures are relatively low.

The Coriolis effect, caused by the earth's rotation, diverts the path of air currents to the left in the Northern Hemisphere, and to the right in the Southern. This results in a permanent movement of the atmosphere westwards, from America to Asia, this in a zone of perpetual fine weather with clement temperatures.

The Polynesians have occupied their islands for only 20 centuries or so. Their civilisation presents certain kinships with those of America. It is logical to imagine that they came from that great continent to the east, from Peru or British Columbia, so as to have the trade winds blowing them as far as Polynesia: this was Thor Heyerdahl's theory, which he tested in his raft *Kon-Tiki*.

Heyerdahl thought that people had been wrong to consign to oblivion the ethnological affinities between Polynesians and, on the one hand, the Ica and Paraca Peruvians, on the other hand the Indians settled between Vancouver and Alaska (Haida, Tlimgit, Isymsian, Nootca, Bella Coola, etc.): sailing vessels, centre boards, fishing instruments, modes of construction, adzes, totems with stacked figures, A1 rhesus + blood groups, and finally, vocabulary.

He had the idea of attracting the world's attention by a spectacular expedition on a raft with sails, the *Kon-Tiki*. Aboard a vessel with minimal seafaring qualities, he showed that it was possible to reach Polynesia from

Peru: he had just to avoid acting as mere flotsam, as in that case the winds and the tides would have carried the raft towards the Galapagos Islands, but thanks to a rudimentary dragline that allowed it to leave Humboldt's current and centreboards allowing the raft to be steered at 30° to the following wind, he was able to land on the Tuamotu Islands.

Heyerdahl's great merit was to write *American Indians in the Pacific*, in which he reiterated the undeniable affinities between Polynesia and America noted by Rivet, Bosch-Gimpera, Mendes-Correa, and a host of other specialists on pre-Columbian America.

Thor Heyerdahl did however try to prop up an indefensible thesis: a fishing expedition off Vancouver had, in his view, been swept away by storms, and been driven to Hawaii, where it landed. This would then have been the point of departure for the colonisation of the Polynesian islands. This goes completely against all the Hawaiian traditions which speak of Polynesian sailors arriving in Hawaii from the Marquesas or Raiatea.

Thor Heyerdahl also suggests that an expedition under Tupac Inca in the fifth century could have brought to Easter Island an advanced civilisation that then spread throughout Polynesia. However, the Peruvian narrative speaks of treasures subsequently brought back to America – two black slaves, a bronze throne, and a stuffed horse's head! Furthermore, this expedition is much too recent to explain all the things – at least twice as ancient – found on Easter Island.

The cultivation of maize which goes back a long way in Mexico has existed in Peru since around 1800 BC. It has been the basic foodstuff in America since the most ancient times. It is absolutely impossible that a small group of individuals could have had the idea of profiting from the favourable winds to embark on an adventure into the unknown, abandoning a rich country and furthermore without taking a provision of maize, which these days grows on the islands without difficulty.

Finally, how could the Polynesians have come from America without bringing vegetables, planting sticks, llamas, vicunas, alpaca, weaving, gold and silver in the shape of a few pieces of jewellery, not to mention scales to enable them to practise commerce? How could they have forgotten gods such as Quetzalcoatl or Viracocha, or the motifs of the snake-llama with marks like eyes, the massive-headed snake with its curly mane and its exorbitant eyes, to list just a few examples among many others? What are we to say of the pierced ears bearing circular objects, and writing, and figures used to count in twenties?

However, a common basis to Mexico and Peru is undeniable, going back to the time before the differences that increasingly separated these two great American cultures: and this very same common basis is found in Polynesia, too, but in new and original shapes.

Orthodoxy insists on the need for the Polynesians to have originated in Asia, without the position or the date of their departure eastwards being made specific.

From China to Indonesia, there have been 25 to 30 centuries in which magnificent civilisations flourished, with artistic treasures that present numerous points in common with Mexico and Peru – and such differences and particularities that it is at once impossible to deny a kinship, and to formulate the idea of a single original birthplace.

As Polynesia possesses several cultural characteristics in common with the civilisations of western America and eastern Asia, people have imagined that cultural influences were transmitted from one coast of the Pacific to the other: the Polynesians, as good sailors, must have helped to carry this knowledge.

But the seafaring problem remains. The Pacific Ocean represents an obstacle three times more insurmountable than the Atlantic. The latter must have been crossed from east to west before Columbus by Africans who left the region of Dakar to reach Central America: Ivan van Sertima shows as much in *They Came Before Columbus*.[4] One or two expeditions must have crossed the Atlantic with a following wind. They never made the journey in the other direction.

The Peruvians under Tupac Inca perhaps crossed the Pacific on their balsa-wood rafts, with a following trade wind, without encountering any

---

4   I. van Sertima, *They Came Before Columbus: The African Presence in Ancient America*, Random House, New York, 1976.

Polynesian islands. It was possible. If they managed the return journey, they must have known about the wind system in the South Pacific: on the way back, they would have reached a latitude close to the 40th parallel south, and been carried back to Peru by westerly winds.

Such an adventure may have happened once in a thousand years.

It is possible, and doubtless probable, that a Chinese junk set sail and ventured from the basin at the mouth of the Hoang-Ho, the homeland of the Chang; that it sailed along the coasts of Korea, the Kamchatka, past the Kurile Islands, the Aleutians, the archipelagos of British Columbia, and Mexico; that it followed the coasts of Central America, and ended up in Peru, never to return. That may have happened once or twice in two millennia, and would explain Chinese signs on pieces of Peruvian pottery, or on tombs in Alaska, if we suppose that the climate was much warmer at the time.

In these exceptional cases, an expedition by sea was not impossible, even if it remains astonishing. Furthermore, it required a powerful motive and the will of a chief to decide on such journeys:

- the prediction of the soothsayer Yupanqui inciting the Inca emperor to set out in search of two islands that he had seen in a dream;
- the desire of a Chinese merchant to open up a new commercial route;
- the will of a black emperor of Bamako to embark with his entire court for the American continent, as spoken of in ancient tradition.

But that the currents could have enabled the two coasts of the Pacific to be linked is frankly inconceivable. This idea is just not practicable. To cross the immensity of the Pacific, three times as wide as the Atlantic, is already improbable even in the favourable direction of America to Asia.

Travelling in the opposite direction, it is perfectly senseless to set out against the dominant winds for an expedition that would have taken several years, without any coasts to follow, and with tiny islands that are both inhospitable and difficult to locate.

The idea that the Polynesians came from Asia is thus unreasonable.

However, two routes have been suggested. Peter H. Buck, in *Vikings of the Sunrise*, sets out the dilemma: could they have travelled via Melanesia, or Micronesia?

The first possibility was rejected by Peter Buck and all the ethnologists. The Polynesians are not black, do not have a matriarchal regime, do not practise commerce or even barter, had neither hens, nor cows, nor pigs in ancient times, and their mythological traditions are increasingly rich once you reach the Cook Islands, Raiatea, the Gambier Islands and the Marquesas.

The notion that the Polynesians crossed via Melanesia has been abandoned. That leaves the idea that they crossed via Micronesia.

Ethnologists have not reached a verdict on this thesis, although it has been officially propounded by popularisers in their accounts of Polynesian origins. Questioned on the subject, Professor Emory, head of the Hawaiian team of the Bishop Museum in Honolulu, said in 1951, "We know nothing about it!"

However, it is absurd to think that a small and developed cultural group could have crossed Indonesia, several centuries BC, without taking from South-East Asia:

- rice, essential as food,
- the betel chewed by the natives,
- the wheel, so common and so practical, as well as the motif of the wheel that is found so frequently,
- weaving, unknown to the Polynesians who plaited,
- the principle of arch construction,
- the representations of the goose Hamsa, for Brahma; the eagle Garuda, for Vishnu; the bull Nandi, for Shiva; the lotus flower on which later on the sitting Buddha would be represented,
- the vegetable motifs with the fig-tree and Bodhi tree, and the extreme complexity of their sinuous lines,
- the animal motifs: bird of paradise, lion, horse, buffalo, mythical snake (*näga*), the elephant Ganesha, the bull-lions facing one another,
- the lingam,

- the different *wayang* figures – leather-based marionettes moved by slender stalks,
- bronze, silver, and gold constituting jewels, necklaces, bracelets, earrings, censers, small bells, trays for sacrifices, and holy water containers,
- weapons such as the *kris*,
- silk fabrics with gold and silver threads,
- *raksasa* statues with giants wielding huge clubs,
- stupas with their extremely strange silhouettes,
- the practice of cremation,
- the Shivaist and Hinduist pantheons,
- the Indo-European languages, in particular Sanskrit,
- blood group B and the predominance of N over M.

None of these are found in Polynesia.

One should add that this journey would have required them to set out blindly, sailing against the dominant winds, across almost empty immensities of sea, with almost no chance of happening upon some minuscule coral island without soil or water, during months of travel across Micronesia.

Instinct impels certain species to troop off in ranks to drown themselves: perhaps they have inherited a migratory habit which is no longer viable. But human beings are not subject to blind animal instincts. The notion that Polynesians one day left South-East Asia without taking anything of its resources, that they slowly crossed Melanesia or Micronesia, is pure abstraction.

Rather than indicating an Asian origin, could the traces of Polynesian civilisation found in Asia stem, conversely, from an immigration of Polynesians? *Vers Nousantara*, by Éric de Bisschop[5] proposes the following simple idea, that after warfare in the Polynesian islands the vanquished had a choice between slavery and exile. Being sailors, they built rafts and set off with a following wind. They brought to the Sunda Islands a whole

---

5   E. de Bisschop, *Vers Nousantara*, Éditions de la Table ronde, Paris, 1962.

vocabulary concerning the sea, fish, seashells, the human body and numbers. Having left without *tahua* and without *arii*, they adopted Asian religions. Discovering the regularity of the twice-annual monsoon, they reached western India, taking with them to Java and Sumatra Indian princes and merchants (unlikely sailors as the *Bhagavat Gita* demonstrates). A few expeditions, in the Indian Ocean, with Mundas on board, reached Madagascar, in the trade winds, and thus could not return to the Sunda Islands: hence that typically Polynesian contribution to Madagascar, with the development of this influence extending, via maritime links, as far as the Red Sea.

The mystery of the origin of the Polynesian peoples is indeed at the heart of the huge problem posed by the civilisations that border the Pacific. It is highly surprising that, dispersed far from the great continents across isolated archipelagos, a people quite different from its distant Amerindian or Asian neighbours would have settled down without borrowing from them rudimentary cultural elements that had appeared among these shore-dwellers some three millennia earlier.

The singularity of the Polynesians thus leads us to the conclusion that they had no contact with America or Asia for some 3,000 years. It then becomes bizarre to discover in Polynesia so many points in common with all the first great civilisations on the planet, as far afield as India, Mesopotamia or Egypt. A common heritage is as undeniable as is this long absence of cultural exchanges.

Since the Polynesians come, as we have seen, neither from America nor Asia, we are led to study the possibility of a different common origin.

It is easy to assume that the mythologies that have reached us do not include many historical truths we can draw on. However, they do represent our sole source of human evidence for past events. It is thus highly important not to disregard them, and through a study of the Polynesian tales we are now going to see that their study can be a veritable mine of information. The truth, however fantastic it may be, can only shine out all the more strongly and surprisingly.

1.1 Polynesia

Polynesian mythology presents us with an important mass of original, unedited memories, religiously preserved and untainted by contact with the great frontier civilisations. For several millennia, the Polynesians remained isolated and untouched by foreign peoples. Their mythology was deprived of information and additions from outside until the arrival of the missionaries and the great waves of Christian conversions in the 18th century. Martha Beckwith of the Bishop Museum in Honolulu isolated later interpolations from the Bible.

We find traces of Adam, the Flood, the Tower of Babel… right in the middle of a mythology that to our eyes is completely novel and unexpected. The Polynesians did of course invent fables and images, they interpreted stories. But they neither speculated nor built up symbols, abstractions, philosophical or metaphysical systems. Their mythology reveals a natural people, very concrete; down to earth, in a manner of speaking.

The ancient tales were preserved with care and transmitted orally. The narrator remained standing and declaimed the myths without stopping, but while swaying on his legs. This rhetorical and physical exercise sometimes lasted a whole night. If the narrator made a mistake in his telling, he could be banished from his clan or even punished with death. Important occasions were necessary for such proofs of public eloquence to be organised.

The immense merit of Polynesian mythology is that it has been preserved intact, apart from later, easily recognisable Biblical additions. The descriptions we find in this richly imagist literature are often unthinkable and unimaginable for a people that live in the tropics!

An endless night

Perhaps the most famous Polynesian god, a great navigator known in all the archipelagos, is Tangaroa, the 'great' or 'distant man', whose name is pronounced Ta'aroa in Tahiti, and Kanaloa in Hawaii. The creation narratives in the Society Islands describe the incredible adventure of this chief, who

Figure 5. *Basalt statue* (Moai) *from Easter Island, called* Hoa Hakananai'a, *circa 1000 AD.*

lived alone, enclosed in the darkness of a cavern, like an unhatched chick in its egg.

Tangaroa the creator sat in a shell the shape of an egg, which was called Rumia (chaos). He remained there for aeons in boundless space, in which there was neither heaven, nor earth, nor sea, nor moon, nor stars. This was the era of night, of impenetrable darkness without beginning or end.

> *The shell was like an egg revolving in endless space, with no sky, no land, no sea, no moon, no stars.*
> *All was darkness. Rumia was the name of the shell of Tangaroa. Tangaroa was quite alone in his shell. He had no father, no mother, no elder brother, no sister. There were no people, no beasts, no birds, no dogs. But there was Tangaroa, and he was alone.*
> *There was sky space, there was land space, there was ocean space, there was fresh-water space.*
>
> *But at last Tangaroa gave his shell a fillip which caused a crack resembling an opening for ants. Then he slipped out and stood upon his shell, and he looked and found that he was alone. There was no sound, all was darkness outside.*
> *And he shouted, "Who is above there, oh?" No voice [answered].*
> *"Who is below there, oh?" No voice!*
> *"Who is in front there, oh?" No voice!*
> *"Who is in back there, oh?" No voice!*
> *There was the echo of his own voice, and that was all.*[1]

Fumbling around in the darkness and finding nothing, Tangaroa took refuge in a narrower shelter, Tumu-iti, without being able to get back to his old grotto, Tumu-nui, and he remained there totally confined in the enveloping darkness. But he grew tired of this shell and, slipping out, he managed to get back to the old one.

1   T. Henry, 'Ancient Tahiti', *Bishop Museum Bulletin*, 48, Honolulu, 1928, pp. 336-7.

And the shell, Rumia, that he opened first, became his house, the dome of the gods' sky, which was a confined sky, enclosing the world then forming. Then Tangaroa dwelt in the confined sky in total darkness, and did not know of the light outside [...][2]

Night, endless, deep and impenetrable, is recurrent in the ancient writings of the Pacific Islands.

Awaiting daybreak

Gods had taken refuge in a grotto (*ana*). Sentinels watched over the entry, awaiting the return of the light, while the chiefs ordered the night to end:

The messengers went at ten-fathom paces, with orders to end the shameful millions of nights. These were orders from the land, orders from the congregated hosts, the orders from those gathered in confined sky. These orders came from the source of the careful and the anxious [...][3]

Several gods follow in succession, struggling to wrench the dark sky from the earth whose prisoner it is, so that light and heat can return to revivify plants and human beings:

There was exploring of the great octopus holding the sky to the earth [...] Tu conjured death upon the great octopus holding the sky to the earth, but it did not die by his agency. All the hosts of gods were raging with anger with Hotu (Fruitfulness) in confined sky. Then Rua-tupua-nui (Source-of-great-growth) conjured death upon the great octopus, and he was the conjuror who caused the great octopus Tumu-ra'i-fenua (Foundation-of-earthly-heaven) to die.
"Tumu-ra'i-fenua is dead! He is dead! He is dead!" This was spoken from south to north, from the east to the west. But he still clung to the sky [...]

---

2   T. Henry, *op. cit.*, p. 337.

3   *Ibid.*, p. 404.

*Cut away the arms of the octopus, give Atea real pain, separate Rumia
behind, separate Rumia before, separate the front pillar, the inner pillar,
the back pillar, the pillar to stand by, and the pillar of exit so that he may
be quite severed!" [...]
But it was only raised, the lifting of the sky was not accomplished by Ru or
Tino-rua, nor by Maui.*[4]

The first glimmers of day

*The night which lingers [Na-po-titi] and extended night [Na-po-tata] had
been created by Tangaroa [...] The duration of night grew shorter, there
were rapid progressions and slow progressions [...]*[5]

Darkness slips into light[6]

This is altogether unimaginable in the tropics. In this region, the sun
rises each day almost vertically and only one and a half hours at most pass
between pitch-black night and the disappearance, or the rising, of the sun.

Men start to emerge from their shelters, jostling in their hundreds
towards the outside, and applaud the marvel of the sky's dome, which is
uplifted, supported on sturdy columns. They encourage the sun's efforts as
it attempts to return. These men are the children of the waning night, which
is creeping away.[7]

Night is pregnant with day. They have to await the delivery and the birth
of the sun before it can again be day. Total darkness gives way to a light
which can just be sensed through the clouds to the north, south, east and
west. This is the announcement of the still invisible sun, Rongo in the

---

4   T. Henry, *op. cit.*, p. 405.

5   *Ibid.*

6   M. Beckwith, *The Kumulipo*, University of Chicago Press, Chicago, 1951, I, 37.

7   *Ibid.*, VII, 598, 643.

southern archipelagos, Ro'o in Tahiti or Lono in Hawaii. This child is lovingly awaited:

You are the little Lono, you are the big Lono.
My eyes! My love! O Lono![8]

It flutters about like a bat and gazes with its two eyes in the four cardinal directions. So the Hawaiian myths refer to 'the bat with eight eyes'. Eight eyes are attributed to the sun in another myth, the one in which he is the son of the moon goddess, Hina. He rummages around like a pig at the four corners of the earth.

Be careful when you give birth, Hina: the pig's eyes are cast towards the
heavens and to the mountains. Hina's son is a pig with eight eyes!
[…] eating from in front and from behind.[9]

The moon has no eyes to see with, in other words, she does not emit any light. On the other hand, she does eat the light of the sun. She shows herself in the north as well as in the south. It is often said that she eats from in front and from behind (*hina maha'i tua mea*).[10] The sun gently sinking down beneath the horizon both to the north and the south shows his face to opposite directions, as is seen in the heads sculpted with two faces:

There was born of the dark depths of the ocean a huge monster with two
faces, as a god for those regions. He had no back to his head, but he had a
forehead before and behind; it was a head with two faces![11]

8   M. Beckwith, *Hawaiian Mythology*, University of Hawaii Press, Honolulu, 1970, p. 211.

9   T. Henry, *op. cit.*

10   *Ibid.*

11   *Ibid.*, pp. 358-9.

Dawn at last

For the Polynesians, the sun was a child who had not yet been born. He bears within him the cherished hope. A messenger brings the good news: the return of day. This message is the light which gently spreads along the edge of the dark firmament and colours successively the clouds on the edge of the sky, as if a shining cloud were travelling tirelessly along:

> *Then was conjured as a messenger for Tane, 'Apo-rau (Catcher-of-many-things).*
> *Give another messenger for Tane! O Tu, fly thou to the sky where the storm is gathering!*
> *There is a cloud, a growing cloud! It is a rising cloud! Fly thou over the tempestuous sea. O the clouds! The dark cloud, the midnight cloud!*
> *Not the shelving cloud,*
> *Not the inflated cloud,*
> *But beyond the drifting cloud,*
> *Beyond the changing cloud,*
> *The red cloud, the yellow cloud,*
> *The clear cloud, the drooping cloud*
> *Beyond the stormy cloud!,*
> *Beyond the furling cloud*
> *And the vaporous cloud!*
> *Fly thou to the lowering sky.*
> *Oh the clouds! The dark cloud, the midnight cloud,*
> *The frozen, gilded cloud!*
> *Faurourou (Darling-child-caressed) is the cloud,*
> *That travels on, travels, grows, and travels on.*
> *Pregnant is the frozen cloud*
> *With Rongo the great messenger of Tane!*
> *Travel on, travel on, grow and travel on.*
> *Great Rongo sleeps in the cloud travelling on.*
> *Rongo turns and caresses,*
> *Rongo sets himself in the cloud*

As he travels on, grows, and travels on.
Rongo feeds upon the cloud
As he travels on, grows, and travels on.
Rongo is nude in the cloud
As he travels on, grows, and travels on.
Rongo causes the cloud to throb
As he travels on, grows, and travels on.
Rongo causes sharp pains in the cloud
The throes of parturiency with Rongo
Overtake the cloud,
Rongo is born of the cloud![12]

The brilliant edge of the first light of dawn is narrow and long. The rest of the sky remains dark and forms a kind of arch encircling the horizon. This is 'Rongo's rainbow', venerated on the Gambier Islands. After the endless darkness, the first dawn was a marvel. So the light had not disappeared for ever! It was adorned with the vivid and transparent colours of southern dawns.

The dawn was wonderful and good,
Adorned with riches!
The dawn was beautiful, fine and sweet!

---

12 T. Henry, *op. cit.*, pp. 369-70.

The sun

The sun still remained low on the horizon. This strange behaviour lies behind many myths. During the long night, the sky is held down to the earth by a great octopus and when darkness yields to light, the gods in turn try unsuccessfully to lift the sky so that the sun can rise high enough and shed its warmth.

> *Prop, now props the warrior,*
> *With the pillar of the friend of the skies.*
> *Cast up by enchantment will be the skies.*
> *Tall Ru, the man,*
> *Propped up by the sky which is propped.*
> *Now propped by the warrior.*
> *Remain up, now sky,*
> *Upon, pia, teve, and the umbrella tree.*[13]

If you want to observe a long night followed by a very gradual return of daylight, where the sun does not simply rise straightaway into the sky, you have to go to a polar region, at least 85° latitude! The bright period then lasts 10 months or so. So it seems that the Polynesians must have lived in such conditions, and not just for the time of a voyage.

Successive years bear the names of heroes who have fought against the sky to hold up the sun. The sun's annual course along the horizon or at a low height above it were symbolised on the sailors' canoes, representing the sun navigating on its own boat. The canoe, stylised, has symmetrically raised prow and stern-post.

The sun rests in the middle, represented by a round head with a simple dot in the middle. The sun is represented the same way in western cosmography: two dots for the eyes, one underneath for the nose, and, at the bottom, a horizontal line for the mouth. The rays emanating from the

---

13   T. Henry, *op. cit.*, p. 351.

26

Figure 6. *Petroglyphs from the Society Islands. They could represent a boat under a shining sun, or else a face topped by a feather head-dress, depending on one's interpretation.*

© Bishop Museum

sun become its hair. Underneath, you can see the paddles of the canoes. The sun navigates across the ocean in its solar bark. A series of men one next to the other represent the sun's successive positions a few minutes apart. Their forearms, when extended downwards, indicate that the sun is still beneath the horizon, and when extended upwards signify that it is above it. This representation shows the necessity of holding up the sky so that it stays as high as possible.

This imploring attitude is traditional. It is that of the praying figure. Finally, the arms become swiftly rounded to form with the forearms an upwards curve, the praying figure transforming himself into a solar bark.

René la Bruyère relates a popular tale in which a stone is thrown towards the dawn of time. The story is referring to the sun: Oro.

> *Cast the stone beyond our archipelago,*
> *To reach the far islands of the lost continent!*
> *This was no joking matter!*
> *Oro reached the horizon and plunged into the ocean depths!*
> *He was numbed by cold! And his disappearance*

Figure 7. *Praying figures – bands of poker work on a bamboo quiver from Tahiti.*
© Bishop Museum

28

Heralded the time of shadows and Great Night!
During this time, the sun which had ever been loyal to the dear earth,
Showed himself to be a capricious and wily god!
He would sometimes abandon our archipelagos
For long months at a time
His red disc would not appear
Above the horizon.
His pale rays were devoid of light
And did not linger, sinking swiftly
Into the mysterious depths of the ocean!
During this time of icy cold,
The local people were downcast!
They were afraid that Oro would never return,
Condemning them to eternal darkness.[14]

The (modern) style completely fails to recall the slow rhythm and typical repetitions of the carefully preserved ancient tales. The memory is so ancient that the sun's caprices obviously did not concern the world of the archipelagos. But there is a persistent horror of the conditions experienced in ancient times.

The Polynesians are known for their courage in combat and their boldness. They have, however, retained a trace of this fear of the approaching night. When you are acquainted with the night of the islands and its perfume, this remains surprising.

Fear falls upon me on the mountain top
Fear of the passing night
Fear of the night approaching
Fear of the pregnant night.[15]

---

14 R. La Bruyère, *Contes et légendes de l'océan Pacifique*, Éd. Pierre Roger, 1930, p. 98.

15 M. Beckwith, *The Kumulipo, op. cit.*, VII, 566.

Indeed, after the continuous daylight, the dark night does not return all at once, but little by little, gently and gradually. The fear will precede and follow this dreadful darkness.

The climate of the original continent

All the mythologies of the Pacific teach us that their origin is on a distant land, in thrall to piercing cold. Referring to the land of their ancestors, the Hawaiians speak of a land without warmth, of cold and shivering.[16] The mythology of the Pacific peoples indicates that they come from a country where the wind was glacial.[17]

The inhabitants of Tonga have preserved the memory of an ice-covered ocean, which they call Tai-fatu, signifying fat-like, congealed or frozen. Their ancestors lived there before they reached the islands.[18]

The original continent of the Polynesians was covered by a strange, thick mud. Its name is *kumulipo*, from heap (*kumu*) and mud (*lipo*). There is no word to designate snow in the tropics; *kumulipo* is the equivalent.

In the Tuamotu Islands where the coral beaches are made of sand as white as snow, the tales use this sand, *one*, to refer to the unusual mud. This sand has strange characteristics. It is sticky, and covers human beings, rivers, trees and mountains. Men have to get rid of it by sweeping it away to get down to the potentially fertile earth. On the sandy ground, no plant could grow. They had to shake the sand that was lying on top of it. By translating *one* as 'snow', the tales start to make sense. You come across a man of the snows, Tiki-one, and a woman who emerged from a pile of snow or dressed in snow, Hina-one.[19]

The man called Tupetupe-one-i-fare-one becomes 'the one who strolls about in the house of snow', in other words 'the one who dwells in an

---

16   M. Beckwith, *Haiwaiian Mythology, op. cit.*, p. 533.

17   J. Macmillan Brown, *Peoples and Problems of the Pacific*, Fisher & Unwin, London, 1931, p. 113.

18   P. Smith, *Hawaiki: The Original Home of the Maori*, Whitcombe & Tombs, Wellington, 1910, p. 177.

19   M. Beckwith, *Haiwaiian Mythology, op. cit.*, p. 294.

igloo'. All sorts of snow fall on Hawaiki, the original continent: "Flying snow, fine snow and cloying snow! Hawaiki was filling up with snow!"[20]

A very strange creature in Polynesian memory

The legends have a great deal to say about the *moko* or *molo* which swarmed on the shores. These words are translated as 'lizard', even though lizards do not have big sharp shiny teeth. In addition, on the Polynesian archipelagos, there is no reptile bigger than the grey *agama*, the common house lizard. But the Polynesian *moko* is *moko-kala, -kaula, -pelo, -olelo, -make-a-kane* (vigilant, prophesying, vagabond or wandering, speaking, deadly or man-eating). The Hawaiian legends frequently refer to *mokos* of extraordinary size, amphibious, that lived in caves and terrorised the local populations.

> "Who dwells in the ocean?" "We who run, who crawl, and who swim about. Tangaroa is master of us all."
> A great spirit ever pervades the sea, his name is Oropa'a (Unyielding-warrior), and he has a roaring voice.[21]

Oropa'a is one of the gods of the Society Islands.

> Rua-hatu-tinui-rau (Source-of-fruitful-myriads) came forth by Tangaroa's incantation; he was god of the Moana-urifa (Sea-of-rank-odor), king of the cast-up ocean. This god had a man's body joined to the tail of a billfish [...]
> The smooth waters within the reefs of the Moana-urifa were his mirrors, and in them were his sleeping pools [...]
> Tumu-nui was the husband, Papa-raharaha was the wife, and there was born to them Oropa'a; that god still exists in the ocean throughout the world. He has no language to tell us what he wants. He lies with his head upwards when the breezes come. The white, foaming breakers are his jaws.

20   T. Henry, *op. cit.*
21   T. Henry, *op. cit.*, p. 344.

He swallows whole persons and fleets of people; he does not spare princes
[…]
The whale was the messenger of Oropa'a.[22]

We can therefore deduce that the reference is not to lizards, but colonies of penguins, roaring sea lions, seals rearing their chests or warming themselves in the sun on sheets of ice, accompanied by the smell of their excrement. There are no seals in northern Polynesia even if you do, exceptionally, find one that has strayed as far as Rapa or the Austral Ridge Islands.

One artistic motif has been preserved to our own day among the Maori sculptors of New Zealand. It represents a body with a man's face and the tail of a marine animal. It resembles a siren, but with this peculiar feature: from its mouth protrude two long tusks, called *ngo-ngo* by the Maori, which extend as far as its middle. It is clearly a walrus. An old man, questioned about this unexpected representation among Maori in the sub-tropics, clearly had it in mind that it was a *maraki-hau*, an animal which he said dwelt in that mysterious part of the world whence their ancestors came.[23]

Engraved on the rocks of Orongo, Easter Island, opposite the three famous small islands, Motu Nui, Motu Iti and Motu Kaukau, you can find an elegant and charming silhouette, an enchanting siren, with a very feminine allure. It is easy to recognise in this figure the curious appearance of the penguin, with its flippers that dangle loosely when it waddles along and then become so agile when it dives. The bifid tail is that of a seal, Ruahatu, king of the seas, the fish-lizard-snake of multiple shapes, with both hair and fangs, diving to the deepest depths of the ocean, with a liking for sleeping on the beaches, human in appearance but with the tail of a swordfish (*rua*).

---

22 T. Henry, *op. cit.*, p. 358.

23 P. Smith, *op. cit.*, p. 176.

Figure 8. *A depiction of Ruahatu, engraved on a rock found at Orongo on Easter Island.*

A startling notion

The names of the original continent are revelatory. It was most commonly called night (Pô). Pô was also the island of death, or the island of the dead. The souls of the dead were thought to return to the great ancestors. The 'earth beneath' or 'underworld' (Rarofenua) are both frequently used terms. Caillot says that the inhabitants of Tonga called their place of origin Lolofonua, which was situated at the remotest part of the lower hemisphere, a "vast land situated in the nether regions, surrounded by the dark waters of the ocean."

The New Caledonians, similarly, spoke of an underwater land called Lolonn, acting as the dwelling place for the souls of the dead. Lolofonua, moreover, was not plunged into total darkness: it was partially illuminated by a strange half-day.[24]

The 'deep south' or 'far south' (*toga-mamao*) are common designations in the Pacific. In the islands of Tonga, to the west of the Austral Ridge Islands, traditions speak of a mysterious earth, that was believed to be very distant (*mamao*). It was given the name Toga, which means 'south'. But in the thinking of the islanders, south was the equivalent of lower down, underneath, and they could use the terms interchangeably.[25]

The original land was often designated as paradise, Purutu. It was synonymous with beauty, happiness, and perfection. In this case, it did not designate this earth on which so many evils were prevalent – darkness, cold, fear, solitude, illness, struggle – but a part that was further away (on the continent or in time) on elevated and once happy regions.

With the arrival of missionaries, Pô and Purutu became the Christian hell and paradise. In paradise, man is immortal. The immortality of the inhabitants of the original continent is often described. The country possessed water and leaves that restored life to anyone who had lost it – which is another way of expressing the idea of a sort of eternity attached to a special rhythm of life in which the year is transformed into a day that lasts several months and a long night.

24   E. Caillot, *Mythes, légendes et traditions des Polynésiens*, Leroux, 1914, p. 244.

25   *Ibid.*

These conditions of life are found only near a geographical pole.

Christopher Columbus himself wanted to discover this land where men did not die. He was familiar with this passage from Pliny, according to whom the poles are inhabited by "a happy race who do not die until they are tired of life":

Below the Tropic of Capricorn [in the Southern Hemisphere] lies the most beautiful inhabited region, because it is located in the finest, most noble surroundings, namely paradise on earth.[26]

The glacial cold, the endless night, the animals referred to by the founding texts of the Polynesian islands are so many descriptions of a life lived in the neighbourhood of the polar regions.

There is of course one great continent to the south, set at the crossroads of three oceans: Antarctica… Is it possible to envisage the Polynesians coming from that region?

There is a coast, at the far end of the Ross Sea, which, at 86° latitude, might correspond to the descriptions that the ancients have left us. This coast is situated opposite Polynesia, with winds from the west all year round to aid navigation from one to the other.

The great sea voyages, in which Polynesian mythology is rich, support our hypothesis, as we shall now show.

---

26   Cited in J. Favier, *Les Grandes Découvertes*, Fayard, Paris, 1991, p. 273.

The quest for an island under the right star

Professor Emory, of the Bishop Museum in Honolulu, noticed that the Polynesians had many more names for stars than we do. The legends of numerous islands would associate a star with a particular place which seemed fitting to it. It became clear that the island's latitude was close to the star's declension, and thus the star would pass vertically over the place associated with it.

Various stories indicate that, in order to reach an island, it was necessary to steer by a particular star: this is a manner of speaking, since any star whatsoever rises somewhere to the east, and sets somewhere to the west, its azimuth varying throughout the night. Éric de Bisschop noted that in general the said star reached its zenith over the island, or would have done two to three millennia ago, if account is taken of the retrogression of the vernal point (the slow and slight variation in the earth's movement).

In order to reach a particular island, the Polynesians sought to get to a position in the wind to the east where the associated star passed vertically overhead – far from easy in a canoe. Then they sailed west with a following wind to reach, in theory, their goal. Since an error of a single degree might lead to an error of more than 100km (60'), they must have relied on the help of some erupting volcano not to land in the wrong place!

Sailors called this method, which did not require a chronometer, 'landfall by latitude'. The Polynesians of course had neither watch nor compass, so navigating was a real art.

One legend says:

I have selected a star, and beneath that star there is a land that will provide us with a peaceful home.[27]

27   P. Buck, *Vikings of the Sunrise*, Frederick A. Stokes, New York, 1938, p. 97.

A Tahitian saga says:

Sail out and sail whither?
Sail north beneath Orion's Belt.[28]

But how did they maintain the right course? At night, navigating by the stars was no simple matter, especially as their courses vary with the latitude. By day it must have been harder still, relying on the sun, which, even at a given position, varies in its course throughout the year. And what when the weather was overcast? Steering by the swell, hoping that it does not change its direction, in an attempt to keep to a course initially found from the stars. And at night, without any moon, when the sky was cloudy? All they could do was to strike sail.

O Tangaroa in the immensity of space,
Clear away the clouds by day,
Clear away the clouds by night,
That Ru may see the stars of heaven
To guide him to the land of his desire.[29]

There is no doubt that the Polynesians were amazing sailors.

Aotea is the canoe,
Turi is the chief,
Te Roku-o-whiti is the paddle.

Behold my paddle!
It is laid by the canoe side,
Held close to the canoe side.

28 P. Buck, *op. cit.*, p. 136.
29 *Ibid.*, p. 98.

Now it is raised on high – the paddle!
Poised for the plunge – the paddle,
Now we leap forward.

Behold my paddle, Te Roku-o-whiti!
See how it flies and flashes,
It quivers like a bird's wing,
This paddle of mine.

Ah, the outward lift and the dashing,
The quick thrust in and the backward sweep,
The swishing, the swirling eddies,
The foaming white wake, and the spray
That flies from my paddle.[30]

The maritime epics of the Polynesians lyrically evoke not the desire for domination, the thirst for gain, or the allure of commercial profits – all of which went against their nature. Their essential passion, especially in ancient times, was always the immense ocean, with its foaming waves, its mighty swell, its storms, its secret riches: fish and islands.

Here, Peter Buck presents a Maori song from New Zealand. The name of the canoe, that of its skipper and even of his paddle, will endure forever.

An attempted expedition across the polar sea

During the period of darkness, the women kept the fires going to provide themselves with light and heat. They made clothes from feathers to protect themselves from the cold. The men felled trees to build great canoes. The expeditions could begin.

At this time, Ru was a valiant warrior. We have already described his efforts to hold up the sky.

---

30 P. Buck, *op. cit.*, pp. 274-5. Maori sea chant translated by James Cowan.

Ru, who raised the sky from the earth, prepared his canoe, Te-apori, to circumnavigate the earth with his sister Hina. As Ru prepared his canoe, he looked around and observed the appearance of the world, and he marked the boundaries in rotation as follows: the east he called Te-hitia-o-te-ra (The-rising-of-the-sun), the west Te-tooa-o-te-ra (The-setting-of-the-sun), the south he named Apato'a, and the north Apatoerau [...] A strong mat for a sail and cords to tie it to a mast were procured, and Ru and his sister embarked on their canoe [...] Ru sat astern with his great paddle for steering and a smaller paddle to use in calms or for plying against the tide in meeting with headwinds; Hina sat in the bows to watch for land, and thus they sailed away.

Ru lay to at night and sailed on in the daytime. They sailed east and arrived at Little-Tahiti, Mo'orea struck by the wind, and at Great-Tahiti with Hiti-i-te-ara-piopio. They sailed around those islands. Ru and his companion sailed on; the islands were all located by them; from south to north, from east to west, they were all located by Ru the dear valiant one, Ru who explored the earth.[31]

The epic of Maui

One of the best known explorers was Maui. A whole side of this hero's character is southern. He was the last child in a family, the sixth, brought up in a submarine grotto.

Here we can see the polar day, which near the pole lasts around six months or moons: the sun remains visible above the horizon all this time, but at the sixth moon, it starts to sink beneath the horizon. It is then deformed by the fogs: instead of being perfectly round, it appears deflated like a jellyfish.

Maui leaves his wife, who returns to live in Pô, the night. He pursues an unsuccessful adventure with his daughter: here, we can see a representation of the polar sun rising above the horizon, while his classic wife, the full

---

31 T. Henry, *op. cit.*, pp. 459-60.

moon, then disappears for months into the night, beneath the horizon. His daughter, the moon's first crescent, rises alone to turn without setting, but never catches up with the sun, becoming more and more slender as she approaches it.

Maui Atalaga is often accompanied by his son, Maui Kisikisi. In a legend from Tonga, related by Caillot (*op. cit.*), the father flies into a rage against this last child: "Who has told this disobedient child to come here? Stop your mischievousness! Go and fetch me some fire." Then the child says to his father: "What is the thing which we call fire?" His father replies: "Go to that hut over there where an old man is warming himself and bring back some fire so that we can cook our food."

So Maui Kisikisi goes off to look for fire, in the place where the old man is warming himself... "The old man took some fire and gave it to him. And the child went on his way with the fire. But on the way, he threw water over it to extinguish it, and the fire went out." The scene repeats itself.

The third time, all that was left in the hearth was an enormous brand, a stump of ironwood, with which the old man was warming himself. For the child had made off with all the rest, to extinguish it en route. So the old man angrily said to him: "If you can carry this log, you can take it away with you." The old man was the child's grandfather – but they did not know each other. The old man Maui said to himself: "No-one could lift this brand. Maybe only Maui Atalaga would be capable of it..."

So Maui Kisikisi goes and lifts the log with one hand. There follows a struggle. The boy lifts the old man in the air, "shakes him violently and throws him down; the old man is all bruised and loses consciousness. Then Maui Kisikisi takes the fire to his father," relating the struggle to him and declaring: "I struck him down and now he is dead."

Then Maui Atalaga becomes furious, since he is full of affection for his father. He "picks up his spade and hits Maui Kisikisi with it. The blow falls upon his head and kills Maui Kisikisi." The grandfather comes round, and reproaches his son: "Why did you kill Maui Kisikisi? It was needless, as he acted only through ignorance. We did not know each other. Go and find the leaf of the *nonu*. With them we can cover the dead, so they will live again."

So Maui Atalaga goes to pick the leaves of the *nonu* and uses them to cover Maui Kisikisi, who comes back to life: "It is only this species of *nonu* which is life-giving, and the tree is not found on earth, but only in the Sky (*lagi*), and in Lolofonua."

Embellishments and interminable digressions adorn this legend, as if in echo of the seemingly endless day and night at the poles, which lasted for a whole year in the sky (*te rangi*), from where men and gods came. Sometimes we hear of a kind of water, sometimes of the leaf of a tree which does not exist on earth, but only in the sky or in that 'lower earth' or underworld, Rarofenua, 'under the sea' or 'beneath the earth'.

It was so cold in the half of the year during which the sun circled beneath the horizon that you had to fight to manage to keep warm. Family affections did not survive the break-up of home life, with the result that people barely knew each other any more, and violence was natural in the struggle to survive. But everything changes the day when father Maui declares to his children:

As for me, I do not want to stay any longer beneath the earth [Rarofenua]
I want to go up there and live in the light.
I will go there with my son, Maui-the-small,
In order to live in the world;
[…] But I will come back to visit you.
So the Maui went up, they went to live in the land of Vavau,
And the part of the land they arrived in was called Koloa,
And it is this land of Koloa which we call Haafuluhao.[32]

Haa means 'the race' and *fuluao*, 'escaped with your skin'. The compound noun might be translated as 'the race of people who have escaped shipwreck with nothing more than the hair on their bodies'.[33] In the high latitudes, day and night do not last the same length of time. Maui is considered to be the one who conquers the sun:

32 E. Caillot, *op. cit.*, pp. 260-1.

33 *Ibid.*

Figure 9 Prow of a Māori…

This legend states that the sun had one long leg and the other short. As it sprang forward with great speed with the long leg, Maui caught it, broke off the extra length of the offending limb, and in that way made it step evenly and go slowly.[34]

It is as he travels up towards the equator that Maui performs this exploit. On reaching Polynesia, his first task is to build *marae*, and to set up on each island a college of priests trained by him.

As he and his people arrived at lands, they built temples conveniently and assigned them to priests.

34   T. Henry, *op. cit.*, p. 468.

Figure 9. *Prow of a Maori war canoe (tuere),*
18th century AD, North Auckland, New Zealand.

They went to the borders. They went to the east, to the Tuamotus and to Mangareva. They went south, to Tubuai, to Rurutu, to the Paroquet Islands, Rimatara and Mangaia and on to Rarotonga, to Rimitera, and to Te Aotearoa of the Maori [New Zealand]. They went everywhere in these directions. They went west, to Tutuila, Upolu, Savi'i [Samoa]; and to Vavau, Atiu [Cook], Ahuahu and Makatea. They went north, to burning 'Aihi [the volcanic islands of Hawaii].[35]

Many stories bring out in great detail how Maui sends his line to the depths of the sea, feels he has got a bite, and draws up to the surface a new island. The myth is easy to understand. By day, if you wish to see land looming on the horizon, all you have to do is scan the distance to right and left and try and detect a shadow, an abnormal accumulation of clouds or a green tint to their underside: then you can guess at a mountainous summit or the reflection of a lagoon on the cumulus you find in fair weather.

You let the fishing line drop, your gaze fixed on the surface of the water: the fish bites. Once the island has been 'hooked', you will see it rising little by little from behind the horizon, and it will 'rise out of the water'. In this way Maui went fishing for islands.

He also uses his nose to locate his quarry: when at night you sail downwind of an island, how can you fail to smell the sweet odour of coral, or the perfume of aromatic plants? Or else Maui tears off an ear to hang it from his hook: again at night, how can you fail to hear the swell breaking on the reefs, breaking with a roar like a drumroll.

Ru and Maui had both gone to fish in the sea.
As bait, they had put human ears
On the hooks at the end of their line: they pulled their line,
And felt something very heavy: it was the lands…
Which they brought successfully to the surface of the water.[36]

35   T. Henry, *op. cit.,* p. 464.

36   E. Caillot, *op. cit.,* pp. 257-8.

Thus they land on a place named Tokelau, occupied by three men. The gods have indeed already been this way:

"Are there any women in your country?"
They responded to this from their canoe: "There are no women here!"
The Maui said: "Where have you come from then?"
And they replied: "It was the gods who created us."
The Maui questioned them further: "Who are these gods?"
And they replied: "The Tagaloa [Ta'aroa]." So the Maui added:
"Stay here, while we go and do our fishing for land,
Then we will go to beneath the earth [Rarofenua]
To seek three women, one for each of you." [37]

Maui gives his name to the island just to the northwest of Hawaii, in the archipelago of the same name. But also to the North Island of New Zealand, called 'Maui's Fish' (Te-ika-a-Maui), the biggest catch he managed to bring up on his line from the depths of the sea. His last adventure starts here.

The myth states that Maui left his brothers with the fish while he returned to the homeland to get a priest to perform the requisite ritual over the new land [...] Many hold that the earliest inhabitants of New Zealand were descended from the Maui family.[38]

What would the logical maritime routes from the Antarctic continent to Polynesia have been?

To emerge from the Ross Sea and rise towards the sun, it was hardly possible to find your bearings, with a celestial pole so close to the zenith: so it was logical to sail along the west coast, lined by the Transantarctic Mountains, and pass between Ross Island and the land. It is probable that

---

37 E. Caillot, *op. cit.*, pp. 257-8.

38 P. Buck, *op. cit.*, pp. 267-8.

this was the key passage, separating two often mentioned reaches of sea known as Tai-koko and Ragi-riri.

The first was narrow, steep-sided near the shore, with squalls which made a choppy sea steam; the second was swept by a powerful swell which broke in huge waves. Moreover, this passage was right next to Mount Erebus, still active, which acted as a beacon, visible from afar, helping mariners to make the right landfall. The name of these two seas could be translated as 'the narrow sea' and 'the enraged sky'.

With the dominant westerly winds, following the passage of depressions, it was then enough to try to head more or less north until you encountered the trade winds. If you got carried slightly towards the east, once you had passed the tropics you were blown back to the west. There was no major difficulty, except of course for the sheer length of the crossing, sailing across vast and dangerous seas prone to sudden squalls and swept by families of meteorological depressions: you could hardly expect to avoid one or more violent storms.

For the return journey to your homeland, it would have been risky to set out due south from Polynesia: there was a strong risk of being driven eastwards and missing the southern continent, ending up instead near Cape Horn. The simplest solution was not to look for the shortest route, but the easiest – in other words, to allow yourself to be blown with free sails by the trade winds westwards, stopping off if possible at the Cook and Tongan Islands, and from there to head south-south-west until you reached the Maui's Fish and could sail down the east coasts of the two great islands of New Zealand. Thereafter you had some 1,400km to go, still trying to keep your bearings southwards, to land on Antarctica which at this point follows the polar circle. The hardest thing still remained: you had to sail down the west coast of the Ross Sea, enter the strait between the Ross Sea and the mainland, and continue right to the head of this immense bay. The two seas that had to be crossed, Ragi-riri and Tai-koko, kept their sternest challenges in reserve: the cold, the terrible katabatic winds and jarring ice floes.

A song, called the *Song of Kahu-koka*, indicates the precise route that needed to be taken to reach Antarctica from the islands:

Now do I direct the bow of my canoe
To the opening whence arises the sun-god,
[…] Let me not deviate from the course
But sail direct to the land, the Homeland.
Blow, blow, o Tawhiri-matea, God of the Winds!
Arouse thy westerly wind to waft us direct
By the sea road to the Homeland, to Hawaiki.
Close, close thine eye that looks to the south,
That thy southerly wind may sleep.
Allow us to sail o'er the Sea of Maui,
And impede us not on our course.
She stirs, she moves, she sails!
Ah, now shall speed Tane-kaha,
The gallant canoe of Kahu-koka,
Back to the bays of Hawaiki-nui,
And so to Home.[39]

South of New Zealand, you run into winds of variable direction –Tawhiri-matea – depressions with strongly dominant west winds. The southern winds were the only ones to fear, since they were blowing straight into the navigator's face. But, if you left at the right season, round the southern summer solstice, you were sure to reach the Ross Sea, setting a course due south by the sun rising towards the south-east on your departure, but getting closer to the south at increasing latitudes.

But Maui ended his work there; he left priests with the new temple named 'Apoo-'ao, and returned to Hava'i with his fleets to consult with the gods and people what to do to prolong the day.[40]

---

39 P. Buck, *op. cit.*, p. 62-3.
40 T. Henry, *op. cit.*, p. 430.

There is no possible doubt: Maui, with his fleets, returned to Hawaiki, the land of the gods, to confer with the human beings who had remained on the distant southern continent, and to tell them that he knew how to capture the sun, and prolong the daylight – he knew the happy regions where the sun shed its warmth and the vegetation bore fruit. On arrival in their native land:

> Maui-the-father [Atalaga] and Maui-the-small [Kisikisi] said to them:
> Come then and and live in your land,
> And tend your crops in all safety.
> Leave the woods and caves where you hide yourselves![41]

His last expedition turned out to be fatal. Maui wanted to "secure immortality for the human race who did not yet know death": he headed off towards the land of everlasting life, a paradise that had become a hell, glacial and deadly. There he found Hina-nui-te-Po, 'Great-Goddess-of-the-Night', and died strangled in her powerful arms.

Tupa the benefactor

The expedition led by Tupa set out from the underworld, Rarofuena. The crew reached Marutea, Aukena and Akamaru and found nothing to eat there. On the Gambier Islands, Tupa was given a warm welcome by the two kings Tavere and Taroi. He offered them seedlings of breadfruit, coconut and fig trees. At this time, the archipelago was short of big trees. Tupa taught them fishing and agriculture, as well as many other useful things.

He promulgated various laws and erected several *marae* on different islands. The biggest were built of stone and the smaller ones made of coral. There were private ones for the use of the men who were destined for the profession of priest. Candidates for the priesthood lived in contemplation and solitude for a long period before being ordained priests of Tu.

---

41 E. Caillot, *op. cit.*, p. 300.

Tupa expatriated the customs of the lost continent. As a 'civiliser' and a 'benefactor' he left the Gambier Islands with his followers, "In the presence of the whole population, who could not prevent themselves from letting out cries of pain" caused by the sadness they felt at his departure. Before he left, he revealed that there was:

Far away, down below, underneath,
A vast land, named Avahiki,
And the Foundation-of-the-earth [Tekere-no-te-henua],
That in this land there are many people,
Ruled over by powerful kings,
And that it was from this land that all their ancestors came.
[…] He soon set out to sea, out of sight of the archipelago […]
To return to the Underworld.[42]

This memory is characteristic of the fabulous journeys embarked on during the years immediately following the first settlements. The conditions of life were certainly poor, seedlings were brought from Antarctica, as well as priests. Indefatigable, these sailor-civilisers returned across the southern seas to the southern continent, only to set off again towards sunny but desolate archipelagos.

42   E. Caillot, *op. cit.*, pp. 174-6.

Tane

Tane seems to have organised several expeditions to return to the ancestral land where the gods continued to live, skilled masters in the various arts and sciences.

But here, the dome of Atea that covers the sky's vault shuts out the full light of day and prevents any real warmth from reaching the earth.

> Tane and Rua-nu'u, and 'Aruru (Collector), Tane's wife, with the two artisans, 'Oina (Swiftness) and Fafa (To feel), set out on a voyage of deity. They sailed in the canoe named Fa'atere-apu [Fast-as-a-fish] […] they passed through all the skies unobstructed until they reached the dome of Atea, when the sailing was retarded, and the canoe became stranded and stood indented!
>
> Then they sailed in a slanting direction, but they were repulsed by the presence of Atea! Enchantments were thrown out to sail by, but derisive flames appeared in the sky of Atea! The artisans, 'Oina and Fafa were consulted; and these artisans struck the outer, right ear of Atea to make him move off, but he was unmoved!
>
> Now Tane stood up in his canoe, which could not go on the voyage to deity! And Tane exclaimed: "This is I, Tane of the living waters! Let this growth of lining be dispersed, let Atea be no more."[43]

Confronted by the ice floe, Tane is obliged to sail along the limit of the ice to find a place where he can take refuge.

> So Tane set sail again in his canoe; he sailed on from age to age, and continued to sail from age to age! They came to an abyss in the east and an abyss in the west; they passed land with rushing tides and lands with light breezes. The canoe beat hither and thither, into contrary currents. Shoals became visible, and a harbor within; at Vavau (Papeno'o) was the harbor,

---

43 T. Henry, *op. cit.*, p. 455.

Vavau in great Tahiti of the rocky caverns! The sails were reefed in and tied, out on the shoals. And now Tane asked his wife, 'Aruru: "O 'Aruru, what shall we do with my canoe in peril out here?"

'Aruru answered:

"What indeed!" Then she looked out well and said: "Turn inland, and turn out and push along with the pole and make one circuit of the sky." And Tane pushed in and out with the pole, and he made one circuit of the sky; then there was a grating sound in the ocean under the lowering sky.[44]

The southern winter was approaching, night fell and their shelter on the ice floe was precarious. They decided to set out again in search of a better resting place, as the ice scraped along the hull.

And 'Aruru said again: "Push on towards that other point in the sky over there; there is a haven, free from the ocean, free from obstacles, free from towering waves." So Tane pushed on thither, and there was the haven, with smooth sea! Then Tane bailed out the sea from his canoe [...] So those gods from the open sky arrived on their journey to deity. They had reached Vavau (Papeno'o).[45]

The crew struck sail and pushed on with poles, eventually reaching a safe haven, sheltered from the huge swell of the southern seas, and the violent tides that created currents which brought dangerous icebergs with them. So Tane was coming back from the Polynesian archipelagos, where the sky was "open"; he was returning to the divine continent from which he had sprung.

Tane was out of breath, and he rested a little while in the bows of the canoe. Tane stood up, Tane whistled, he whistled and breathed heavily! Ro'o, the famous, and all the host of gods of this world welcomed them that had come on a voyage of deity.

44 T. Henry, *op. cit.*, pp. 455-6.

45 *Ibid.*, p. 456.

Tane and Hoani proposed going down below, to Ta'ere, and so they flew there. Then Ta'ere welcomed them, and said: "Is that thou, great Tane, god of all things beautiful?"

Tane answered: "This is indeed I, great Tane, whose eyes measure the skies, whose eyes unite with those of Ro'o, the famous." [...]

Tane dwelt with Ta'ere for a period, and he obtained all the science of Ta'ere-of-all-skill in himself. Then he returned to this world. Thus ended the visit of deity, of those gods of the skies, and Tane's canoe set out to sea again.

Vavau receded, the shoals were left behind. And Tane guided his canoe again along the land of light winds, by the way of the land of rushing tides. They sailed again by the abyss in the west and the abyss in the east, and continued to sail from age to age, until they reached Vai-ora (Living-water) in the sky of Tane![46]

Tane leaves the ice, and once again sails along the southern continent westwards and eastwards, to reach the free and life-giving waters of the open sea.

---

46   T. Henry, *op. cit.*, pp. 456-7.

'Ui-te-Rangiora in Antarctica

His name seems to mean: 'of-the-generation-of-those-who-were-delivered-from-the-sky'. He thus belongs, apparently, to that first generation of the gods who set sail from the sky, from that land situated in the extreme south, where the sun stayed absent for long months, where the sea was turned to ice, where the beaches and the waterways were invaded by seals, where icebergs floated, where the rocks are not black, but white with snow.

His ship *Te Ivi-o-Atea* can be translated as: 'It's-him!-The-widower-of-the-Brightness-which-opens-up'.

> Rarotongan mythology includes tales of remote ancestors who ventured forth on the seas in the dim past. Amongst these was 'Ui-te-rangiora [...] in his ship Te Ivi-o-Atea [he] sailed to the far south where he saw rocks that grew up out of the sea named Tai-rua-koko, the long hair that floated on the surface, the sea covered with foam like arrowroot, the animal that dived down under the sea, a dark place where the sun was not seen, and the high white rocks without vegetation upon them. These wonders have been interpreted as the sea south of Rapa, bull kelp, the frozen sea, sea lions, the Antarctic night, and icebergs.[47]

'Ui-te-Rangiora thus sets sail from the place where a coastal sea (*tai*) is closed by a double passage (*rua koko*), perhaps the one that can be surmised beyond the channel separating Ross Island and the coast, in the middle of the western coast of the Ross Sea.

An improbable epic towards the deep south

An old king, Taratahi, originally from Hawaiki, lands on the Gambier Islands (Mangareva) with his followers. Nothing is known about his crossing from the ancestral continent, nor about his expedition from Hawaiki to the Gambier Islands. Fierce and cruel, the king quarrels with their teeming

---

47 P. Buck, *op. cit.*, p. 111.

inhabitants and is driven away from the Gambier Islands. Eventually, he reaches Easter Island, with a small group of faithful followers.

Anua-Motua son of old Taratahi is, however, well loved and stays on the Gambier Islands to become king in his turn. He had come from the distant south with his father. His own son, Te Agi-Agi, was a soothsayer and high priest who had a vision of Taratahi being in danger and reproached his father for having expelled the old king. Anua-Motua decides to set off in search of him. He had, anyway, been seized by a renewed longing to travel.

He has two large voyaging canoes built and embarks with some of his family and his followers. All in all, the expedition numbers about 1,500 souls.

Then, when they have covered about a third of the distance separating them from Easter Island, their last call being Ducie (Kooa), a small island between the Gambier Islands and Easter Island, he "set out towards the south"!

Here begins a great adventure, the most amazing ever to have occurred in that distant time.

The crossing was long, days followed days.
And no land appeared.
The people of the two ships were exhausted.
Only Anua-motua was not,
And also his sons, who had confidence in him.
They knew that their father had travelled the world,
And that, consequentially, he should know the way…
Anua-motua and his three sons, Te Agiagi, Puniga and Marokua,
Were on the same boat, which governed these last ones.
However, the crossing went on too long.
The great priest Te Agiagi ended up
Consumed by worry at the length of the journey.
Though he did not dare tell his father
Who he would usually sit close to in the bottom of the boat.
However early one morning,

He went up to the highest point on the ship.
And, o surprise! On the horizon he saw a big patch of black,
Which was nothing other than a great land seen from afar!
Immediately he went down to tell his father
Who, followed by his other children, came straight away,
His head wrapped in a bag called tupata,
Saw in turn what had appeared in the distance.
Anua-motua was cold, everyone was trembling.
Looking at the stars, Anua-motua,
After a moment's reflection, said to his children:
Let us go back, we will soon arrive in Taikoko.
In this place, the sea was very bad,
And the air was more than chilly: it was very cold!
His children having asked him why they ought not go on,
Anua-motua replied that the further they went, the colder it would
become!
That in front of them were two lands,
And between them a perilous sea,
That this sea is called Taikoko,
And that the part of the sea where the waves,
Small, but strong and vicious,
Constantly break, is called Ragiriri:
That no vegetation could be seen there on the land by the sea;
The Sun was not high, that is to say
Never rose high in the sky;
That there are high arid mountains, narrow strips of land,
A pool with many whales in it,
And strange fish not found in Mangareva.
He added that he had passed by it, to get to Avahiki from Mangareva,
But he had believed at one point he might leave his life there:
That it was for this reason, because of the danger,
That they must turn back.
Then he was quiet. And his children obeyed him

And hastily turned the ship around;
Seeing this, the people on the other ship did likewise.
And the migrants, changing direction,
Started a new voyage in the other direction.
This one was, happily for them, much shorter than the first journey.
The winds of the East pushed them rapidly towards the island which they
wished to reach.
Finally, after quite a good crossing,
They arrived at the islands of Matakiterangi [Easter Island] […]
They were worn out with fatigue and at the end of their resources.[48]

Another version of the story relates that Anua

Turned the canoe back from the route they had been following,
And that soon, from the polar region
They reached the temperate zone.[49]

Having left Ducie Island, Anua-Motua heads south to find the Ross Sea, or more precisely to land on the volcanoes which illuminate the sky at night and darken it by day, acting as a beacon to sailors. He hopes to find the passage between Ross Island and the mainland, to reach those seas called Tai-koko and Ragi-riri.

Anua-Motua knows that at the head of the Ross Sea there is the place of origin of his family, with its high Transantarctic Mountains, whales and innumerable varieties of seals unknown on the Gambier Islands.

But instead of reaching New Zealand before heading south, he set out from a much too easterly longitude. After a long and hard voyage through storms and hurricanes from the west, unable to sail far enough back upwind with two heavily laden ships, once in Antarctic waters he headed towards the Amundsen Sea or even the Bellinghausen Sea.

---

48   E. Caillot, *op. cit.*, pp. 198-201.
49   P. Laval, *Mangareva*, Librairie Geuthner, 1938, p. 14.

He had to abandon the attempt, turn round and sail north. The little fleet, after a fabulous expedition over a distance equivalent to a third of a round-the-world journey, with 1,500 people on board, without compass or any metallic object, had succeeded in finding the pinprick of Easter Island.

Anua-Motua doubtless had *mana*, the ability to command authority over people and things, but he was in addition enough of a sailor to make landfall at the right latitude, by observing the height of transit of the stars. Without instruments and in spite of the vessel's movements, it is not impossible that he managed to reach considerable precision in degree – say a 100km or so. Reaching the desired latitude, and keeping to it, the two ships must have been favoured by easterly winds and judged their route by sight, with lookouts at the mastheads scanning the sea. This requires great skill, as those who have navigated across the vast expanses of the southern seas to make similar landfalls will appreciate.

The stories that have been gathered, both from the Gambier Islands and the Tongan Islands so widely removed, are sufficiently in agreement for us to eliminate any amalgam of fable or later memories made up by sailors passing through. The latter did not know of the existence of Antarctica, and millennia spent in the locality of the tropics did not encourage the imagination to dream up a great land far to the south, with whales and seals, where the sun never rose very high in the sky. A vivid memory remained of Hawaiki, the ancestral land, near the South Pole.

Anua-Motua is said to have died on Easter Island, sharing out his goods, and reserving for his favourite son, Te Agi-Agi, part of the original continent, where he had already given some islands to his first son, who had stayed in the deep south. One story says that Te Agi-Agi set off to take possession of his inheritance. Another story says that Anua set off with him and died there too, being buried by his friends and relatives in accordance with the prescribed rites.[50]

---

50   E. Caillot, *op. cit,* pp. 205-7.

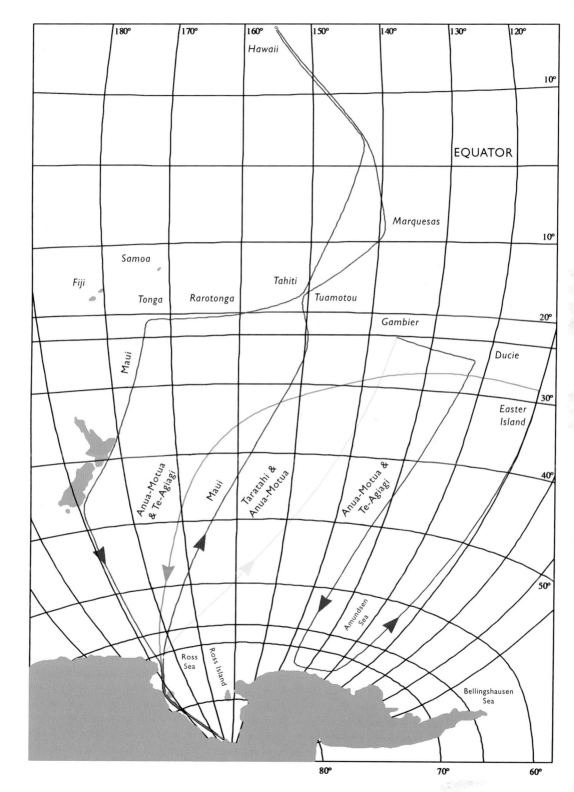

Our idea of the Polynesians having come from Antarctica is thus strongly supported by all these fabulous crossings of southern seas which constitute some glorious pages in the greatest maritime epic of ancient times. They tell us, for instance, that contacts between the homeland and the new colonies may well have continued for some time. Eventually, the climate of Antarctica became so inhospitable that all its inhabitants had to flee north. All they are left with from this continent are memories preserved in oral history.

Of course, when positing this theory of the Polynesians' Antarctic origins, we are immediately confronted by a great number of difficulties.

How had the future Polynesians managed to settle on the great frozen continent? Doubtless, when they settled there, the climatic conditions were quite different. How can we conceive of Antarctica as being a land sufficiently warm to sustain life?

Before we start speculating, let us study without further ado the memories of the peoples whose shared characteristics with the Polynesians we have already listed, and see if these memories describe the same landscapes as theirs do.

We will be travelling in China and Japan, around the Mediterranean, and in India and Mesopotamia.

If their descriptions agree with those of the Polynesians, we will be able to attribute to them a greater degree of plausibility in that it is unthinkable that a single one of these regions can have left its mark on the others and can thus claim paternity.

Could the traces of the earliest civilisations now be covered by a thick layer of eternal ice?

1.2 China

Before our era, in northern China, in the lower plain of the Huang He, at the head of the Gulf of Petchili, a fabulous civilisation developed. This was in the distant period of the Xia, then the Shang – or Yin and later Zhou – often called the 'Warring States'. This advanced and refined culture owed nothing to Central or Western Asia: the first caravans to be organised to eastern Turkestan, and further westwards or southwards, started very soon before our era. In fact they came into existence at the same time as the first maritime expeditions towards the south-east of the Pacific. Before that time, we can uncover evidence for only one or two voyages undertaken by Chinese merchants or adventurers.

The *Shu Jing* of Confucius

Around 500 BC, Confucius assembled the narratives of historians in the *Shu Jing*. In the third century BC, Shi Huang Ti ordered the burning of this work which the scholars in each family hid. Then, from the copy found under Vou-Ti, circa 140 BC, 58 of the 100 initial chapters were taken up and commented on. The didactic and moral preoccupations found in it allow us to glimpse some venerable opinions on ancient times, even if the *Shu Jing* "is not an ancient or totally reliable document."[1]

It traces the chronology of an era separated by periods, or *ki*. "The Sovereign King in the middle of the Sky" is Tian Huang, the "intelligent Sky." He was born on Mount Vou-vai, the mountain which "encloses everything", which is in the "south-east, twelve thousand leagues from the mountain Kouen-Louen."

Tian Huang was accompanied by 11 dragon-kings, or *Io*, which means 'mountain'. Together, they "had governed over all the universe in peace. Men under their reign had an abundance of all things without having to procure them through work."

---

1   G. Pauthier, *Livres sacrés de l'Orient*, Firmin Didot, 1840, pp. 15-9.

Tian Huang "taught the people and gave them the rules of wisdom and good government." Indeed, "there was nothing he did not know and nothing he could not do." In the first *ki*, nine brothers travelled "on a chariot of clouds drawn by six birds." They constructed cities surrounded by walls. All the different peoples in the universe were content with their lot and no one thought of his or her own interest.

For some reason, the kings of the fourth *ki* "taught men to go back into caves in the rocks. They mounted winged stags to rule." It is possible that this is a reference to sailing boats. A king of the seventh *ki* "turned over the mountains and turned back the rivers." So "the universe had not yet been tempered."

The eighth *ki* was a disturbed, cold period, in which "men covered themselves with grass." "The swollen waters had not yet flowed away." "There was extreme misery." To protect themselves from the cold, and the hoarfrost, men covered themselves with animal hides. "They used their furs as a kind of cloth to cover their heads." Men ceased to live in caves in the 22nd and final *ki*.[2]

Thus, while men originally lived in peace and plenty, one event transformed the world into a hostile place. They had to learn to protect themselves from the cold and to live in caves until the return of more favourable conditions. How can one fail to think of the Polynesians, obliged to leave the original continent because its climate had suddenly become too inhospitable?

The original mountain

From the most ancient times, the Chinese seem to have attached a great importance to mountains, to which they offered solemn sacrifices. Mountains are close to the sky, they give birth to the rain-bearing clouds and are closed worlds, since there is no essential difference between mountains and islands.

Among the cardinal mountains, the Tai Shan is particularly venerated. It

2   All the quotations are taken from G. Pauthier, *op. cit.*, pp. 20-7.

was popularly believed that after death, all souls return to a sort of Hades situated at the foot of Tai Shan. As it is in the east, it is at the origin of all things and all beings, the source and master or life, of destiny and death.

Other mythical mountains at the extremities of the world play the role of poles, pillars of the sky. The most well-known is Kouen-Louen. It is extremely high, according to some so high that it touches the sky.

> The approach is protected by a mysterious Water,
> Which circles the Mountain three times before returning to its source.
> Whoever drinks of it attains immortality.[3]

Kouen-Louen is not just a mountain: there is a nine-storey temple on its summit and those who succeed in climbing the successive stages of Kouen-Louen raise themselves to immortality. There are hanging gardens whose trees bear pearls or produce jade, all sorts of rare and precious plants, and many divine beings (*chen*).

Kouen-Louen is the earthly capital of the Lord of the Sky. However, a goddess-mother, Xi Wang Mu, according to the *Shan Hai Jing*, "lives in a mountain of jade to the north of Kouen-Louen." "She stays at the bottom of a rocky cavern," with "the body of a human, but the tail of a leopard and tiger's teeth." "She rules the spirits of Plague and Catastrophe."

All kinds of monsters are found guarding the entry to these domains. The one that is sometimes called the Lord of the Earth (Tu Bo) is a nine-headed snake which keeps guard over one gate, wrapping itself nine times round itself. It spreads infection by vomiting out whole swamps. Above the gaping abyss rise the nine gates of the sky guarded by wolves. Those who wish to pass through these gates are hurled into the chasm.

The Chinese texts are much too late not to have been interpreted a thousand different ways, with a profusion of symbolic figures and fables. But we do find a distant echo:

3   M. Granet, *La Pensée chinoise*, Albin Michel, Paris, 1950, p. 354.

- of the original mountain, with a famous temple, at the summit of a series of terraces, the model of truncated stepped pyramids;
- of a special body of water barring access, encircling this land several times over;
- of the evils that assail this hellish region, where once there was beauty and refinement. It is now impossible to get there.

Immortality

The Chinese, like the Polynesians, imagined a sort of immortality for their ancestors. Thus there are the cycles of Yin and Yang. An allusion to the polar night may be seen in this symbol: the Yin is insensibly transformed into the clarity of the Yang with the sun's disc. The Yin corresponds to the cold polar night, the Yang is the polar day. The sun reappears, shedding light and a little warmth into the sky.

> *Very far to the east of the Oriental Sea*
> *Lies a bottomless Abyss: the Kouei-hiu*
> *Where all the waters of the world mingle.*
> *Above the Kouei-hiu*
> *There are five magical islands*
> *Where the Immortals reside,*
> *Dressed in feathers and equipped with wings,*
> *Where the plants of immortality grow on which they feed.*[4]

The eastern sea is the Pacific Ocean, the Kouei-hiu is the Southern Ocean where all the waters of the world rotate. It is possible, in my view, to conclude that the Chinese migrated from islands near the southern continent to set sail for Asia. Life there seemed to last so long that its inhabitants doubtless seemed immortal. It was so cold there that they must have dressed in garments of feathers, like the Polynesians, which made them look like birds. The wings represent the sails that propel their

4   M. Granet, *op. cit.*, p. 357.

enormous junks. These islands later disappeared, having been rendered inaccessible by distance and ice.

The terrible Shi Huang Ti, an emperor from the third century BC, haunted by death, launched expeditions to seek for the plant of immortality that grew on those original islands. The young men who went on board had to fast in order to set off for countries where one died of hunger and cold.

According to the ancient Chinese texts, no one has found these islands since.

Figure 11. *Yin and Yang.*

1.3 Japan

According to Shinto creation myths,[1] in the beginning was chaos, like an ocean of oil, or an egg. From this confusion was born a divinity, then other divinities who soon disappeared. There were in all seven generations of these secondary divinities, who appeared in couples of brother and sister.

The eighth and last pair comprised Izanagi, 'the man who invites', and his sister Izanami, 'the woman who invites'. On the order of the heavenly divinities, they advanced on the floating bridge of the sky, and plunged a heavenly spear bedecked with jewels into the chaotic waters that spread out beneath them. They stirred it until the liquid coagulated and thickened.

In this way the island of Unogoro came into shape. Its name means the island 'which coagulates by its own means'. Izanagi and Izanami made of this newly-appeared island the central pillar of the Earth. Then the two divinities decided to explore this island-pillar.

We encounter the classical themes: chaos, the ocean, confusion, the egg, the island which you cannot go round. This is situated at the Pole, for the water is as thick as oil, 'coagulates', and thickens, turning to ice. Furthermore, the island is close to the Pole where the 'central pillar' is found, the axis of the vertical world, around which all the stars are to turn.

From the union of the two gods sprang several islands and several divinities: as in the Chinese myths, we have the same coastal archipelago in the southern continent. An infirm child is born, who at the age of three could still not stand upright. During the dark polar night, he had to grope his way through the caves that served as a refuge – or to 'swim' as it is related in the Polynesians myths, in which Ru became a hunchback.

Izanami continued to bring forth the sea, the waves, the mountains, then the god of fire. Izanagi decided to visit his sister in the world of darkness, where she had built herself a castle. Izanagi endeavoured to persuade her to return to the world above. But she hesitated, claiming that it was too late,

1   *Nihongi* (Chronicles of Japan), circa 720 AD.

as she had taken food in the land of darkness. She adjures her brother not to follow her, and withdraws into her palace.

Izanagi breaks off a tooth from the left extremity of his comb, and sets fire to it to provide himself with light in his sister's dark shelter, and he finds her in an atrocious state of decomposition, gnawed by worms; her putrefying flesh spreads a sickening stench. Horror-stricken, he flees.

But she, displeased at this, sends after him the demons of the world of darkness. Izanagi fights an army of 1,500 warriors. Finally, at the passage separating the world of light from the world of darkness, he bombards his pursuers with three peaches, blocks the passageway with a great rock, and hurls invectives at his sister:

> [...] he will set up one thousand five hundred maternity houses,
> every day will see one thousand five hundred births,
> in this way a fair balance will be established between births and deaths.

'Tasting' the food of the world of darkness, and ingesting the harmful fruits of the long polar night, makes you ill and sterile, and leads to death. After this contact with death and the infernal regions, Izanagi embarks on self-purification. He strips off his clothing and plunges into a river.

Thus, finally, are born from his left eye Amaterasu, the goddess who makes the sky shine, and from his right eye the god of the Moon. From his nose springs Susanowo, the 'impetuous male'.

Amaterasu is resplendent and luminous. Izanagi places under her domination the plain of the high heavens and presents her with a gift of a necklace of precious stones. Susanowo is impetuous and dark: he is to reign over the marine plain.

But Susanowo is inconsolable. He weeps and laments aloud, unceasingly. At the sound of his voice, the mountains soon wither and the seas dry up. He wants to visit his mother – Izanami – in the land of darkness. The southern storms rouse winds and waves whose powerful voice is an incessant lament. The forests perish on the heights. The sea freezes and dries up.

Susanowo then decides to bid farewell to his sister, the sun goddess, and starts walking towards her kingdom in the skies. But his approach is so tumultuous that the sun goddess fears he may intrude on her own domains. So she prepares to go forth and meet him. She throws over her back a quiver with 1,000 arrows in it, and another with 500; she seizes her bow and takes up her position so vigorously that her legs sink up to her thighs in the ground.

The ocean sets out around the summer solstice, when the sun turns without setting in the sky, a short way above the horizon, thawing the ice that had kept the waters prisoner. Then, around the equinoxes, the sun goddess turns close to the horizon in which she seems half sunk.

A titanic combat ensues. It soon relents, and the adversaries present each other with gifts: a sword and jewels, which they put in their mouths and chew. Peace returns. However, the 'impetuous male' does not give up his bad manners: he breaks up the divisions between the rice fields that Amaterasu had drawn up, fills in the irrigation ditches and soils her dwellings with excrement.

The sun goddess, Amaterasu, is vexed. To show how displeased she is, she withdraws into a rocky grotto and blocks its entry. The myriads of divinities are greatly troubled. So they all gather in the dried-up bed of the celestial river to deliberate.

The sun has disappeared. It refuses to return. So it is polar night. The celestial river is, as in other mythologies, the various waters around the original continent. So the divinities are here gathering on the ice floe that has formed. Jewels and mirrors are set out at the cave mouth: their magic is useless.

The fable imagines a lascivious and provocative dance that finally persuades the sun goddess to reappear. Then light shines again on the earth. Banished from the sky, Susanowo descends on to the land of Izumo, situated in the western part of Japan, opposite Korea, at the mouth of the most important river, the Hii: "He goes back upstream."

All maritime migrations that land on a continent, or on big islands, have naturally sought a harbour at the mouth of a river, where they can obtain shelter and freshwater, as well as a navigable access to the interior.

In general, Japanese legends are both refined and crude, salacious and yet melancholic. At no point does tragedy prevail. One is never overwhelmed by the weighty sense of catastrophe belonging to other mythologies. Perhaps this is owing to the profound harmony between the Japanese and the natural environment. They have placed an emphasis not only on an everyday functionalism, but also on qualities like fertility, purity and beauty.[2]

2   Citations taken from P. Grimal (ed.), *Mythologies des montagnes, des forêts et des îles*, Larousse, Paris, 1963.

1.4 Iceland

Written in Iceland in the 14th century, the *Edda* is the origin of a great deal of Germanic mythology and has managed to preserve, over 600 years, previous traces of the origin of the peoples of Iceland. Their magnificent isolation has allowed this text not to be diluted by contact with other civilisations.

Rendered in the vernacular by the Icelandic historian Snorri Sturluson at the beginning of the 13th century, the *Edda* constitutes the most complete, coherent and intelligible collection of Nordic mythology bequeathed to us by medieval Scandinavia.[1]

A world emerging from the void

The *Voluspa*, the anonymous prologue to the *Edda*, thus informs us of the origin of the world in its Icelandic version:

It was Time's morning,
When there nothing was;
Nor sand, nor sea,
Nor cooling billows.
Earth there was not,
Nor heaven above
The Ginnugagap ['yawning gap', abyss] was,
But grass was nowhere.

The myth recounts that earth and the heavens were created before the sun, moon or stars were set in the sky. Night precedes day and vice versa! So why is night prior? The sun, during the course of the year, stays above the true horizon for as long as it sinks beneath it. It is even visible for a little

1   Introduction by F. X. Dillmann to Snorri Sturluson, *L'Edda : Récits de mythologie nordique*, Gallimard, Paris, 1991. All of the subsequent citations are taken from Snorri Sturluson, *The Younger Edda* (trans. R. B. Anderson), Scott, Foresman & Co., Chicago, 1897.

longer than it is invisible. In addition, when it has set, it is only really dark night when it moves more than 18° below the horizon. Finally, the moon sheds its light half the time: in total, the period of darkness is much less than that of brightness.

Now it is very common among the Nordic peoples to grant a major importance to the night. Why? The sun remains for 24 hours below the horizon only if you go beyond the polar circle, where there reigns a glacial cold, which makes agriculture, livestock farming, and any normal life impossible.

In the *Edda* the land of the dead, Niflheim, is ruled by the goddess Hel and guarded by the terrible hound, Garm. It is described as being beneath the world of men, covered in ice and darkness.

Is it not perfectly obvious that this icy country lies within the polar circle? The Arctic? So one might think.

A land surrounded by water

There is enough evidence, however, to allow us to think that the country described here is none other than the southern continent.

> [...] before the races came into existence, and men increased and multiplied [...] [the Gods] made the ocean; they fastened the earth together and around it they laid this ocean in a ring without, and it must seem to most men impossible to cross it. [...]
> The earth is round, and without it round about lies the deep ocean, and along the outer strand of that sea they gave lands for the giant races to dwell in; and against the attack of restless giants they built a burg within the sea and around the earth. [...] they called the burg Midgard.

Within the Arctic Circle there is an ocean turned to ice and surrounded by dry land. The description of Midgard, conversely, fits the description of Antarctica, the southern continent surrounded by a marine abyss. The eastward current flows right round it and passes as often as you like round its base, wrapping itself round the land in the middle like a great snake.

The ancestors from the southern continent, Erebus, were 'gods'. Their immortality came from an annual and interminable rhythm: uninterrupted brightness and prolonged, terrifying darkness alternated. It seemed to last an eternity. One year among ordinary human beings was a day and night for these gods.

A strange fruit grew in this land outside time – a golden apple conferring a virtue of immortality on those unfortunate gods who were suffering and dying much more than usual.

Idun was the wife of Brage, the god of poetry, "He is famous for his wisdom, eloquence and flowing speech." She "keeps in a box those apples of which the gods eat when they grow old, and then they become young again," the golden apples of youth.

The terrible dog Garm keeps watch, guarding the approaches. He barks and howls like the storms at high latitudes, like sea lions, like craters belching out fiery floods. He bites and seizes his prey in the same way as the wind, the biting wind, or the coming of the polar night. He keeps watch over a universe buried under snow and darkness, where people hide in the depths of their shelters, numbed, famished, asleep.

1.5 Egypt

Pre-dynastic Egypt presents us with a flowering of engravings and drawings representing river boats, made of reed, or seafaring boats. The exchange of circular, cylindrical, oval and rhomboid seals show that there was navigation, at a distant period in the past, between Egypt, the Persian Gulf and the Indus Valley.

The Sumerian cultural contribution seems to have shortly preceded the sudden appearance of sailors, grouped into nomes (administrative divisions) with totems, peaceable and living on hunting and fishing, manufacturing pottery and finely carved flints into worked stones polished to perfection.

The two first dynasties of the Old Empire constructed huge and admirable mastabas (sloping sided tombs). From the third dynasty onwards, we find a mastaba, at Saqqarah, which marks the beginning of a flourishing period of classical, smooth-sided pyramids, accompanied by basins for boats.

One of these, at the foot of the Pyramid of Khufu, preserved a seafaring boat of generous proportions, 43m long, with planking of cedar sewn together. Cedar trees do not grow in Egypt, so they must have been imported. The constructors built with consummate art. The elegant hull shows that the ancient Egyptians were then capable of importing enormous tree trunks, and building fleets of 50–60m long ships. The sea level seems to have been higher then that it is now, since the ships could sail down the Nile and reach the Red Sea by an arm of the delta. They must also have been able to sail up the Gulf of Aqaba, the Dead Sea and the Jordan as far as the Lebanon, to obtain cedar.

The Middle Empire seems more ephemeral, racked by warfare. The New Empire is better known thanks to numerous excavations: the famous 18th Dynasty; the voyage onto the Red Sea launched by Queen Hatshepsut; and, later on, the battles fought by Ramses against the Sea Peoples, circa 1200 BC.

Egypt developed a magnificent and autonomous civilisation, with coastal expeditions to the south-east of Africa, and to the Syrian coast, Crete and the Aegean Sea. Around 600 BC, Necos II sent a fleet to sail round Africa, a voyage which, according to Herodotus, took three years.

Egyptian hieroglyphics, partly translated, are a valuable source of information, but the most ancient texts were studied, interpreted symbolically and commented on in several religious centres. The *Pyramid Texts* and the *Book of the Dead* constitute a major, though anonymous, basis, with a religious, but in no way historical set of preoccupations. All the ancient Egyptian dates rest on a fragile scaffolding of careful studies and suggestions that are generally accepted but which are impossible to verify.

The primeval ocean

Before the creation existed a vast watery region which was completely still and covered by total darkness.

> *"I was alone with the Primeval Ocean, in the inertness, and could find no place to stand … (the gods of the) first generation had not yet come into being."*[1]

This complete night recalls the night that can be observed only in the polar circle. This vast expanse, the primeval ocean, surrounds a land which is not firm. Mention is made of subterranean creatures which know nothing beyond this darkness. They are snakes. They "served notice that the mound would emerge from the waters, and they were also its first inhabitants [...] they would die [but] their earthly posterity has not come to an end."[2]

The southern seas driven by the west winds form a snake, a river that turns on itself several times over to return to its source where all the waters of the world congregate:

> Far away – all unknown, beyond the range of mortal minds, scarcely to be approached by the gods, is a cavern of immense age, hoary mother of the years, her vast breast at once the cradle and the tomb of time. A serpent

---

1   Extract from *The Coffin Texts* cited in D. Meeks and C. Favard-Meeks, *Daily Life of the Egyptian Gods* (trans. G. M. Goshgarian), John Murray, London, 1997, pp. 13-4.

2   *Ibid.,* pp. 15-6.

surrounds this cave, engulfing everything with slow but all-devouring jaws; never ceases the glint of his green scales. His mouth devours his back-bending tail as with silent movement he traces his own beginning.[3]

The original island

In Middle Egypt, at Hermopolis, the theogony begins with the *Ogdoad* – eight gods.

> At Hermopolis, it [the Primeval Hill] was an island in a lake – which symbolized the primeval waters – and was called the "Isle of Flames" with a clear allusion to the glow of that momentous sunrise of the First Day. In the pyramid texts a curious writing of the "island of appearance (or 'of sunrise') of the earth" obviously reflects the same line of thought.
>
> The waters surrounding the Primeval Hill were, naturally, the waters of chaos; these, personified in the god Nun, were still supposed to surround the earth, an inexhaustible reserve of latent life and fertility. And the subsoil water, as well as the Nile flood, was thought to flow out from Nun. Since the Primeval Hill was the place of the sunrise and creation, and hence the place of rebirth and resurrection, the waters of Nun which surrounded it became those waters of death […].
>
> Here chaos had been conceptualized in eight weird creatures […]. Nun was the formless primeval ocean and his female counterpart, Naunet, was the sky over it. […] The next pair of the Ogdoad were Kuk and Kauket, the Illimitable and the Boundless. Then came Huh and Hauhet, Darkness and Obscurity; and, finally, Amon and Amaunet, the Hidden and Concealed ones.
>
> On the Isle of Flames the eight mysteriously made the sun-god come forth from the waters […]. The sun child is suckled by a cow; the sun is a powerful bull; the sky itself is a cow. […] So we may see the cow of heaven studded with stars and with the sun-boat sailing along her body.[4]

3   D. Meeks and C. Favard-Meeks, *op. cit.*, p. 19.

4   H. de Frankfort, *Kingship and the Gods*, The University Press of Chicago, Chicago, 1948, pp. 154-5.

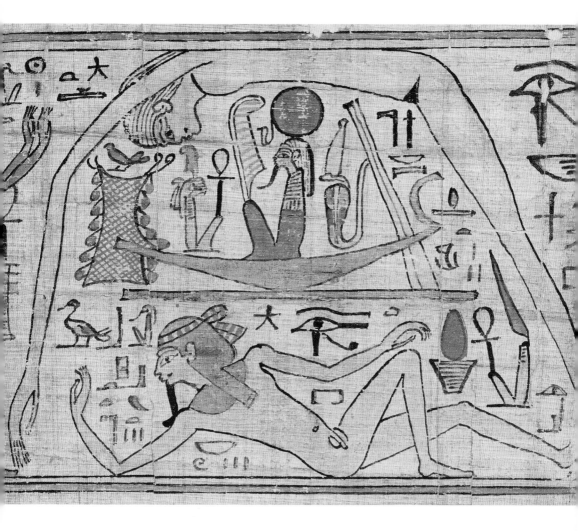

Figure 12. *Detail of the Ancient Egyptian* Papyrus of Neskapashuti, *dating from the 21st Dynasty. The god of the earth, Geb, lies under the vault of heaven represented by the body of Nut, across which Ra navigates his barque.*

"You have sailed the length of this river as a star sails on the Great Green [the ocean] which is under the body of Nut." (*Pyramid Texts* 802).

We thus find in these texts many points that remind us of Antarctica:

- A primeval ocean surrounds the original land of the gods.
- The sunrise, so commonplace and familiar for the most ignorant person, would not merit any particular attention, its memory would have no reason to be preserved or considered a singular event, if it had not been longed for.
- A day cannot be called the 'First Day' unless it is exceptional and memorable, opening up the era of what is essentially a new epoch. There is no 'First Day' without a previous 'Chaos' that brings to an end a previous epoch that was happy and tranquil enough to have passed almost unnoticed. This 'Chaos' is an important turning point, the bringing to an end of a life – a human life as well as a material life, that of water in particular, which ceases to be a living thing to congeal into "the waters of Death"! The curiously inert, "completely still" waters correspond in reality to the ice floe that imprisoned all those who were under the earth, on the 'Isle of Flames', with its active volcanoes.
- The Egyptians were aware of the daily rising and setting of the sun. Now, the appearance on the horizon of a star that was believed to be dead and which had just been reborn was something quite different.

The solar barque does indeed seem to sail along the horizon under a cloudy sky, Nut, the 'Cow of the Sky'. The course of this infant Sun assumes more and more strength each day, after the spring equinox, and daily hovers up and down just above the horizon, like a ship.

This reminds us quite straightforwardly of Polynesian mythology in its description of the sun's journey through the clouds around the horizon.

Punt, the lost continent

The story of the shipwrecked sailor, found in a papyrus written in the 12ᵗʰ Dynasty, and deciphered by the Russian Egyptologist M. Golenischeff, relates the story of a sailor who claims to have seen Punt, to have lived there, and to have witnessed its disappearance. This evidence from another age is of great value in situating this mysterious land geographically.

The sailor had been sent by the king of Egypt to the mines of the Upper Nile in a barque with a crew of 150 men. After "having passed the cataracts and the land of Ouaoua," they eventually end up on the sea. "There, a tempest swallowed up the vessel, destroyed all the sailors, and he himself was thrown, by the waves, alone and naked, on to the shore of one of those happy isles where the shades of the dead reside."

This island is guarded by a gigantic snake 30 cubits long, with a beard two cubits in length, and walking on two legs like a man. Its limbs are covered in gold, its eyebrows in lapis lazuli, that intensely blue-coloured stone composed of lazurite. It speaks, and tells the shipwrecked man that it is the sovereign of Punt. Seventy-five other snakes live with it, probably its children or its companions. It "graciously accepts the supplication of the Egyptian grovelling before him," then questions the stranger on his birth and the aim of his journey, advising him not to lie, since it "knows everything of the divine sciences."

After the explanations of the shipwrecked man, the snake announces that he will stay for four months on the island. He will go short of nothing. It promises him that a ship will come by looking for him and he will be able to return to his country. This is indeed what happens. After wishing him a safe return, the snake offers the Egyptian a rich cargo of the most precious herbs and spices. Suddenly, a star fallen from the sky "becomes the source of a blaze." The shipwrecked man finds that all that is left of the snakes is "a mess of cadavers." Once he has embarked on the ship, he turns back to look at the marvellous island. It had disappeared from view.[5]

---

5   Fr. Lenormant, *Histoire ancienne de l'Orient*, vol. III, A. Lévy, 1882, p. 67; J. de Morgan, *La Préhistoire orientale*, vol. II, Librairie Geuthner, Paris, 1926, p. 251.

Originally, Punt was indeed a great island in the Indian Ocean, with "a degree of advanced development." This birthplace of culture cannot be situated in Somalia, southern Arabia, Abyssinia, Nubia or the Upper Nile. Nor is it to be found in Mozambique or South Africa, even if these countries collectively kept the name of Punt. The magic island where you land only by the hazard of storms was the divine land of the Egyptian gods, surrounded by the primeval ocean.

Punt continued to be inhabited

"After the act of creation, the waters of the original chaos did not remain completely uninhabited." Nun "lived in a cavern of abysmal depth [...]. It was there that the gods went to see him."[6]

These subterranean dwellings make one think of the southern continent, subject, at least partly, following a yearly rhythm, to the darkness of the polar night. The southern seas and the ice floe surrounded the land, where the gods live in wretchedness, having little to eat for lack of harvests or livestock: "Periodically, under the impulsion of a prolonged fast, they shattered the immobility of chaos and flew off to the regions beyond it." Dressed in garments of feathers, on broad-winged sailing vessels, "The moment they crossed the border dividing the uncreated from the organized universe, they were struck by the sun's rays. They then transformed themselves into real birds in order to swoop down on Egypt. These were the migratory birds." [7]

Leaving the polar circle, these migrants are like ghosts or shades. However, "they had human heads and conversed in human language." The appearance attributed to the dead, and the life beyond the grave that is imagined for them, is closely based, naturally enough, on the appearance of these gods, who look as if they had disembarked from another planet. And yet, they come from Punt, the cradle of the world, and from Nun, the primeval ocean, which surrounds it, having become the waters of death.

6   D. Meeks and C. Favard-Meeks, *op. cit.,* pp. 92-3.

7   *Ibid., p. 92.*

Figure 13. *Egyptian rock painting from the 18th Dynasty, representing in relief soldiers sent by Queen Hatshepsut on an expedition to the land of Punt to bring back the ingredients necessary for the temple ritual. Mortuary temple of Hatshepsut, Deir-el-Bahari, Thebes (circa 1503–1482 BC).*

"The first known references to Punt date from the 5th dynasty. The most recent attestations of expeditions date from the 26th dynasty."[8] In the 5th Dynasty, the Palermo Stone recorded that Our-djed-ba brought a dwarf back from Punt.

Several expeditions to Punt took place with the aim of bringing back various luxury substances, indispensable for the worship of the gods, such as incense, myrrh and olibanum. On a vase inscribed with the name of King Teti, dating from the 6th Dynasty, circa 2280 BC, conserved in the Berkeley Museum, we find an elegant figure representing Punt. Mention is made of *antyou*, incense.

Punt is referred to mainly in royal inscriptions and private autobiographies relating different expeditions. Some authors boast, like a certain Khu, "of having followed his master eleven times to the land of incense."

Modest expeditions did thus take place, as did more significant ones involving up to 3,000 men. In the accounts, mention is always made of the riches of that continent. One returns from it laden with precious products – livestock, long ivory tusks, blocks of wood, gold dust, panther hides, ostrich eggs and feathers, rare animals, numerous felines.

We are told that the vegetation there is abundant and varied. The inhabitants of Punt live in huts on stilts. They have fine features and the men wear little goatees.[9]

The Egyptians gave the name 'Punt' to the set of distant regions situated in the direction of the South Pole, on the eastern and southern coast of Africa: they carried out voyages during the Old Empire, and even the Middle Empire, and then the memory of the place finally faded away.

Egypt long maintained commercial relations with several distant lands in the Indian Ocean, where the climate was tropical or temperate, before the New Empire.

---

8   P. Vernus and J. Yoyotte, *Dictionnaire des pharaons*, Éditions Noêsis, 1998, pp. 131-2.

9   « À la quête de Pount », *Archaeologia*, 96, July 1976.

The real Punt, the southern continent, had become cold enough to mean that it had long been impossible to find incense, ivory, ostriches or panthers there.

But life remained possible, in spite of the cold and the absence of agriculture or livestock, at least on a small surface area of the Antarctic continent – that situated far from the Pole.

> The sole exception to the rule was the country Punt, located somewhere to the south-east. A land of aromatic spices, the place where the phoenix came from, a region of light where the sun rose [...] Punt was more or less conflated with the "land of the gods".[10]

---

10 D. Meeks and C. Favard-Meeks, *op. cit.*, p. 91.

1.6 Greece

The myths related by authors such as Hesiod, Homer, Euripides and Aeschylus, the products of a long process of oral transmission, also include references to an original land that are close to those seen in the texts we have just been studying. Night, cold, and the vast ocean surrounding a land peopled with immortals are the most striking elements of these resemblances.

Dark night

When Hesiod and Homer refer to night, they mean black night, deep and dark, like that of the polar regions.

Hesiod was born, it is thought, in the 8th century BC. For him, a catastrophe known to the Greeks as 'Chaos' was the necessary forerunner of the first black night, without sun or daylight.

"In truth at first Chaos came to be."[1] First appears black night, then Erebus, an unfathomable abyss where death reigns. Then come the 'aether' and the light of day.

In Polynesian mythology, the gods were angered at Atea, the dark sky held down by the earth, preventing light and heat from establishing themselves and enabling life to grow. Conversely, in the *Theogony*, it is the Sky, Ouranos, who hates his sons, born from the Earth, the oldest of which is Cronos, who is not yet the master of time.

> [...] *they were hated by their own father from the first. And he used to hide them all away in a secret place of Earth so soon as each was born, and would not suffer them to come up into the light: and Heaven rejoiced in his evil doing. But vast Earth groaned within, being straitened, and she thought a crafty and an evil wile.*[2]

---

1   Hesiod, *Theogony*, in *Hesiod: The Homeric Hymns and Homerica* (trans. H. G. Evelyn-White), William Heinemann Ltd, London, 1914, line 116.

2   *Ibid.*, lines 156-60.

The earth was in the depths, too low to see the sun. The earth was 'below', 'underneath' for the Polynesians. For Hesiod, the earth is 'inside'.

The famous myth of the castration of Ouranos can also be interpreted in terms of a 'polar' reading. When Ouranos, the starry sky, stretches out his body over that of Gaia, the earth, Cronos, in complicity with his mother, cuts off his genitals so as to put an end to his tyrannical reign.

> And Heaven came, bringing on night and longing for love, and he lay about Earth spreading himself full upon her. Then the son from his ambush stretched forth his left hand and in his right took the great long sickle with jagged teeth, and swiftly lopped off his own father's members and cast them away to fall behind him. And not vainly did they fall from his hand; for all the bloody drops that gushed forth Earth received, and as the seasons moved round she bore the strong Erinyes.[3]

In reality, the children of the night sailed off, carried away by stormy winds, in a sea swollen with furious waves. The bloody remains of the father's genitals are red, like the lava of active volcanoes. The inhabitants abandoned an inclement sky that had lost its fecundity. They made their way back up towards the light to flee the harsh disadvantages of a land that had become infernal, and to escape death.

The starry sky above his arms

Atlas gave his name to the mountains of North Africa and, beyond them, to the Atlantic Ocean. Hesiod says of him:

> And Atlas through hard constraint upholds the wide heaven with unwearying head and arms, standing at the borders of the earth before the clear-voiced Hesperides.[4]

---

3   Hesiod, op. cit., lines 173-85.

4   Hesiod, op. cit., lines 516-8.

Atlas is the world axis. He is the vertical pivot around which the heavenly sphere turns each day. This ideal sphere is linked to the stars, to the heavenly bodies, whose course is horizontal. A little later, in the 6th century BC, for Aeschylus, Atlas is the one who "stands bearing on his shoulder the pillar of heaven and earth." He is "Atlas, pre-eminent in mighty strength, who moans as he supports the vault of heaven on his back."[5]

The earth's axis of rotation, and so, apparently, that of the starry sky, is almost vertical in proximity to the poles. It is called a "column" bearing the sky and acting as its pivot, at a point that is indeed called the "celestial pole" in cosmology.

Euripides was a Greek tragedian of the 5th century BC. He in turn refers to the Hesperides, daughters of Atlas and nymphs of the setting Sun. For the Mediterraneans, the sun sets in the Atlantic, beyond Gibraltar, in other words beyond the Pillars of Hercules. The Hesperides designated the Cap Verde islands.

For most ancient Greek authors, other islands were situated at the limits of the ocean and the starry sky. The celestial pole was there in an almost vertical position, with the result that sailors no longer had any possible route to steer by the stars. These Hesperides are described as sonorous because of the violent west winds, in latitudes that are said to be roaring, bellowing, howling. More poetically, Euripides calls them "musicians":

And he [Heracles] came to those minstrel maids, to their orchard in the west, to pluck from golden leaves the apple bearing fruit, when he had slain the tawny dragon, whose terrible coils were twined all round to guard it; and he made his way into ocean's lairs, bringing calm to men that use the oar. And he stretched out his hands to uphold the firmament, seeking the home of Atlas, and on his manly shoulders took the starry mansions of the gods.[6]

5   Aeschylus, *Prometheus Bound*, from *Aeschylus* (trans. H. Weir Smyth), Harvard University Press, 1926, lines 351, 429-30.

6   Euripides, *Heracles* (trans. E. P. Coleridge), in *The Complete Greek Drama* (eds W. J. Oates & E. O'Neill Jr) Random House, New York, 1938, lines 395-405.

The underworld

Homer was immortalised by his two epic poems, the *Iliad* and the *Odyssey*, in the 8th or 9th century BC, around the same time as Hesiod.

Homer's underworld is the kingdom of Hades. In order to reach it, you must go down, which means to 'go beneath the earth' but also to 'go south'.

Before Odysseus can reach the underworld, Circe guides him through a perilous maritime route. She advises him: "be in thy mind no concern for a pilot to guide thy ship, but set up thy mast, and spread the white sail, and sit thee down; and the breath of the North Wind will bear her onward."[7]

He must cross the ocean to reach a land with dark forests:

> *There into Acheron flow Periphlegethon and Cocytus, which is a branch of the water of the Styx; and there is a rock, and the meeting place of the two roaring rivers.*[8]

The rock referred to here resembles an active volcano that pours into the water a stream of fiery lava, amidst a terrible hubbub.

Before plunging into the heart of the dark kingdom, the crew is struck by a terrible sadness. They tear their hair, uttering loud groans of despair and giving way to cries and tears, overwhelmed by the desolate aspect of this region.

In the *Odyssey*, the approach to the underworld is also characterised by a thick fog, and a deep darkness. The underworld is a sunless land, at the far side of the sea.

> *So when we had made fast all the tackling throughout the ship, we sat down, and the wind and the helmsman made straight her course. All the day long her sail was stretched as she sped over the sea; and the sun set and all the ways grew dark.*

---

7   Homer, *Odyssey* (trans. A.T. Murray), William Heinemann, Ltd, London, 1919, Book X, lines 505-7.

8   *Ibid.*, Book X, lines 514-5.

*She came to deep-flowing Oceanus, that bounds the Earth, where is the
land and city of the Cimmerians, wrapped in mist and cloud. Never does
the bright sun look down on them with his rays either when he mounts the
starry heaven or when he turns again to earth from heaven, but baneful
night is spread over wretched mortals.*[9]

The reader will doubtless grant that the arrival of Odysseus' boat in the
underworld bears many resemblances to a vessel landing in Antarctica, in
the middle of a polar night.

Here is a description of the underworld by Hesiod:

*And there, all in their order, are the sources and ends of gloomy earth and
misty Tartarus and the unfruitful sea and starry heaven, loathsome and
dank, which even the gods abhor. It is a great gulf, and if once a man were
within the gates, he would not reach the floor until a whole year had
reached its end, but cruel blast upon blast would carry him this way and
that. And this marvel is awful even to the deathless gods.*[10]

It is a terrible place, where it is impossible to live, a dismal region where
the sea provides no nourishment; it is an immense continent where the
inclement weather and the violent winds, forever blowing, sweep everything
away in their path. Even the immortals are powerless in these dark lands.

Night "holds in her arms Sleep the brother of Death, even evil Night,
wrapped in a vaporous cloud."[11]

Within the polar circle we find this dark night that lasts for several weeks
or months every year – a night unknown on the rest of the Earth. At the
pole, night lasts until the winter solstice, then retreats. A darkness like that
of fog then lifts, giving way to a sun that gives light but no heat, without any
night.

9   Homer, *op. cit.*, Book XI, lines 14-20.

10   Hesiod, *Theogony, op. cit.*, lines 736-43.

11   *Ibid.*, lines 755-9.

The glowing Sun never looks upon them with his beams, neither as he goes up into heaven, nor as he comes down from heaven. And the former of them roams peacefully over the earth and the sea's broad back and is kindly to men; but the other [the night] has a heart of iron, and his spirit within him is pitiless as bronze: whomever of men he has once seized he holds fast: and he is hateful even to the deathless gods.[12]

Cold and immortality

For Hesiod, the children of the polar night, again called "the dark night," personify the evils due to the catastrophe and to the glacial night that ensued. Gaia is the land of the immortals who are masters of the mountain peaks of snowy Olympus.

Aeschylus' Prometheus stays bound to the foot of the Caucasus, until he is delivered by Hercules. His liver is gnawed by an eagle in a cold and impetuous climate that reminds one of that of Erebus. The inhabitants of these regions "dwelt beneath the ground like swarming ants," in "sunless caves." They do not experience the seasons, since they never leave their shelters because of the inclemencies and the deep darkness. "They had no sign either of winter or of flowery spring or of fruitful summer."[13]

And just as we here again encounter the theme of cold, so we also meet that of immortality. Thus the Gorgons "dwell beyond glorious Ocean in the frontier land towards Night where are the clear-voiced Hesperides." They are eternal. They "were undying and grew not old."[14] Their teeth are as long as a boar's snout. Here we should remember the descriptions of Polynesian walruses.

The mere fact of looking Medusa in the face turns whoever dares do such a thing to stone. Transformation into stone can here be interpreted as the stiffness characteristic of death by cold.

Medusa resides not far from the kingdom of shadows.

12   Hesiod, *op. cit.*, lines 760-7.

13   Aeschylus, *op. cit.*, lines 450-6.

14   Hesiod, *op. cit.*, lines 274-8.

The ocean

The Oceanides are daughters of Oceanus, the god who personifies the river that encircles the whole world. Through their names the Oceanides evoke swift and elegant sailing vessels, capable of confronting every sea. They are probably boats that enabled men to flee far from the dark and icy lands referred to in the description of the underworld.

Among them, Hesiod refers to Electra who bears to Thaumas "swift Iris and the long-haired Harpies, Aello (Storm-swift) and Ocypetes (Swift-flier)", daughters "who on their swift wings keep pace with the blasts of the winds and the birds; for quick as time they dart along." Another daughter of the sea, Ceto, gives birth to the "fair-cheeked Graiae," the sisters "Pemphredo well-clad, and saffron-robed Enyo." We can see in these descriptions a reference to the billowing sails of a ship, puffed out like cheeks and dyed a yellowy-orange

The Oceanide Doris has 50 daughters by Nereus, known as the Nereids. Hesiod describes them as "lovely" and "gracious," "rosy-armed," "of charming figure." They are "fond of laughter," and "divine." Of one of them, Cymodocea, it is said that she "easily calms the waves upon the misty sea and the blasts of raging winds." They probably personify the rich, peaceful, artistic colonies established in the islands or on different bays.

For a Greek who viewed the sea with horror, as Hesiod did, it is not the Mediterranean that is being evoked here, or even coastal trade in the Aegean, but most probably the Atlantic, that ocean which is also "the perfect river" as far as its extreme southern limits, i.e., as far as the polar circle.[15]

The river that flows back towards its source

Hesiod refers to 25 daughters who sprang from the ocean-river. They are established on the mouths of the Nile or the Po. The last-named and the first of all is Styx, the sacred sea of Erebus. The dead return there to join their ancestors. Styx is the original sea.

---

15 Hesiod, *op. cit.*, lines 240-75.

And there [in hell] dwells the goddess loathed by the deathless gods, terrible Styx, eldest daughter of backflowing Ocean. She lives apart from the gods in her glorious house vaulted over with great rocks and propped up to heaven all round with silver pillars. [...] Far under the wide-pathed earth a branch of Oceanus flows through the dark night out of the holy stream, and a tenth part of his water is allotted to her. With nine silver-swirling streams he winds about the earth and the sea's wide back, and then falls into the main; but the tenth flows out from a rock, a sore trouble to the gods.[16]

The southern ocean surrounds the Antarctic continent. A powerful current, flowing with a volume a thousand times that of the Amazon, drains it from west to east, so that it behaves like a river wrapped round the continent. The land guarded by the Styx is a rocky coast, bordered with icebergs, with ice that shines like silver.

When she sees her son, Odysseus' mother, now a shade in the kingdom of the dead, is amazed at his presence in this place:

"My child, how didst thou come beneath the murky darkness, being still alive? Hard is it for those that live to behold these realms, for between are great rivers and dread streams; Oceanus first, which one may in no wise cross on foot, but only if one have a well-built ship. [...] But haste thee to the light with what speed thou mayest, and bear all these things in mind."[17]

The secret of these mysteries was the object of various initiations, with various symbols being brought into play. The reality of the existence of the gods of the polar regions was probably difficult to imagine in Greece.

But their influence seems to have been significant.

---

16 Hesiod, *op. cit.*, lines 755-94.

17 Homer, *op. cit.*, lines 155-60, 204.

Diodorus Siculus

For his part, Diodorus Siculus, a Greek historian of the 1ˢᵗ century BC, relates in his *Historical Library* the history of the Atlantans. They lived in a rich country, and formed the most civilised of the lands next to the oceans. "It is among the Atlantans […] that the Gods were born." The Atlantans were frequently attacked by the hideous Gorgons. These were finally "destroyed by Hercules when, during his journey in the west, he erected a column in Libya."

According to Diodorus, near Libya, beyond the Pillars of Hercules, "is found an island on the high sea, of a considerable size, and situated in the Ocean. It is several years' journey from Libya, and located to the west. The land is fertile and mountainous." It is a land "of great beauty," "navigable rivers flow through it." There are many gardens there, as well as all sorts of trees and orchards. "The air there is so temperate that fruit grows in abundance throughout most of the year." The Greeks of later antiquity kept a vivid memory of a distant ancestral continent, woody and mountainous.

This country had once been happy. More recent tales became mixed up with it. That of the Atlantic colonies, with their pleasant climate, so desired by Perseus, Bellerophon, and Hercules, and glimpsed by Odysseus. Was this the site of the original land of the Atlantans, on the shores of the ocean? In other words, was this unknown southern land, so ardently sought for, the birthplace of the gods, as it was claimed to be?

18 Plutarch, *On the face which appears on the Orb of the Moon* (trans. A. O. Prickard), Warren and Son Ltd, London, 1911.

The cradle of humanity

In the *Odyssey*, Homer calls Ogygia the distant island in the Atlantic Ocean that is governed by Queen Calypso. As we know, Odysseus stayed there for 10 years, captivated by her charms.

Between 83 and 75 BC, the Greek historian Plutarch mentions Ogygia in a dialogue between scholars who are debating whether it is possible or not to see the inhabited moon.[18]

The Carthaginian Sylla declares, "in Homer's words, 'Far o'er the brine an isle Ogygian lies', distant from Britain five days sail to the West." If you continue even further west, you reach "the great continent [...] inhabited by Greeks," the one called Nyctoros. The god who resides on this "island of night" is Cronos. Young men are sent to him as an offering every 30 years.

> *They put out, and naturally do not all fare alike; but those who come*
> *safely out of the perils of the sea land first on the outlying islands [...]*
> *There they spend ninety days, meeting with honourable and kindly*
> *treatment, and being addressed as holy persons.*[19]

Then, sailing with a favourable wind, they finally reach the island of Ogygia. No one inhabits this sacred spot except for the *daimones* who are immortal. The obligatory length of stay for travellers here is 13 years. Those who decide to stay lead a contemplative life amidst marvellous natural scenery, the presence of the god having transformed this lost corner of the ocean into a paradise.

Cronos, or Saturn, is entrapped here in the bonds of sleep – he rests in a cavern where the walls look like gold. The men who decide to sojourn on Ogygia all have an abundant supply of the goods they need for their sacrifices. They are safe from all material concerns. The man who told this story to Sylla spent 30 years there studying astronomy and the physical sciences.

---

18 Plutarch, *op. cit.*

19 Plutarch, *op. cit.*, XXVI.

The issue raised by the island of Ogygia is not that of characterising Plutarch's ideal society – an academy of sages and philosophers honouring the divine and taking pleasure from the good things of the world – but rather of knowing what the author's sources could have been. He gives a precise description of a polar night, which could not have sprung from pure imagination.

Is it Ogygia that the mythical Orpheus is speaking of when he talks about the cradle of humanity?

O Mighty Titans, who from heav'n and earth
Derive your noble and illustrious birth,
Our fathers' fires, in Tartarus profound
Who dwell, deep merg'd beneath the solid ground:
Fountains and principles, from whom began
Th' afflicted, miserable, race of man:
Who not alone in earth's retreats abide,
But in the ocean and the air reside;
Since ev'ry species from your nature flows.[20]

20   The Hymns of Orpheus (trans. T. Taylor), Philosophical Research Soc., 1987, XXXVI To The Titans.

1.7 Rome

Ovid

In the Metamorphoses,[1] when Ovid, a Latin poet of the 1st century AD, recounts the birth of the world, the chaos he describes is also quite similar to the southern polar lands.

Firstly, nothing seems to exist other than a "rude and undeveloped mass," where "all discordant elements confused, were there congested in a shapeless heap." The sun does not yet brighten the earth with its rays so the air is "opaque," deprived of light. The earth trembles without finding its equilibrium. It is unstable, just as an ice floe can be.

The earth surrounding this unstable land is itself "unfit to sail" because of the ice floating on its surface. The sea was enclosed by the land, without any definite coastline. The elements that were present at the creation of the world were in perpetual metamorphosis. They were constantly subject to the change caused by the struggle between extreme cold and intense heat.

> *[…] to naught was given*
> *a proper form, in everything was strife,*
> *and all was mingled in a seething mass –*
> *with hot the cold parts strove, and wet with dry*
> *and soft with hard, and weight with empty void.*[2]

Glacial cold was juxtaposed with burning volcanoes. The water was transformed into soft snow, or else into a lifeless block of hard ice. Nothing could preserve its shape until a god imposed order on these mixed-up elements by banishing the shadows of darkness.

Night and day thus have their own distinct places granted to them. "The tranquil peace" in which they henceforth exist will prevent them from occupying the same sky at the same time.

1 Ovid, *Metamorphoses*, (trans. Brookes More), Cornhill Publishing Co., Boston, 1922.

2 *Ibid.*, Book 1.

But God, or kindly Nature, ended strife –
he cut the land from skies, the sea from land,
the heavens ethereal from material air;
and when were all evolved from that dark mass
he bound the fractious parts in tranquil peace.[3]

After this period of chaos with its dark night, Ovid unambiguously indicates that the original Antarctic continent was an island. Its shores are enfolded in the southern seas which are subject to extremely violent winds.

He rounded out the earth
and moulded it to form a mighty globe.
Then poured He forth the deeps and gave command
that they should billow in the rapid winds,
that they should compass every shore of earth.[4]

Ovid, when he separates the entire earth into five regions, knows that at the poles, snow invades the land. He is a good enough geographer to recognise the world's different climatic zones:

Such heat consumes
the middle zone that none may dwell therein;
and two extremes are covered with deep snow;
and two are placed betwixt the hot and cold,
which mixed together give a temperate clime.[5]

So Ovid was aware that a frigid Antarctic zone was the counterpart to the northern Arctic region. Ovid's description of Mercury's journey to Atlas is of interest to anyone looking for mention of polar lands in ancient texts.

3   Ovid, *op. cit.*, Book 1.

4   *Ibid.*

5   *Ibid.*

The rapid vessel, with its golden sails, makes its way down the African coasts, and the mountains that will later be named after Atlas. In fact, the ship reaches the southern continent in the southern seas, through which the world's axis passes – described as being full of dark vapours, bristling with ice, white with heaped snow, battered incessantly by the winds.

Here, Ovid is referring to the sun – the monster Argus – illuminating everything on the horizon, around the summer solstice, inside the polar circle; then its slow descent, close to the horizon, until its complete disappearance that entails the polar night:

> Argus, Aristorides, whose head
> was circled with a hundred glowing eyes;
> of which but two did slumber in their turn
> whilst all the others kept on watch and guard.
> Whichever way he stood his gaze was fixed
> on Io – even if he turned away
> his watchful eyes on Io still remained. [...]
> Io, Mercury, the favoured son of Jove,
> descending to the earth from heaven's plains,
> put off his cap and wings [...]
> then soothly piped he on the joined reeds
> to lull those ever watchful eyes asleep;
> but Argus strove his languor to subdue,
> and though some drowsy eyes might slumber, still
> were some that vigil kept.
>
> Low lies Argus: dark is the light of all
> his hundred eyes, his many orbed lights
> extinguished in the universal gloom
> that night surrounds.[6]

6   Ovid, *op. cit.*, Book 1.

Pomponius Mela

Pomponius Mela, a Spanish author of the 1st century AD, gives a description of the region around the pole, deep inside the polar circle. Indeed, his precision is quite remarkable:

> [...] *under the very pole of the stars, where the sun rises, not every day as it does for us, but for the first time at the vernal equinox, and where it eventually sets at the autumnal equinox. Therefore, for six months daylight is completely uninterrupted, and for the next six months night is completely uninterrupted.*[7]

In order to make such a statement, the author must necessarily have benefited from direct evidence of these extraordinary conditions of life. Since neither he nor any of his compatriots went to the pole, this evidence can have come only from the past.

---

7   F. E. Romer, *Pomponius Mela's Description of the World*, University of Michigan Press, Ann Arbor, 1998.

1.8 India

Since we have exhumed without too much difficulty so many traces of a southern origin in Greek and Latin culture, it is unsurprising to discover others in Indian and Mesopotamian cultures.

The Indus Valley is located in the tropics. The sun rises and sets each day, its trajectory intersecting with the horizon at an angle of 60° to 70°. The texts that speak of the land of the ancestors nonetheless contradict this familiar observation: "That which is a year is but a single day of the Gods."[1] "There are uncreated lights and created lights. There the stars, the moon, and the sun are only once (a year) seen to rise and set, and a year seems only as a day."[2]

The Airyana Vaejah, the original land of the Iranians, was a place rendered uninhabitable by glaciation: "in this original home the sun rose and set only once in the year, and [...] the year was like a day to the inhabitants of the place."[3]

The place in question can only be within the polar circle. In India as in Persia, the swarm of gods invented for the needs of endless fables contrasts with an underlying simplicity: the terrifying polar night alternates with the polar day that is, all the same, reassuring, since it follows on from an interminable darkness. A short recapitulation of the most important divinities will allow us subsequently to follow the mythological tales from this part of the world.

The sea of Kouro-Vasha is the name of the primeval ocean and Airyana Vaejah that of the original continent which was once a paradise. Vritra is the warrior god of violent geological upheavals, the snake lurking beneath the waters, holding them in a grip of ice. Vritra is also the chief of the night demons, the Rudra and the Marut who are the terrible warriors of active

---

1   *Taittirīya Brāhmana*, III, 9,22,1, cited in L. B. G. Tilak, *The Arctic Home in the Vedas*, Poona, Bombay, 1903, p. 70.

2   *Vendidad*, II, 40 (trans. J. Darmesteter) in *Sacred Books of the East*, vol. 4, OUP, Oxford, 1880.

3   L. B. G. Tilak, *op. cit.*, p. 98.

volcanoes. Indra, the day that conquers night, is the adversary of Vritra. Other names exist to designate the same things. Thus Varuna is the god of the long night, alternating annually with Mitra, the long day that insensibly follows it, or else Angra Mainyu, the destroyer, the chief of the Daevas – the enemy of Ahura Mazda is the day that follows night and vanquishes it.

Night and darkness

O spacious, darksome Night!
May we, uninjured, reach the end of thee, reach,
O thou blessed one, thine end![4]

Aditi, Mitra, Varuna, forgive us however we have erred and sinned
against you.
May I obtain the broad light free from peril: O Indra, let not during
darkness seize us.[5]

Dawn

Chitrâvasu is [means] the night; in old times, the priests were afraid that
it [night] would not dawn.[6]

In the polar regions, the dawn, far from leading to dazzling sunshine, is endlessly prolonged and remains in a permanent state of latency:

These very Dawns are those that first shone forth, the Goddesses make five
forms; eternal [they] are not separated, nor do [they] terminate.[7]

4   *Atharva-Veda*, XIX, 47, cited in L. B. G. Tilak, *op. cit.*, p. 128.

5   *Rig Veda* II, 27, 14 (trans. R. T. H. Griffith), E. J. Lazarus and Co., Benares, 1896.

6   *Taittirîya Samhitâ*, I, 5, 7, 5, cited in L. B. G. Tilak, *op. cit.*, p. 129.

7   *Taittirîya Brâhmana*, II, 5, 6, 5, cited in L. B. G. Tilak, *op. cit.*, p. 100.

When the light of day appears, it is not very different from the darkness of the night. The day star does not pierce the horizon with its rays. The sky's light is neither bright nor dark.

The dawn, turning daily under the horizon, is slightly brighter to the north than to the south. Thus, dusk and dawn are two twin sisters, Ushâsanaktâ and Naktoshâsa, and the gradual repeated advances of the dawn are compared with the successive advances of love:

> *Great is, in truth, the number of the Mornings which were aforetime at the Sun's uprising.*
> *Since thou, O Dawn, hast been beheld repairing as to thy love, as one no more to leave him.*[8]

> [...] the verse states in unmistakeable terms (1) that many days passed between the appearance of the first morning beams and sunrise, and (2) that these days were faithfully attended by the Dawn, meaning that the whole period was one of continuous dawn which never vanished during the time.[9]

The sun turns tirelessly below the horizon for anyone who lives a few degrees away from the pole. This marvellous dawn turns like a potter's wheel around an axis close to the vertical: it turns around the world axis. "Thou, Morning, turning thee to every creature, standest on high as ensign of the Immortal, To one same goal ever and ever wending now, like a wheel, O newly-born, roll hither."[10]

The return of day

The reappearance of daylight and then of the sun is the victory of Indra (or Mitra) over the glacial darkness, Vrtra (or Varuna). The rivers and the ocean

8   *Rig Veda, op. cit.,* VII, 76, 3.

9   L. B. G. Tilak, *op. cit.,* p. 90.

10 *Rig Veda, op. cit.,* III, 61, 3.

are freed from the ice. The ice is compared to butter, as a counterpart to curdled milk, representing an ice floe breaking up into small sections that melt in the heat.

> To Mitra the cream which forms on the milk and to Varuna, the butter made by churning.[11]

> I will declare the manly deeds of Indra, the first that he achieved, the thunder-wielder. He slew the Dragon [Vrtra], then disclosed the waters, and cleft the channels of the mountain torrents.
> He slew the Dragon lying on the mountain: his heavenly bolt of thunder Tvastar fashioned. Like lowing kine in rapid flow descending the waters glided downward to the ocean [...]
> When Indra, thou hadst slain the dragon's firstborn, and overcome the charms of the enchanters, then giving life to Sun and Dawn and Heaven, thou foundest not one foe to stand against thee.[12]

You will recall that for the Polynesians cows symbolised the shining clouds that accompany the sun, Rongo, still weak, but growing slowly. So we find they exist only during the month-long polar day.

According to Tilak, the cows do indeed symbolise the months of the polar day. Thus the *dashgvas*, 10 cows, and the *navagvas*, nine cows, are the main families of the Angiras.

> ...the number of the sun's horses is said to be not only seven (*Rig-Veda*, I, 50, 8), but also ten in IX, 63, 9; and if the first be taken to represent seven months, the other must be understood to stand for ten months as well.[13]

---

11   G. Dumézil, *Les dieux souverains indo-européens*, Gallimard, Paris, 1977, p. 66.

12   *Rig Veda, op. cit.*, I, 32, 1-2, 4.

13   L. B. G. Tilak, *op. cit.*, p. 159.

The missing months are those of the polar darkness. Varying with the distance from the pole, a greater or lesser number must be subtracted from the total of 12. The cows that are still there when the light returns are the months in the year when the sun shows itself.

Thus Indra is praised for having slain the demons, defeated darkness with light, and for having found cows, the dawn and the sun.

Subsequently, two months of dense night are subtracted from the annual tally and this is the case until the foundation of Rome, with Numa's reform, in the 8th century BC, December being until then the tenth and last month of the year. The Romans later made up the year with January, dedicated to Janus, and February, devoted to the dead.

There are many texts that praise the thawing of the ice and many, too, which proclaim the annual death of the dragon hidden in its depths.

The isle of the blessed

In *La révolte contre le monde moderne*, Julius Evola quotes two passages from the *Rig Veda*, in which King Yima, the child of the Sun, is he "Who travelled to the lofty heights above us, who searches out and shows the path to many."[14] He is the one who has "come through the air's wide ocean."[15] In fact, he managed to cross the primeval ocean.

Evola mentions another aspect of the Hindu tradition: the symbolic habitat of the blessed and the land of the living, an island where Narayâna reigns, a lord of fire and splendour.

Here, as in other civilisations, we find a reference to a lofty mountain, Mount Meru. This mountain, covered with reflective ice, benefits more than the plains from the sun's low rays. It reflects them even when the sun itself disappears from sight and sinks just below the horizon. Situated on the original island, it, too, makes us think of Antarctica.

---

14 *Rig Veda, op. cit.*, X, 14, 1.

15 *Ibid.*, X, 10, 1.

1.9 Mesopotamia

It would be quite wrong to leave Mesopotamia, the cradle of different civilisations, out of our investigation into the southern continent and its vanished inhabitants. The Sumerians appeared there mysteriously, bringing with them an astonishing and refined culture, altogether foreign and unprecedented in these regions of western Asia.

Where did this civilising people come from? Did it cross the primeval ocean referred to in the historical texts? Did it originate in the continent of Dilmun, recognisable from its high mountains and its vast forests?

The influences of a people that came from afar

Art and architecture, as well as the cultural centres discovered on archaeological sites between the Tigris and Euphrates, reveal the invasion of a gifted and advanced people. The great cultural development that happened in this region was as sudden as it was prodigious.[1]

The objects that have been discovered are decorated with figurative and nonfigurative themes, stylised with elegance, sobriety, life and movement. No scenes of combat are to be found on them. There are innumerable representations of ships, with great wooden vessels, totems bearing solar or lunar discs, decks and sails, and round anchors. The pots show schematically rectangular hulls. Stems and sternposts are symmetrical, oars are shown vertically. These oars have been mistakenly interpreted as combs or clouds of rain. Even if it is difficult to believe that an entire people crossed the ocean,[2] we can only deduce that sailors disembarked here.

These foreigners were hunters, herdsmen, farmers, artists and builders. Their clothing was designed to protect them from the cold of their region of origin: they wore robes and woollen bonnets, and skirts fringed with layers of feathers. The small 'bespectacled' figures showed serious, pious faces. Their enormous eyes with their dilated pupils evoke the darkness of night.

---

1   H. Frankfort, *Kingship and the Gods*, The University Press of Chicago, Chicago, 1948.

2   *Ibid.*

The Anunnaki are undoubtedly this civilising people that suddenly arrived in Mesopotamia:

> *The Anunnaki, the great gods,*
> *In your midst have taken up their dwelling place,*
> *In your large groves they consume (their) food.*
> *O house of Sumer, may your stables be many, may your cows multiply,*
> *May your sheepfold be many, may your sheep be myriad [...]*
> *May the Anunnaki decree the fates in your midst.*[3]

On their continent of origin, these gods lived without bread for nourishment or garments to clothe themselves. They ate plants with their mouths, like sheep, and drank water from ditches. And yet they landed in the "house of Sumer" with a civilisation of astonishing richness and great refinement. Their land of origin no longer afforded them the living conditions they had known hitherto. They must have left it after a climatic change rendered life difficult if not impossible in their homeland.

Enki, the creator of humankind

Enki for the Sumerians, Eâ for the Babylonians and Oannes for the priest Berosus, in his history of Babylon, circa 325 BC: in all these guises, is represented on sculptures wearing a fish-head head-dress that covers his back. This is the classical attire of officiating priests.

According to Berosus:

> At Babylon there was (in these times) a great resort of people [...] [who] lived in a lawless manner like the beasts of the field. In the first year there appeared, from that part of the Erythræan sea which borders upon Babylonia, an animal destitute of reason, by name Oannes, whose whole body [...] was that of a fish; that under the fish's head he had another

---

3   Extract from the poem, *Enki and the World Order*, cited in S. N. Kramer, *History begins at Sumer*, Thames and Hudson, London, 1958, p. 145.

Figure 16. *Sumerian sculpture (circa 2750–2650 BC) representing a man praying and a woman holding goblets, from Tell Asmar, Iraq.*

head, with feet also below, similar to those of a man, subjoined to the fish's tail [...].

This Being was accustomed to pass the day among men; but took no food at that season; and he gave them an insight into letters and sciences, and arts of every kind. He taught them to construct cities, to found temples, to compile laws, and explained to them the principles of geometrical knowledge. He made them distinguish the seeds of the earth, and shewed them how to collect the fruits; in short, he instructed them in every thing which could tend to soften manners and humanize their lives. From that time, nothing material has been added by way of improvement to his instructions. And when the sun had set, this Being Oannes, retired again into the sea.[4]

This is probably a sailor, wearing a seal-skin to protect against the cold.

The arrival of boats from the southern continent is designated by an expression that recurs again and again: "Royalty came down from the sky," i.e., from the celestial mountain, Kur.

Kur, the original mountain

Seven ancients (*apqalû*) had come down from the sky. They had gone on to found several of the great cities in Sumerian history: Ur, Nippur, Eridu, Kullab, Kesh, Lagash and Shuruppak. Sanctuaries were also constructed – ziggurats, in the image of Mount Kur.

To Ur, the shrine, he came,
Enki, King of the abyss, decrees the fate [...]
Dais of abundance of the land, [...] green like the mountain,
[...] May your perfected divine laws be well directed,
The great mountain, Enlil, in heaven and earth has uttered your exalted name;

---

4   Berosus, according to Alexander Polyhistor, from I. P. Corey, *Ancient Fragments*, William Pickering, London, 1832.

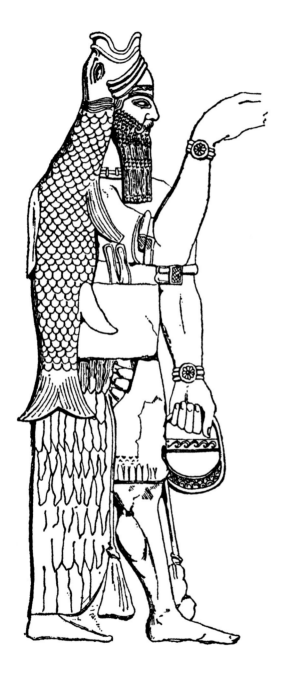

Figure 17. *The god Enki / Eâ, on an Assyrian bas-relief from the palace at Nimrud.*

City whose fates have been decreed by Enki,
Shrine Ur, may your rise heaven high.[5]

In Mesopotamia, at Eridu, the present Tell Abu Sharaïn, a cemetery was discovered consisting of 1,000 or so tombs facing south-east, as well as a two-storey ziggurat, 24m high.

These religious buildings, built up in stacked platforms of decreasing size are numerous in Mesopotamia. Among the most notable is the ziggurat of Uruk, modern-day Warka, which is 56m by 50m and surrounded by 800 circular towers, over an extent of some 10km. That of Ur measures 43m by 65m and that of Kish, 90m by 50m.

These ziggurats are of the same family as the Saqqarah pyramid of the 3rd Dynasty in Egypt, the Mexican *teocallis*, the Peruvian *wakas*, or the Polynesian *marae*. All these buildings are in the image of Mount Kur (or Ekur) on the original continent.

Nippur – the shrine where dwells the father, the "great mountain",
The dais of plenty, the Ekur which rise…
The high mountain, the pure place…
Its prince, the "great mountain", Father Enlil,
Has established his seat on the dais of the Ekur, lofty shrine [...].
Enlil, the worthy shepherd, ever on the move [...].
Enlil, whose command is far-reaching, whose word is holy,
The lord whose pronouncement is unchangeable, who forever decrees
destinies,
Whose lifted eye scans the lands,
Whose lifted light searches the heart of all the lands,
Enlil who sits broadly on the white dais, on the lofty dais,
Who perfects the decrees of power, lordship, and princeship,
The earth-gods bow down in fear before him,
The heaven-gods humble themselves before him [...].

---

5   Extract from the poem, *Enki and the World Order*, cited in S. N. Kramer, *op. cit.*, p. 146.

Ekur, the lapis-lazuli house, the lofty dwelling-place, awe-inspiring,
Its awe and dread are next to heaven,
Its shadow is spread over all the lands
Its loftiness reaches heaven's heart,
All the lords and princes conduct thither their holy gifts, offerings,
Utter there prayer, supplication, and petition.[6]

Kur is a sacred place because it was there that the divine laws were given to the Father, Enlil. The lofty mountain has become the 'heart' of the sky, the axis of the world, passing through the zenith. Enlil, who is also the sun, turns in the sky above the horizon and reigns over terrorised gods.

The sun's descent into the underworld

The sun's disappearance is described in the symbolic form of the descent of the solar goddess to the underworld. This movement corresponds to the total disappearance of the sun around the winter solstice, in regions close to the South Pole. The same phenomenon recurs each year and is followed by a long period of daylight in the course of which the sun not only resurfaces, but starts to turn in the sky without setting.

The memory of this happening, experienced by the ancestors in their land of origin, was to remain engraved in the scriptures.

The Mesopotamians called the sun Enlil or Ninlil, or else Inanna or Ishtar. The misadventure experienced by Inanna speaks volumes on several points.

From the "great above" she set her mind toward the "great below", […]
Inanna abandoned heaven, abandoned earth,
To the nether world she descended, […].
The seven divine laws she fastened at the side,
Gathered all the divine laws, placed them in her hand,
All the laws she set up at her waiting foot,

6   S. N. Kramer, *op. cit.*, pp. 143-4. Extract from a hymn to Enlil.

The shugurra, *the crown of the plain, she put on her head,*
Locks of hair she fixed upon her forehead,
The measuring rod and line of lapis lazuli she gripped in her hand,
Small lapis lazuli stones she tied about her neck,
Twin nunuz-*stones she fastened to her breast,*
A gold ring she gripped in her hand,
The breast plate "Come, man, come" she bound about her breast,
With the pala-*garment of ladyship she covered her body,*
The ointment "Let him come, let him come" she daubed on her eyes.
Inanna walked toward the nether world [...].[7]

All these precious attributes symbolise the power and brilliance of the sun before its descent into the underworld.

When Inanna arrived at the palace, the lapis-lazuli mountain,
At the door of the nether world she acted boldly,
In the palace of the nether world she spoke boldly,
"Open the house, gatekeeper, open the house,
Open the house, Neti, open the house, all alone I would enter."
Neti, the chief gatekeeper of the nether world,
Answers the pure Inanna:
"Who, pray, are you?"
"I am the queen of heaven, the place where the sun rises."
"If you are the queen of heaven, the place where the sun rises,
Why, pray, have you come to the land of no return?
On the road whose traveler returns not, how has your heart led you?"[8]

As one might expect, the land from which man was driven out because of its polar night which made vegetation and life impossible, and to which no one could go back, became the land to which the souls of the dead returned.

7   S. N. Kramer, *op. cit.*, p. 216.
8   S. N. Kramer, *op. cit.*, p. 218.

To the pure Inanna he says:
"Come, Inanna, enter."
Upon her entering,
The shugurra, *"the crown of the plain" of her head, was removed.*
"What, pray, is this?"
"Be silent, Inanna, the laws of the nether world are perfect,
O Inanna, do not deprecate the rites of the nether world."
Upon her entering the second gate,
The measuring rod and line of lapis lazuli was removed.
"What, pray, is this?"
"Be silent, Inanna, the laws of the nether world are perfect,
O Inanna, do not deprecate the rites of the nether world." [9]

The story incessantly takes up the same theme for the following gates.

The small lapis-lazuli stones of her neck were removed [...]
The twin nunuz-*stones of her breast were removed [...]*
The gold ring of her hand was removed [...]
The breast plate "Come, man, come" was removed [...]
Upon her entering the seventh gate,
The pala-*garment of ladyship of her body was removed.*
Bowed low, she was brought naked before her [Ereshkigal]. [10]

The dazzle, the colours of the sky and of the mountains with their icy glow, tinted by the gleam of the snow, have disappeared with the departure of the sun. The solar disc has inexorably slipped beneath the horizon as it enters into the realm of darkness. Inanna seems to have fallen into a trap where she has found herself to be powerless and absolutely vulnerable. She has allowed herself to be well and truly manipulated by Neti, who has taken away her royal attributes and her clothes one by one, so that eventually she is totally naked.

9   S. N. Kramer, *op. cit.*, p. 219.

10 *Ibid.*

We reach the centre of the polar night. The solar goddess is at the lowest point in her course beneath the horizon: she is naked and without radiance. The innumerable representations of Inanna as a naked goddess were to experience an incredible spread from the Near East to Europe. They circulated in the form of amulets, statuettes, engravings, paintings, or menhir-statues. Small marks around her neck and her wrists show where her lost jewels had once been.

The unhappy fate of the Anunnaki

Demons persecute Inanna as well as her companions and protégés, the Anunnaki gods. These demons are cold, darkness, hunger, illness and distress. The Anunnaki call on the solar goddess and describe to her the miseries and the sufferings they have undergone because of her disappearance:

> *Inanna is about to ascend from the nether world,*
> *The Anunnaki seized her (saying):*
> *"Who of those who have descended to the nether world*
> *ever ascends unharmed from the nether world?*
> *[…] They who accompanied her,*
> *They who accompanied Inanna,*
> *Were beings who know not food, who know not water*
> *Eat not sprinkled flour,*
> *Drink not libated water,*
> *Take away the wife from the man's lap,*
> *Take away the child from the nursemaid's breast.*[11]

The Anunnaki have come to experience the depths of the night of the underworld, stripped of everything, of family and food. No more family life or conjugal life: all that remains is the basic instinct for survival. They were without any hope of being reborn to the light of the sun.

11   S. N. Kramer, *op. cit.,* p. 221-2.

The sun's return

Inanna finally rises up from the underworld. All her resplendent, glowing attributes are returned to her. Her adornments, her jewels, her colours and the gleam with which the sun decked the icy mountain, the snow-covered plain and the lofty clouds are restored to nature – a nature full of magnificence that had been dispossessed of these, its belongings. On her return to the sky, the Sun changes name: Inanna or Ishtar becomes the god Inti. The goddess of the underworld becomes the god Nergal and the lunar god Dumuzi becomes the goddess Sin.

The style in which the cataclysm is described is that of ritual lamentations. The passages are repetitive and interminable and in this respect they are in the image of a darkness followed by a dawn which in its turn is never-ending, the dawn of an endless day.

In the Babylonian version of the descent to the underworld, Inanna is Ishtar, who reigns in the sky in joy and glory, at least during the polar day. Suddenly:

> Towards the land of no return, the goddess Ishtar,
> Daughter of Sin, turns her ear.
> Towards the house of Shadows, the abode of Nergal,
> Towards the house which he who enters does not leave,
> Towards the road with a departure but no return,
> Towards the house where those who enter lack light,
> Towards this place whose inhabitants have only dust for food, and mud for nourishment,
> Where they do not see the sun but live in shadows,
> Where they are clothed like a bird in a garment of wings…[12]

The description is clear: cold obliged the Anunnaki to make clothes from feathers, so that they seemed to have wings, just like birds.

In Mesopotamia, the gods continued to be represented in this way, with

---

12   G. Contenau, *Le déluge babylonien*, Payot, Paris, 1952, pp. 219-20.

one or two pairs of wings. The costumes of the gods are clearly drawn or sculptured with superimposed rows of horizontal feathers, each row covering that beneath it in such a way as to ensure that the result is waterproof, as well as warm.

Ishtar is brought before the queen of the underworld, Ereshkigal. In this now wretched country, "one eats dirt ... in place of food," the wife is "taken away" from her husband, and children from their parents. Like Inanna, Ishtar crosses through seven gates in succession. Each time, the Chief Porter strips an item of clothing off her, and she ends up naked.

> *As soon as the goddess Ishtar went down*
> *Into the land from which there is no return,*
> *And she saw Ereshkigal, her presence made her lose her mind.*
> *Ishtar, without thinking, throws herself at her.*
> *Ereshkigal speaks, addressing Namtar her attendant,*
> *Giving her this order: "Go! Namtar! Lock her up in my Palace!*
> *Release the sixty diseases and set them against Ishtar!" [...]*
> *Since the goddess Ishtar has been in the Land from which there is no return,*
> *The bull no longer mates with the cow, the donkey no longer mates with the she-ass,*
> *The boy in the street no longer approaches the girl,*
> *The boy sleeps in his room, the girl sleeps by his side.*[13]

Contenau, in his book *Le déluge babylonien*, and Kramer in *History begins at Sumer*, demonstrated how very varied the accounts of this event are, cropping up as they do throughout Mesopotamian literature.

13   G. Contenau, *op. cit.*, pp. 219-20.

The primeval chaos

The belief according to which the universe emerges from a primeval ocean is one of the most widely spread across the whole earth, among the most diverse peoples and in every age.

In the Mesopotamian creation epic, the primordial pair, the god Apsu (fresh water) and the goddess Tiamat (salt water), are mixed together in the primeval chaos. Their mingled waters form the first element – the infinite primeval ocean.

Apsu is usually translated as 'fresh water'. The word is also written *absû*, which gives us our word 'abyss'. It in no way designates rivers, streams or lakes. This fresh water is specific to the ancestral land.

Stories tell of the spell cast on it which eventually destroy it. Journeys are prevented, or made difficult, by Apsu, which becomes the 'waters of death', to be confronted with rods which are irretrievable if they fall in.

It seems, given all this, that Apsu represents a water in which ice is starting to form. As for Tiamat, it relates to the bloated dragon which personifies the saltwater ocean. Tiamat is specific to the ancestral land, and it is necessary to struggle against it: it seems to designate the southern seas that are subject to storms, and very dangerous.

Lahmu (mud) and Lahamu (silt) appear and are named. Growing through the ages, they cover more and more. In reality, this is a reference to snow. At the extremities of the vast liquid expanse, all around the horizon, a deposit of mud slowly rose, forming a great double circle, constituting Kishar, the terrestrial horizon, and Anshar, the celestial horizon.

This mud which appears in the land of the gods, and starts to grow, to increase year by year, reminds one of the Polynesian myths: it is snow, so difficult to describe after centuries in Mesopotamia, but having left a memory of itself nonetheless.

In a later version of the primordial epic, a time of darkness is described, populated by hideous monsters. The *Enuma elish*, a Babylonian creation myth from the second millennium BC, describes them invading the coasts and terrorising the population:

They were furious; they devised mischief without resting night and day.
They prepared for battle, fuming and raging;
They joined their forces and made war,
Ummu-Hubur [Tiamat] who formed all things,
Made in addition weapons invincible; she spawned monster-serpents,
Sharp of tooth, and merciless of fang;
With poison, instead of blood, she filled their bodies.
Fierce monster-vipers she clothed with terror,
With splendor she decked them, she made them of lofty stature.
Whoever beheld them, terror overcame him,
Their bodies reared up and none could withstand their attack.[14]

Here we can recognise a reference to the Polynesian *mokos*. These are sea lions, animals with tusks, crawling on their stomachs like snakes and able to raise their heads but not to turn them…

The sight of active volcanoes led to them being imagined as having the power to spit flames, something that continued to be represented through the image of a dragon.

The *Epic of Gilgamesh*

The *Epic of Gilgamesh* dates from the second millenium BC. It is the most famous of the Mesopotamian legends and tells us a great deal about the nature of the country that our hero visits twice after long ocean crossings. During his wanderings, Gilgamesh discovers places and people that, symbolically, indicate the presence of the southern continent. Gilgamesh was the king of Uruk, one of the holy cities in Mesopotamia, situated not far from the mouth of the Euphrates.

14   *Enuma elish* (trans. L. W. King), from *The Seven Tablets of Creation*, vol. 1, Luzac, London, 1902.

The wild friend

In Uruk, Gilgamesh gathers 50 companions who no longer have house or family and are ready to follow him to the ends of the earth, wherever he goes and whatever he does.

When Gilgamesh meets the man who is to become his best friend, Enkidu, the latter is living as a wild man, dressed like the animals he lives among. "Matted hair was all over his body, like the skins of the cattle." He is "innocent of mankind," living amongst the wild animals of the plain.[15]

Enkidu is representative of the gods who have just disembarked from Dilmun, the original continent. "Born in the mountains", he is covered with a fur-lined coat and "roams the steppe".[16] In fact, we are to understand that he makes great sea journeys.

Countless versions and additions to the original Sumerian text have rapidly transformed marine terms into terrestrial terms: the steppe replaces the sea with the same desert-like intensity; the storms and the difficulties of the journey are transformed into mountains that need to be crossed.

Gilgamesh and Enkidu set off on an expedition to find the wood necessary to build Uruk. They have to cross seven mountains before reaching the land of the living.

The big sleep

The scene of their arrival is the foot of a huge mountain which has all the appearances of Kur. It is a sacred mountain on which Gilgamesh and Enkidu offer sacrifices of "fine-meal". To do this, they dig a well for Shamash, the Sun. They just have time to jump into it to avoid the storm. Enkidu places Gilgamesh within the shelter of an enchanted circle, and "sleep which falls upon mankind fell upon Gilgamesh."

During this time, a squall passes over them, heads off and then returns. Outside, the sky is raging.

15 R. Temple, *He Who Saw Everything: a verse version of the Epic of Gilgamesh*, Rider, London, 1991.

16 *Ibid.*

After travelling, after roaming the steppe,
Shall I merely lay my head
Down into the earth's guts?
And then sleep –
Sleep forever?
No! Let me see the Sun!
See the Sun and be sated with light!
If there is light enough,
Then the darkness shrinks away
May the light of Shamash the Sun
Be seen even by he who is dead! [17]

The sun has plunged below the horizon: Utu, the Sun, has sunk down into the bosom of his mother Ningal. Once the sun has hidden itself, the climate in this region forces Gilgamesh to cover himself in his mantle while his teeth chatter.

The land of the living, in the region where Gilgamesh lands, does not seem to be close enough to the South Pole to experience a real, continuous polar night. But it must have been well within the polar circle.

They saw also the Cedar Mountain, where lived the gods
And Irnini, Goddess of Love, holy Inanna had her throne seat
The cedar raised aloft its great luxuriant growth:
What cool shade, what delight! […]
And it rained the presage of death on them
Like a light rain in a mist
But Shamash raised up great winds against Humbaba:
The South Wind, the North Wind,
The East Wind, the West Wind,
The Blowing Wind,
The Squally Wind,

17 R. Temple, *op. cit.*

The Shaparziqqu Wind,
The Evil Storm,
The Sihurra Wind,
The Wind of Frost,
The Storm,
The Thunder Storm –
13 winds he raised against him
And Humbaba's face was darkened.
He cannot push forwards,
He cannot run backwards.[18]

The Sun – here, Shamash – combats Humbaba, the guardian of the forest. The latter personifies the terrible southern storms heavy both with snow and volcanic ash.

Humbaba, apparently victorious, suggests to Gilgamesh that they take myrtle shrubs from the forest, as well as all the wood destined to embellish the city of Uruk.

The tyrannical hero, following his logic – that of killing all the enemies of humankind – refuses these presents and kills Humbaba.

Then Humbaba himself uprooted for Gilgamesh
The first of his trees.
The sons of the city who had come
Come with Gilgamesh from Uruk
Cut down the tree's crown, bundled it,
Lay it at the foot of the mountain.[19]

"The high-grown cedar's tip would have penetrated to heaven."[20] In it, we can recognise the axis of the world, vertical at the pole.

18   R. Temple, *op. cit.*

19   *Ibid.*

20   *Ibid.*

Gilgamesh refuses the advances of Ishtar, the solar goddess who reigns in the sky for half the year, and descends into the underworld for the other half, her burning fire losing all its gleam, and the day star remaining buried under the snow and the ice, stripped of all its vestments during the polar night.

Gilgamesh rejects this mortal aspect and hurls at Ishtar these explicit words in which we find two characteristics of the country in thrall to the long night: the icy cold and the southern storms:

> Like a pan full of burning coals which go out
> You are but a back door which does not stay shut
> But flies open in the raging wind.[21]

The return journey to Gilgamesh's own country takes place amid the snivellings of Enkidu, who betrays his fear so as to bring out the superior courage of the hero voyager:

> Oh my master, journey you to the 'land', I will journey to the city.
> I will tell your mother of your glory, let her shout,
> I will tell her of your ensuing death, let her shed bitter tears.
> For me another will not die, the loaded boat will not sink,
> The three-ply cloth folded will not be cut.[22]

The ship that returns to Uruk must confront the southern storms that have torn the sails: it needs to be three times as thick.

Enkidu "cast down in sorrow, drifts into a sad and lonely sleep." In a dream, he sees a "young man, whose face was dark."

> He transformed me into a double of his body
> So that my arms were now clad in feathers like those of a bird.
> Fixing his gaze on me, he led me to the House of Darkness

21 R. Temple, *op. cit.*

22 S. N. Kramer, *op. cit.*, p. 236.

There where Irkalla lives, He, the God of the Dead.
No one who enters that house comes forth again.
It is the one-way road from which there is no return;
Those residing there are bereft of the light for ever,
Where dust is their food and mud their sustenance.
They are dressed as birds, with garments of wing feathers.
They see no light but crouch in darkness.[23]

This dream of Enkidu's enables the Sumerian bard, the unknown author of the astonishing *Epic of Gilgamesh*, to evoke the wretched life of the gods of Dilmun, the original continent. As with those of the Polynesians, the feather garments were at once light, warm and impermeable. They were ideal for an icy region but fragile and difficult to make. Latterly, this costume was made of wool, but fashioned in such a way as to imitate the successive rows of feathers arranged in bands.

Enkidu finally dies and all must lament his passing. Gilgamesh knows that the sufferings endured on the frozen continent have finally overwhelmed his friend.

Gilgamesh's second journey to Dilmun

Gilgamesh's second expedition to the original land is undertaken with the aim of finding the secret of eternal life. With this in mind, he wishes to meet his ancestor Ziusudra, or Uta-napisti, an inhabitant who lives on in Dilmun, eternally, as befits him.

In Sumerian, Zi-ud-sudra means 'Life-of-prolonged-days'. This name was translated almost literally into Akkadian by Um-napishti or Uta-napisti: 'Day-of-prolonged-life'.

Day and night are so prolonged in the region of the pole that they constitute a whole year. So it seems that it is life, and not the day, which is prolonged. This slippage in meaning was universal as well as natural, since man has always coveted the secret that would prevent him from growing old.

---

23   R. Temple, *op. cit.*

To arrive in Dilmun, Gilgamesh crosses the primordial sea, the waters of death. When he arrives before the man who survived the Flood and is protected by the gods, Gilgamesh is a frightening sight. His hair and his beard are shaggy and he is covered with animal skins. He reaches Mount Mashu at the moment when the sun started its nocturnal journey, beneath the horizon when the polar night sets in.

Gilgamesh meets the guardians of the great gate, the Scorpion Men. Usually, a mere glance from one of these guardians is fatal, but they allow Gilgamesh to live. He announces:

"I have come in search of life,
To see Ziusudra, my forefather –
He who survived the Flood
And joined the Assembly of the Gods."[24]

The reply comes:

"There never was a mortal, Gilgamesh,
Never one who could do that.
No one has travelled the mountain's path.
For twelve double-hours its bowels…
Dense is the darkness and there is no light."[25]

In spite of everything, Gilgamesh plunges into the darkness:

He travelled from the east to west
Along the road of the Sun.
When he had gone one double-hour
Dense was the darkness and there was no light.
This permitted him no sight of its front or his rear […]

24 R. Temple, *op. cit.*

25 *Ibid.*

When he had gone three double-hours
Dense was the darkness and there was no light.
This permitted him no sight of its front or his rear.[26]

The story continues, with the same insistent repetitions, with an occasional slight variant:

When he had gone nine double-hours, he felt the morning breeze.
It was fanning his face [...]
When he had gone ten double hours
He knows the moment of rising is near.
When he had gone eleven double hours
He rose just before the Sun
When he had gone twelve double hours
Day had grown bright.[27]

The repetitive style, expressing the sheer length of eternity, is perfectly well adapted to the interminable wait experienced in the polar night. The Polynesian poem of creation, in the Hawaiian *Kumulipo*, displays exactly the same characteristics: 'It is night', instead of 'there is no more light'; and, right at the end, 'it is day', instead of 'it is light'.

And this dawn so long awaited and expected is quite magical, with the subtle nuances of precious stone colouring the snow, the ice and the clouds.

Gilgamesh comes across "wondrous trees, with fruit of carnelian and lapis lazuli."[28] The hues of these two stones are very similar to those of ice. They display sumptuous colours, characteristic of polar regions.

The beauty of the polar landscapes is not due only to the reflections of ice and snow, but also to the transparency of the air. The latter brings out the infinite nuances of the sky and the lofty clouds. Expeditions to the South

26   R. Temple, *op. cit.*

27   *Ibid.*

28   *Ibid.*

Pole have often produced enthusiastic descriptions. One Mesopotamian text says that Gilgamesh "went back and forth among these marvels" which looked like agate, obsidian, and turquoise, decorating "this garden of cedars."

> *Upon seeing the bejewelled shrubs, he approaches them*
> *The carnelian bears its fruit*
> *And hung it is with goodly vines,*
> *The lapis lazuli bears leaves*
> *Lush fruit also hangs from it*
> *It is fine to the eye.* [29]

Utanapisti offers the plant of eternity to Gilgamesh

Utanapisti is revolted by Gilgamesh's stench, his mop of hair and his animal skin. After giving him some encouragement, he asks the boatman Ursanabi to bring the traveller out of the ice and allow him to set sail. They have already left when Utanapisti's wife turns to her husband and asks him to grant Gilgamesh a favour:

> *"Gilgamesh has come hither,*
> *He has wearied himself,*
> *He has exerted himself,*
> *What gift will you make him*
> *That he may return to his land?"* [30]

Utanapisti offers Gilgamesh the mysterious plant for which Gilgamesh had undertaken this long voyage. This plant is "a secret of the gods." It is specific to the polar circle where people are annually plunged into darkest night: they will have to arm themselves with big stones, like a diver, to pull this prickly reed from the bottom of the sea.

29 R. Temple, *op. cit.*

30 *Ibid.*

125

Figure 18. *A winged genie with the tree of life represented on a bas-relief in alabaster from Nimrud, Assyria (circa 883–859 BC).*

Gilgamesh pulls out "the plant that is different from all others. By its means a man can lay hold of the breath of life." The hero intends to take it back home to Uruk with him.

On the orders of Utanapisti, Ursanabi the boatman helps Gilgamesh to cross the waters of death. The latter, on his way, encounters stone statues and breaks them into pieces, for no apparent reason. As with the Polynesian Ru, what in fact is happening is that he is breaking up blocks of ice.

Before climbing aboard Ursanabi's boat, Gilgamesh has to cut the poles that will serve as gaffs, or oars, enabling him to cross the waters of death on the other side of the ocean. During the crossing, when one gaff has been worn down by use, Gilgamesh abandons it and takes up another, so as not to have any contact with the deadly waters.

The description of the work which consists of pushing away the floating ice with gaffs is most striking. If the gaffs fall into the water, you must not try to fish them out in case your arms or hands freeze. After he has travelled 500km, a snake steals his plant from him, "sloughing its skin" as it does so. Eternal life cannot exist far from the pole. At the pole, you have to go under the earth like a snake during the long polar night, after slipping on the 'skin' which protects you from the icy cold.

On his return to Uruk, Gilgamesh, dispossessed of immortality, finds his old, normal conditions of life again. He washes, sheds his savage attire and becomes a happy, civilised human being, worthy of leaving his name to posterity.

1.10 The Bible

The Bible is a valuable source of information, since the Hebrews constituted, right from the start, a separate, chosen people, which has always endeavoured, with rare obstinacy, to resist outside and foreign influences. We can thus anticipate that the Scriptures will in their turn be free of outside influences.

Genesis

Everything begins as a consequence of a catastrophe in which we again find the end of a happy, paradisical period in Eden, with three universal characteristics: the darkness of the polar night, the ocean flooding the primeval earth, the return of the sun and the moon that had fallen into non-being, with the separation of heaven and earth, thus of light and darkness.

> *In the beginning God created the heaven and the earth. And the earth was without form, and void; and darkness was upon the face of the deep. And the Spirit of God moved upon the face of the deep [...] And God made the firmament, and divided the waters which were under the firmament [...] And God said [...] let the dry land appear [...] And God said, Let there be lights in the firmament of the heaven to divide the day from the night [...] and to divide the light from the darkness. [...] And God created great whales [...].*

Eden is not described in Genesis, as the story is centred on the creation insofar as it is the responsibility of Yahweh alone. And in Eden, it is essentially humankind which was created, i.e., Adam and Eve.

Innumerable allusions were made to the "holy hill," the "high hill," where the people of Israel are summoned to climb up and serve God.

---

1   Gen. 1: 1-21.

128

The original earth, Eden

Adam and Eve are the first human beings on earth. They were created by Yahweh and live in a garden where the trees produce fine fruit. Their existence is happy, they lack nothing and are in a state of innocence, in perfect intimacy with God.

Two trees grow in Eden: the tree of life and the tree of good and evil. The tree of life is well known in Mesopotamia. It grants a relative eternity to those who live on the original continent. Driven out of Eden, Adam and Eve can no longer eat of its fruits. The tree of good and evil, or the 'tree of the knowledge of good and evil', is however found nowhere apart from the Biblical story of Genesis.

Despite God's command, Adam and his helpmeet taste of its fruit and lose their state of grace. God sends them away for having eaten this mysterious forbidden fruit. The Old Testament is the only text of antiquity in which this irreversible punishment is mentioned. The passage devoted to Eden is very short, even if it has provoked much ink to flow subsequently!

In the Bible, Eden is a real country, where man and woman live in a primitive state of happiness.

Thou sealest up the sum, full of wisdom, and perfect in beauty.
Thou hast been in Eden the garden of God; every precious stone was thy covering, the sardius, topaz, and the diamond, the beryl, the onyx, and the jasper, the sapphire, the emerald, and the carbuncle, and gold: the workmanship of thy tabrets and of thy pipes was prepared in thee in the day that thou wast created.
Thou art the anointed cherub that covereth; and I have set thee so: thou wast upon the Holy Mountain of God; thou hast walked up and down in the midst of the stones of fire.
Thou wast perfect in thy ways from the day that thou wast created, till iniquity was found in thee.
By the multitude of thy merchandise they have filled the midst of thee with violence, and thou hast sinned: therefore I will cast thee as profane out of

the mountain of God; and I will destroy thee, O covering cherub, from the midst of the stones of fire.[2]

I covered the deep for him, and I restrained the floods thereof, and the great waters were stayed:[…] and all the trees of Eden […] shall be comforted in the nether parts of the earth.[3]

Ezekiel makes it clear that in Eden:

- the rivers were "restrained" by ice, frozen over;
- the same thing happened to the ocean, the "great waters" being stayed, immobilised;
- the darkness of the polar night "covered the deep";
- the holy mountain, referred to so often, was in Eden;
- the earth was erupting, it was necessary to walk up and down "in the midst of the stones of fire," burning rock or flowing lava;
- the trees were "comforted in the nether parts of the earth," and several of the numerous children of Adam and Eve likewise: for that, there must have been chaos: a violent geological cataclysm.

This state of happiness proper to Eden, the active volcanoes and the precious stones are recurrent motifs in Mesopotamian literature. Cornelian, amethyst and lapis lazuli all express the translucent, dazzling and varied gleam of ice.

David refers to Eden and its holy mountain, the eternal mountains as well as the primordial darkness. He glorifies the divine justice of the "land of forgetfulness" (Ps. 88: 12), which cannot fail to remind us of other ancient texts.

---

2   Ezek. 28: 13-18.
3   Ezek. 31: 15-16.

Job

In his wretchedness, Job evokes the long darkness in Eden.

> *Let that day be darkness; let not God regard it from above, neither let the*
> *light shine upon it.*
> *Let darkness and the shadow of death stain it; let a cloud dwell upon it;*
> *let the blackness of the day terrify it.*
> *As for that night, let darkness seize upon it; let it not be joined unto the*
> *days of the year, let it not come into the number of the months.*
> *Lo, let that night be solitary, let no joyful voice come therein.*
> *Let them curse it that curse the day, who are ready to raise up their*
> *mourning.*
> *Let the stars of the twilight thereof be dark; let it look for light, but have*
> *none; neither let it see the dawning of the day.*[4]

This reminds us of the way days are reckoned in India, where several months are left out, since they correspond to the polar night. So Job is clearly speaking of this particular night, specific to the original continent.

Dante situates Eden at the South Pole

Maps of the Middle Ages are in general still oriented with the east and Jerusalem at the top, which places north on the left. North is sometimes known archaically as 'septentrion' because of the seven stars in the Great Bear and the Little Bear, which remain visible as they turn round the celestial North Pole. The south, or *meridies*, is thus on the right, with another circumpolar constellation constituted by the four stars forming the Southern Cross.

Dante Alighieri, the famous Florentine poet of the 13th century, whose *Divine Comedy* describes hell, purgatory and paradise, is in spirit led through these realms in the company of Virgil, and imagines that he meets there the souls of the damned, those who await heaven, and the saved. He places Adam and Eve in purgatory. In the first canto:

4   Job 3: 4-9.

To course across more kindly waters now
my talent's little vessel lifts her sails,
leaving behind herself a sea so cruel [...].

Then I turned to the right, setting my mind
upon the other pole, and saw four stars
not seen before except by the first people.

Heaven appeared to revel in their flames:
o northern hemisphere, because you were
denied that sight, you are a widower![5]

Here we must point out that the Southern Cross is not visible in the
Northern Hemisphere, at least north of the Tropic of Cancer. Likewise, the
Great and Little Bears cease to be visible in the Southern Hemisphere, at
least from the Tropic of Capricorn.

Then Dante imagines his meeting with Cato of Utica:

The rays of the four holy stars so framed
his face with light that in my sight he seemed
like one who is confronted by the sun.

'Who are you – who, against the hidden river,
were able to escape the eternal prison?'
he said, moving those venerable plumes.

'Who was your guide? What served you both as lantern
when, from the deep night that will always keep
the hellish valley dark, you were set free?

---

5   Dante Alighieri, *Purgatorio* (trans. A. Mandelbaum), Bantam Books, Toronto / New York, 1982, Canto I,
    tercets 1, 8, 9.

The laws of the abyss – have they been broken?
Or has a new, a changed decree in Heaven
let you, though damned, approach my rocky slopes?'

These tercets 13–16 of Canto I emphasise the importance of this Southern Cross, which shone on Adam and Eve, over their heads, near the celestial South Pole. The gleam of these four stars was above all spiritual: they were holy, since the first couple was, in the view of Christians, holy too, before original sin. We find:

- "a sea so cruel": as you would expect of the southern seas that encircle the Antarctic continent;
- "the deep night" of the polar circle;
- the "hidden river" encircling the "eternal prison," the river ocean, Tartarus, which flows through icy wastes;
- the feathers which the inhabitants use to cover themselves and protect themselves from the snow and the cold;
- the "laws of the abyss," the "decree in Heaven," which are normally immutable but are strangely susceptible to change in a short space of time;
- the rocky slopes, finally, remind us that the great southern continent possesses particularly high and steep mountains.

In the 13th century, Dante was perfectly well acquainted – doubtless more than might appear – with the science of his time. It is not surprising that he situates the earthly paradise beyond the seas, in the Southern Hemisphere. Not in proximity to the North Pole, where the constellation of the Great Bear swings, but close to the South Pole, where that constellation was no longer visible and where, not far from the zenith, the four stars of the Southern Cross could be seen.

Saint Brendan

An educated monk of Irish origin, Brendan had in the 6th century founded the Abbey of Clonfert, of the Order of St Benedict. He died there on 16 May 578.

The Fabulous Voyages of Saint Brendan, rejected by the Bollandists from their *Acta Sanctorum*, appear in other collections of texts from that period, less severely expurgated. They are the object of many legends. He "embarked with twenty seven believers, including the future St. Malo," on "a ship of willow covered with carefully greased leather [...] The team first took the route of the tropic [...] In the seventh year [...] they sailed further to the south, for the whole of Lent [...] the route led them into the area of darkness which surrounds the Island of the Saints". When they had crossed it, they found themselves flooded with light, on the shores of the island they had sought for so long. "It was a vast land, scattered with precious stones, covered with autumn fruit and illuminated by a day without end." [6]

---

6   « Les Îles perdues de Saint-Brandan », pp. 120, 122, and « Cités englouties », *Les Dossiers de l'Histoire mystérieux.*

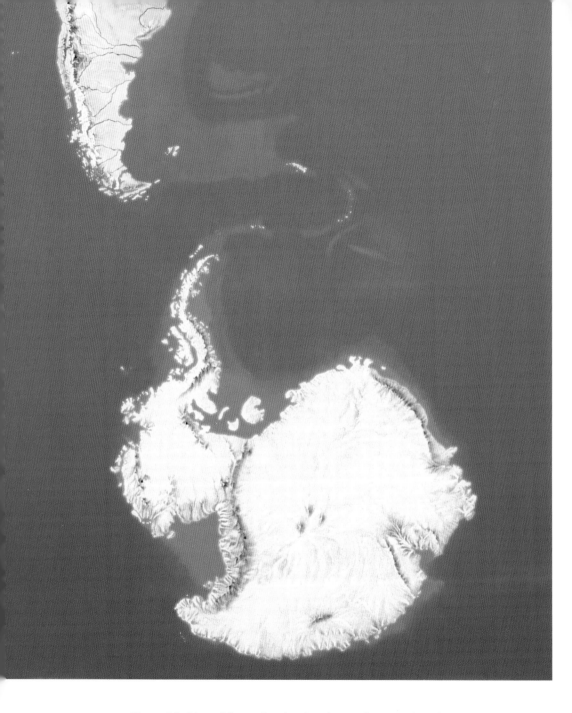

Figure 19. *Map of Antarctica showing the southern continent's proximity to South America.*

Whether we are talking of Polynesia, China, Japan, Egypt, Greece, India or Mesopotamia, the foundation myths of different civilisations share common features that indicate their origin is to be found near one of the poles. This recurrence is enough to suggest a basis in reality.

The only land of any importance in the polar regions is Antarctica. As for the variety of the genetic and cultural stock we find in the great civilisations, it can perhaps be explained by differences that were there from the start on that great continent.

It is time to take a closer look at the particularities of this place, since it seems difficult to believe that life could be feasible there.

After equipping his ships in search of Terra Australis Incognita, the great navigator James Cook finally 'proved' in the 18th century that this legendary continent in the polar region did not exist, and indeed never had existed… It thus disappeared from Buache's map, which was still being used as a reference work, and on which it had been clearly charted.

In 1820, the British naval officer Edward Bransfield sighted the mainland of Antarctica, setting in motion the 'rediscovery' of this vast land. In 1821, an American sealer John Davis finally set foot on the continent. By the 20th century various government-funded explorations had superseded the individual attempts of the previous century. These expeditions have become, up until our own day, a matter of fierce competition between different states which all want a piece of this frozen continent for themselves. Technological developments have allowed scientists to set themselves up in the field, something which could not have been envisaged a few decades before, when death had often been the only tangible discovery of explorers.

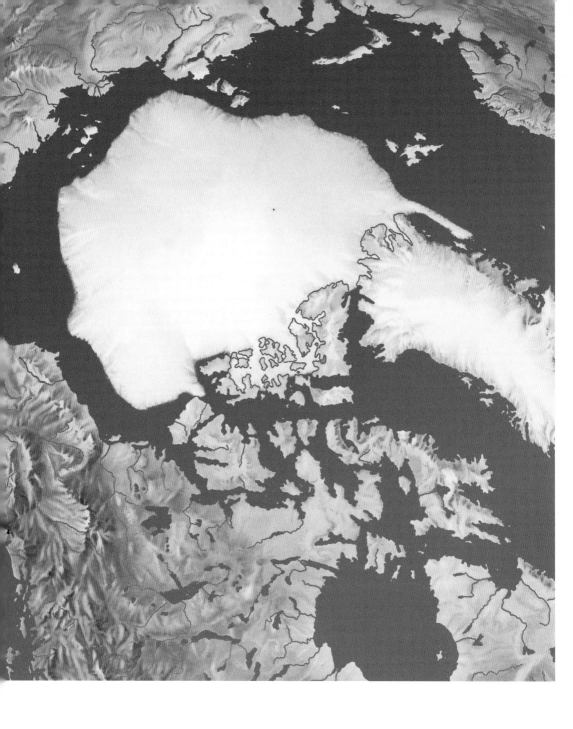

Figure 20. *Map of the Arctic with neighbouring land masses.*

2.1 The poles

The poles of our globe are strangely different, which does not make our attempts at forming a clear and distinct idea of them any easier.

The North Pole is situated on a sea which reaches a depth of 3,000m, and is occupied by an ice floe of varying thickness which is slowly drifting. In addition, this Arctic Ocean is closed off, for thousands of kilometres, by Eurasia, including its extension, the Kamchatka Peninsula, then, after a brief interruption – the Bering Strait – by North America with Alaska and the Canadian archipelagos. On the other hand, this frozen ocean opens onto the North Atlantic. Although navigable only with difficulty, it remains temporarily reachable through the famous North-West Passage off America, and the North-East Passage off Eurasia, these two sea routes being in general open a few weeks every year thanks to powerful icebreakers.

The South Pole is more or less at the centre of the southern continent of Antarctica. Antarctica is itself encircled by a huge mass of water, including as it does the Pacific, Atlantic and Indian Oceans.

The Antarctic extends over approximately 14 million km^2 (whereas Europe covers only ten, and the United States 9.3 million km^2). Stripped of its ice, it would itself rise to a height of almost 600m, according to some estimates. The ice reaches a thickness of up to 4,800m – 1,600m on average. This ice makes it into the highest continent in the world with an altitude of 2,300m, on average, whereas Australia reaches only 340m.

In addition, immense platforms of ice extend out into the water, occupying part of the Ross and Weddell Seas; their thickness varies from a few dozen metres to 400m, floating with the rhythm of the tides.

To this freshwater ice we need to add the ice floe proper, whose surface area varies from summer to winter, from between some four to 25 million km^2. Even today, no satellite photograph makes it possible for us to define the exact outline of the coasts.

However, two to three percent of the land is known to be exposed, either due to warming caused by local volcanic activity or by steep mountainous uplift, as in the Transantarctic Mountains. According to the latest surveys, the highest summit of the Antarctic continent is Mount Vinson with a height of about 4,900m (and not 5,100m as was previously believed).

For convenience, a distinction is drawn between East Antarctica, bigger and older (dating from the Pre-Cambrian shield) and geologically stable, and West Antarctica, more mobile and recent, the highest summit of which is Mount Vinson. These two zones are separated by the Transantarctic Mountains, a mountain range more than 4,000km long, several summits of which reach heights of more than 4,000m.

The record for cold, registered at the Vostok base situated at 3,800m altitude, is – 89.3° C. The violent winds known as the 'katabatic' winds can blow at more than 300 km/hour. As a result of these climatic conditions, that make life nigh impossible, the exploration of the Antarctic requires the most heroic efforts.

Traces of life

It was easy to imagine this frozen continent to be devoid of all trace of life. But this belief proved to be mistaken: its fossils reveal fern-trees, forests and coral. You can even find dinosaurs taken by surprise as they eat their last meal at an altitude of 4,000m.

A brief historical outline of the discoveries will enable us to gain a more precise idea of this continent that remained unknown for so long. In 1911, on the Beardmore Glacier at the foot of Mount Buckley, Scott found a rocky peak emerging from the ice, with strata of carbon that contained fossilised leaves. You can see the imprint of wonderfully well preserved stalks in them, their cell structure clearly visible. In 1914, A. C. Seward, of the British Museum, described these fossils and reached the following conclusion: "By all accounts, Antarctica must have undergone a brutal climate change."

In 1935, geologists on the Byrd expedition brought back from their trip a rich collection of fossils, with the imprint of petrified leaves and branches, from the Weavey Mountains, at a latitude of 86°58' south.

In 1952, Dr Lyman identified species of fern-trees called *glossopteris* that exist in Africa, South America and Australia, as well as a fern-tree of another species, and finally a petrified imprint of what is probably a reptile.

In the Horlick Mountains, at the so-called 'Dirty Diamond Mine', 85° south and 110° west, wood fossils were discovered in 1959, and not just any types of wood: swamp palms, laurels, fig trees, beeches, sequoias, giant ferns, trees with indeciduous leaves…[1]

Frozen fish (*nototheniis*) were discovered on the summit of the Ross Ice Shelf, as well as clams, snails, sponges and coral…[2]

In 1969, on the slopes of Graphite Peak in the heart of the Transantarctic Mountains, the fossilised fragment of a lower jaw bone was found. It belonged to an amphibian from the labyrinthodontes group, one of the first vertebrates ever to live on earth, some 230 million years ago. That same year the trace of a lystrosaurus turned up imprinted in the rocky gangue, a species very common in Africa and India.

In 1994, on the Kirkpatrick Mountains, at 84°20' south and 166°19' east, they unearthed the fossils of two dinosaurs, seven to eight metres long: a carnivorous cryolophosaurus taken by surprise while eating a herbivorous prosauropod, whose bones were found in a jumble.[3]

W. R. Hammer discovered four dinosaurs and 2.5 tonnes of fossils on the Beardmore Glacier, at an altitude of 4,000m and at a distance of 650km from the pole.

A luxuriant vegetation

Despite all these remains, the life that can be observed in these regions these days is concentrated in the marine zones. The present vegetation of Antarctica consists essentially of a lichen that sticks to the rocks, and some 70 species of moss. There are only two root plants that have been noted up until now. One is from the family of Graminaeae (*Deschampsia antarctica*) and the other is a carnation (*Colobanthus crassifollus*). If you ignore the coasts, home to birds and mammals, Antarctic fauna is extremely limited:

1   *National Geographic Magazine*, Oct. 1959.
2   *Ibid.*, Apr. 1963, p. 268.
3   *Ibid.*, Oct. 1994.

insects, protozoa, acari and collembolans are the only representatives of the animal kingdom. The largest of these creatures is no bigger than 5mm.

This circumstance highlights the importance of the fossils discovered by scientists, for these reveal that there was indeed on this continent a luxuriant vegetation and an equally varied fauna. We are led to the conclusion that the Antarctic experienced a period of clement weather, favourable to the development of complex organisms.

How long did it last? More than a few years are necessary for a beech to mature and a dinosaur such as the cryolophosaurus to measure 7 to 8m.

It is difficult these days to imagine the Antarctic without its icecap. After all, the poles bring together all the climatic conditions that favour a permanent freeze. Despite a recent and quite partial melting of the ice, perhaps owing to the phenomenon of global warming, this environment precludes any elaborate biological developments.

In 1773 in the journal of the *HMS Resolution* James Cook himself had no hesitation in stating:

> I had now made the circuit of the Southern Ocean in a high Latitude and traversed it in such a manner as to leave not the least room for the possibility of there being a continent, unless near the pole and out of reach of navigation. [...] should anyone possess the resolution and fortitude to... [push] yet further south than I have done, I shall not envy him the fame of his discovery, but I make bold to declare that the world will derive no benefit from it.

As we know today, on this point at least, the famous navigator was quite simply wrong.

The slow migration of the celestial poles

Various theories have been aired to account for these traces of life, some frankly defying common sense. For example, the theory put forward by Milankovic, a Yugoslav reinforced concrete specialist who explained these significant climatic deviations with the aid of astronomy.

Our planet can be represented as a sphere, the terrestrial geode being close to a somewhat flattened ellipsoid of rotation. To represent the stars of the sky, we use a globe, called a 'celestial sphere'. Its radius is not important, since the distances are measured in angles.

On the celestial globe, the stars are situated according to the terrestrial reference system: the equator for the latitudes, the Greenwich meridian for longitudes.

The earth turns round the sun in a fixed plane among the stars. This is the ecliptic, whose poles are unchanging. The earth's axis of rotation is known not to be perfectly fixed vis-à-vis the stars:

- The celestial North Pole oscillates around a mean position, describing a small ellipse, $9.2°$ half major axis and $7°$ half minor axis, in 18.61 years. This is called nutation.
- The mean position of the celestial North Pole itself describes a small circle of a radius of approx. $23.5°$ around the North Pole of the ecliptic in 25,760 years. This is the conical movement of the axis.

Of course, the co-ordinates of the stars slowly change. But the stellar migrations are so slow that their effect is tiny. Sailors use the celestial poles to check their direction, despite the fact that they vary from age to age. They simply use different stars as reference points. In fact, on a day-to-day basis, vast, slow stellar migrations have no effect on the earth's latitudes and even less on its climate.

So we can conclude that to resort to them in order to explain significant climatic modifications with sudden paroxysms in the history of the earth is ludicrous.

Likewise, however numerous and dramatic they may be, volcanic eruptions alone cannot explain the presence of forests of huge beeches. Nor can they heat a territory of 14 million km^2 long enough to allow such a development of plant and animal life.

The interglacial period and climatological logic

To explain the presence of the fossils discovered in Antarctica, some scientists have developed the idea, now officially accepted, of a so-called interglacial period. To believe them, the planet must have undergone a process of warming that allowed the development of a luxuriant nature pretty much everywhere, in particular at the poles.

In this theory, the ice, formed during a glacial period, suddenly retreated to East Antarctica to the south of the Transantarctic Mountains. An inland sea must have invaded the Wilkes Basin. Aquatic flora developed. Beeches grew on the shores. The flora and fauna would have been able to spread and flourish in a favourable climate, 500km from the South Pole.

But just as rapidly as it arrived, this interglacial period was brought to an end by a new glacial period which swelled the volume of the glaciers that swept down into the marine basin.

All the animals and plants, already fossilised or not, would have been enveloped, right to the tops of the mountains at a height of over 4,000m.

This idea rests on a sudden climatic phenomenon that scientists can simply not explain, even now, and so it acts as a sort of *deus ex machina* that answers questions which until then had remained unanswered.

How, after all, can we believe that it was ever warm at the poles?

Several elements combine to determine climate, but the two main factors are obviously altitude and latitude. Already in antiquity, Ovid had divided the world into three zones. A 'torrid' zone around the equator, a 'glacial' zone near the poles; and a 'temperate' zone situated between the two. So latitude determines the climate in accordance with whether we are in the equatorial, polar or temperate zone. Indeed, at all points of the terrestrial globe, the sun remains annually on average just as long below as it does above the horizon. Conversely, its maximum 'height' when it is above the horizon is linked to latitude:

- At the equator, this height reaches a value varying from 66.5° at the solstices to 90° at the equinox.

- Between 23.5° and 66.5° latitude, this same height reaches a peak at the summer solstice, the longest day, and diminishes 47° at the winter solstice, the shortest day.
- Near the poles, the sun's height never extends to more than 23.5° and its rays have a very low angle of incidence. For this reason, six months of continuous sunshine are not enough to heat these icy regions.

The altitude of geological relief is the second determining factor on climate. As everyone knows, the higher you go, the lower the temperature gets. On the highest mountains, the ice does not melt, and the same is true in the equatorial regions.

The North Pole is in the middle of the basin formed by the icy Arctic Sea. It is permanently covered by a vast ice floe, which is sea water that has frozen over, and occupies almost the entire Arctic Circle. Its height does not in general extend above a few metres of altitude. It is thus not comparable with the Antarctic glaciers, which, resting for the greater part on a raised continent, reach an average thickness of 2,300m. It is this very elevated altitude which leads to the Antarctic harbouring more than 90% of the planet's ice and the temperature at the South Pole being on average between 10 and 30° lower than that at the North Pole. The Antarctic is the most icy region on the globe.

Apart from latitude and altitude, other factors contribute to modifying climate. On the one hand, we have the great sea currents that sweep across the globe, in particular the Gulf Stream, the Kuroshio or Japanese Current, and the Humboldt Current, which can significantly heat up or cool down enormous areas. But no warm current reaches the shores of Antarctica.

Also, in a more localised way, the proximity of the sea contributes to moderating the climate. But the Antarctic, with its ice floe, has such a big surface area that in no way can the sea warm its interior climate.

Finally, we must bear in mind that the snow and the ice reflect a great part of solar energy and thus contribute to cooling. This is especially true in Antarctica where the snow cover reflects almost 80% of the incoming shortwave radiation, whereas land without ice reflects only 35%, and the oceans 15%. This is why, paradoxically, if you rise 1,000m into the atmosphere above the frozen continent, the temperature warms up almost 30° whereas practically everywhere else, at such an altitude, the temperature is of course noticeably less than that of the ground.

This climatic logic ensures that, within the polar circle, at less than 2,600km from the one pole, no flora or vegetation of any complexity can exist. Even at lower altitudes, it is impossible to imagine a forest, traces of which have nonetheless been discovered in the Arctic and Antarctic. So we can say with the geologist H. J. Harrington that the presence of normal climatic conditions and normal biotypes at the South Pole is fundamentally anomalous.[4]

As we can see, it is impossible to envisage that any global warming could explain a warm period in the Antarctic in its present position, with the South Pole more or less at its centre. We are driven to the conclusion that this continent was not always near the Pole...

The dinosaur fossils found on the Kirkpatrick Mountains, at 84°20' south and 166°19' east, are in themselves enough to summarise the situation.[5] William R. Hammer, of Augustana College in Illinois, was collecting fossils with his team near the Beardmore Glacier. It was on this occasion that one of his colleagues discovered the remains of two dinosaurs. One of them was a carnivore, cryolophosaurus ('frozen-crested lizard'). It belongs apparently to the *ellioti* species and dates from the Jurassic, i.e., between 185 and 200 million years ago. It is thus more ancient than the other carnivorous dinosaurs that have been found in other regions of the world.

This cryolophosaurus measured around 7.5m. It looked quite alarming, with its sharp pointed teeth set in its jaws like butcher's knives. Its skull was adorned with a complicated crest that could be erected in a fan, like the tail of a peacock. Hammer says that it played a role in courting rituals.

4   H. J. Harrington, 'Antarctica', *National Geographic Magazine*, suppl., Apr. 1987, vol. 171, no 6, p. 556.

5   *National Geographic Magazine*, Oct. 1994.

146

Might it not have been erected in this way when the animal was fighting? At death, it was in the act of devouring a herbivorous dinosaur, smaller in size, called a prosauropod. Some sudden event occurred which put an end to the feast. If this had not been the case, the cryolophosaurus would have finished its meal.

We cannot in fact explain the fossilisation of the two dinosaurs as the result of a slow process. The victorious dinosaur would have found it difficult to kill its victim and start to tear it apart and devour it while succumbing to the results of falling accidentally into a marsh, a peat bog or pool of sludge.

We must remember that fossilisation can be very abrupt in the case of volcanic eruption. Under a burning rain of ash, entire forests can be petrified in a few minutes. This phenomenon occurred at Saint-Pierre in Martinique, where in 1902 everything was swept away by a burning cloud. Trees and branches became as heavy as stones.

The unfortunate prosauropod must have been metamorphosed into a fossil before its limbs could be devoured or before they decomposed. The victorious cryolophosaurus did not even have time to flee. It died with its prey between its teeth.

We should point out that this petrified drama was discovered at an altitude of 4,000m. Now it is highly improbable that the herbivorous dinosaur could have found abundant grass at such an altitude. Furthermore, we cannot accept the conclusion that these animals lived at the South Pole, where the climate never reached a high enough temperature to enable vegetation to grow that could sustain such highly developed animals.

Everyone knows that the hypothesis of a massive fall of bolides – meteorites or even planetoids – has been advanced to explain the end of the dinosaurs. A similar event is far from being able to serve as an explanation in the case we are examining.

Our scenario, indeed, demands the combination of three exceptional circumstances:

- firstly, a volcanic eruption must have led to a brutal fossilisation of the two animals;
- secondly, the ground must have risen dramatically by 3,000 to 4,000 m;
- thirdly, the Antarctic continent must have drifted by 3,000 to 4,000 km.

It is this last point that is the most remarkable.

2.2 Cartography

I feel it is necessary at this point to go back to the earliest maps of the Antarctic continent. The accounts provided by the ancients may once again give us an answer, where science finds a stumbling block.

Maps through the ages

Cartography is the response to a very ancient need in man to represent his environment, to learn about it and find his bearings. Today, we have at our disposal means that no one could have imagined a few decades ago. Civil and military satellites placed at the service of the wider public allow us to observe land and sea at a scale of 1 in 50,000 (1cm on the map represents 500m on the ground). It will soon be possible to have three-dimensional visual representations of the road traffic on the Place de la Concorde, or volcanoes before and after eruption, at a few hundred metres' altitude – all on your own PC.[1]

It is well known that the most remote civilisations favoured shipping. Moving heavy loads by land was indeed more complicated, given the rudimentary character of roads and vehicles. It was more practical to load your cargoes on ships than to cross forests, mountains and other watercourses. Furthermore, there was less risk of encountering the hostility of warlike populations. But you had to be able to find your way around, a requirement inseparable from cartography. To make a good map, you must not lose your bearings. How did the ancients find out where they were?

Greek antiquity contributed a great deal to the progress made in the calculation of terrestrial and maritime surface areas. The astrolabe measured latitude. The height of the sun or another star was indicated on the instrument's graduated dial. Measuring longitudes was much more complex and more unreliable since the ancients lacked precise clocks that could be easily transported at sea. So they used the clepsydra, the hourglasses or water clocks which were later to serve Christopher Columbus. The latter's

---

1   *Science et Vie*, Dec. 1999, pp. 54-60.

erratic functioning – to put it mildly – shows how much steering techniques left to be desired. So the first navigators found their bearings from the position of stars and constellations. The Pole Star was the main reference point by which sailors in the Mediterranean or on the Atlantic coasts could find their location. Climatic conditions determined whether or not it could be observed: in a sky covered by clouds, the Pole Star was of no help to navigators. They needed a tool capable of steering them that was independent of the weather.

In the 12th century, European sailors used the water compass introduced by the Chinese and the Arabs: a magnetised needle, mounted on a straw floating in a bowl of water. Unfortunately, though relatively good at indicating north on land, it showed itself to be inefficient on board ship. It was only in the 1260s that the needle was fixed on a pivot. From then on, the marine compass was adopted and continued to gain in precision. Nonetheless, the Pole Star remained, even in the 15th century, more reliable on expeditions; the navigators placed more confidence in the Pole Star and the sun than in the magnetic pole. In the Northern Hemisphere, the celestial pole is near Ursa Minor. In the Southern Hemisphere, it is near the Southern Cross. It is not always easy to find them. It always depends on the weather.

It is probable that the first maps precede even the invention of writing. Thirty centuries BC, the peoples who had taken to navigation were already endeavouring to draw the outlines of coasts and routes on clay tablets. Attempts to represent the world are frequently encountered in the history of mankind. They are as varied as they are emblematic of the milieu from which they sprang. Astronomical expertise enabled explorers to find their way, and merchants to develop the economy by sea, at a time when they still did not have any reliable instruments by which to navigate. From the 13th century and throughout the Middle Ages, portulans became necessary to navigators, merchants and fishermen. These nautical charts indicated capes and the distances between different ports. These charts had a much more practical than scientific advantage. The best routes, the quickest ways of getting from one port to another, were noted in manuals, often on vellum. The portulans, thanks to the accuracy with which they traced the outline of coasts, constituted a solid working basis for the mathematicians and astronomers, who could, thanks to the new scientific advances, busy themselves with cartography.

Amazing maps

A first symbolic representation of the Antarctic region can be found in the map that is considered to be the oldest in the world, since it supposedly dates from the first Babylonian dynasty (1830–1530 BC). Babylon is represented in the middle. The 'bitter river' or ocean surrounds the land.

The neighbouring lands of Mesopotamia are indicated in cuneiform writing. Beyond the zone of the waters, i.e., the ocean, seven triangles indicate other regions. The term describing these territories is *na-gu-u*, which could be translated as 'island'. They lie "outside the continent inhabited by men."[2]

Next to one triangle, we find this note: "Country where the sun no longer rises." The fifth triangle bears the annotation: "Where the sun cannot be seen." The archaeologists Unger and Contenau here correctly see an allusion to the polar night.[3]

On the fourth rectangle can be read: "Brightness greater than dusk and starlight." This is presumably a region of the polar circle, situated in Antarctica, more than 500km from the South Pole. The seventh triangle reads "Heavenly Ocean," and "the animals that the god Marduk created."[4]

Behind the monsters imagined in the mythologies we can recognise the innumerable seals of the Antarctic coasts.

The ocean surrounds all the different lands, but also encircles the country "where the sun rises," which is far from insignificant since there is also a country "where it no longer rises." Indeed, and it is important to notice this, it is said that, in this particular region, the sun *no longer* rises, and not merely that it does not rise.

---

2   G. de Champeaux and D. S. Sterckx, *Le Monde des Symboles*, Éditions Zodiaque, St-Léger Vauban, 1966, p. 67.

3   G. de Champeaux and D. S. Sterckx, *ibid.*; G. Contenau, *Le déluge babylonien*, Payot, Paris, 1952, p. 78.

4   G. Contenau, *ibid.*

Figure 21. *Babylonian tablet (circa 700–500 BC), probably from Sippar, southern Iraq. This tablet has a cuneiform inscription on it, above a unique map of the Mesopotamian world.*

What are we to conclude from this? Quite simply that there was a time when the sun's risings and settings happened in the familiar way. Then an event occurred which disturbed the seemingly immutable course of nature. Now, if the sun no longer rises during six months of the year, ice has all the time it needs to invade the continent.

If it had not done so, are we to seek the reason in the fact that this continent was further from the South Pole than it had been when the region was mapped?

The Saint Gall palimpsest

Considered to be the most ancient map of the world still existing in the West, the Saint Gall palimpsest apparently dates from the 9th century AD.

Schematised to an extreme degree, like the Babylonian tablet, the earth is represented by a circle, surmounted by a Christ on the cross, so that the top points east. On the lower left, i.e., to the north-west, we find Europe, *EVROPA, JAPHET*. On the upper left we find Asia, *ASIA, SEM*. In the lower middle, i.e., to the west, lies Africa, *AFRICA, CAM*. The three parts of the world are thus all in place, attributed to the three sons of Noah, who were deemed to be the ancestors of the entire ancient world.

In the upper middle, an empty rectangle, with an unknown land on the eastern side – the Orient. A sea corridor separates the two, horizontally: the Red Sea, stretching out along a north-south axis, *HILYS*. A second vertical strip to the right of all this represents the South Atlantic and the Indian Ocean, running from the south-west to the south-east.

Finally, a third of the circle, on the right-hand side, and thus all situated in the south, is a vast continent: *TERRA INHABITABILIS*, an important land, one that must have been known but had become uninhabitable: Antarctica.

Figure 22. *Saint Gall map from a manuscript held at the Stiftsbibliothek St Gallen, Switzerland.*

Macrobius

In the 15th century AD, a commentary on the *Dream of Scipio* appeared with a representation of the world inspired by the cosmography of Macrobius, a 5th century compiler (Bibliothèque Nationale, Paris). The five climatic zones described by Ovid in his *Metamorphoses* are clearly indicated. Going from the North Pole to the South Pole, we have:

- an icy northern zone, *FRIGIDA*;
- a temperate northern zone, *TEPERATA*;
- a central tropical zone, *PERUSTA*;
- a temperate southern zone, *TEPERATA ANTIPODUM*, nobis Incognita;
- an icy southern zone, *FRIGIDA*.

Europe and Asia straddle the two first zones. Africa straddles the two following zones, with the Red Sea and Persian Gulf opening up on to the Indian Ocean.

The southern continent is represented as being as big as the first three continents put together, and includes the three climatic zones beyond the southern seas. This incontestably shows that people retained the memory that this southern land had in the recent past experienced climatic conditions much more clement than those of today!

Saint Isidore of Seville

Isidore was the last father of the Western church. As Bishop of Seville (601-636 AD) he played a dominant role in Visigoth Spain. As a compiler, his most famous encyclopaedic work is the *Etymologies* or *Origins*.

They contain "everything you need to know," according to a contemporary, and "devote several books to cosmography as well as physical and political geography." Isidore accepts that the earth is round, but while rejecting the hypothesis of antipodean men, something he considers to be a mere fable, he comes close to believing in a land at the antipodes of ours.

It is in his description of Libya that we find a surprising statement, often repeated by cosmographers and cartographers of the Middle Ages:

Figure 23. *Macrobius's map – a depiction inspired by the cosmography of Macrobius, a 5th century compiler.*

SEPTEN · TRIO

BORIAS AQUILO.

TIMISERICI CAPI DESERTI·

DESERTA ARINOSA·

ALBANIA·

GENS COLO

GALAGIA
LI CARI
PAMFI
LIA
FRIGIA
SIA MINOR

CAPADOCIA

CILICIA

DICI
NAS
A SI
NA

BITI

HIC APUD
EUROPAE
ALANIA

DACIA

SAR
MA
TICA

MAGEDONIA

ALIS PONT

TESSALONICA
EPIRUM

BAL
MATIA

A CAIA

TRISTAI

PANNONIA

NORICU
RETIA
GER
MANIA

MOESIA

MOESIA
DUR
PANI
TRA
CIA RICIA

CALABRU
APULIA
SPOLITE

SINUS ADRIATICI

ROMA
ROM

FRANCIA·

GALLIA BELGICA

PROUINCIA

GALLIA LUGDUNI

SI

SIPTIMANIA

AQUITANIA

TUUAS CO

NIA

GALLICIA

KORUS AGRESTIS·

OC
IAUONIUS

QUINTUS A SEPTEN TRIO

TRASCIUS CIRCIUS

As well as the three parts of the world, there is a fourth part beyond the ocean in a southern direction, unknown to us because of the sun's heat. In these regions it is claimed in fable that the Antipodeans live.[5]

This text is also found, in bad Latin, on the very fine oval-shaped map by Beatus of Liebana, known as Beatus of Saint-Sever, dating from the middle of the 11th century.

EXTRATRESAUTEMPARTESORBISQUARTAPARSTRANS
OCEANUMINTERIORESTIMMERIDIEQUAESOLISARDOR
INCOGNITANOBISESTINCUIUSFINIBUSANTIPO
DASFABULOSAEINHABITERE«POUNT»

The text rewards a more careful translation than the one cited above.
EXTRA TRES AUTEM PARTES ORBIS: "Outside the three parts of the (terrestrial) globe," i.e., outside Europe, Asia and Africa. Indeed, circular maps of the Macrobius or TO (*Terrae orbis*) type, between the 5th and the 12th century, are ignorant of the existence of America. They comprise Europe and Asia as one block, and Africa, separated from the first two by the Mediterranean. There is no attempt at proportion or precision, but the arrangement is clear and elegant. It summarises in a simple way a far-reaching body of information.

QUARTA PARS, TRANS OCEANUM, INTERIOR, EST, IMMERIDIE: "a fourth part, beyond the ocean, within the interior, east, in a southern direction." *Immeridie* means 'to the south': the maps take care to indicate, on their margin, the four cardinal directions, north (*septentrio*), south (*immeridie*), east (*oriens*) and west (*occidens*).

QUAE SOLIS ARDOR INCOGNITA NOBIS EST: "Where the heat of the sun is unknown to us." Most of the translations get this completely wrong: the sun's heat renders the equatorial regions difficult to live in, but in no way impossible. As they remained unknown to these cartographers, it was

---

5   *Cartes et Figures de la Terre*, Centre George Pompidou, CCI, Paris, 1980, p. 138.

Preceding page: Figure 24. Beatus Map, *drawn from the commentary on the Apocalypse attributed to Beatus of Liebana, also known as Beatus of Saint-Sever, mid 11th century.*

believed that an excessive temperature made them uninhabitable and thus uncrossable.

IN CUIUS FINIBUS: "In these extremities." How can you talk about extremities on a sphere? The earth turns on an invisible axis, passing through its centre, and crossing its surface at the poles: everything is rotating, apart from at these two points.

A Hindu poem says, "O Wheel, how would you be effective without your two poles? If they did not remain motionless, how could everything turn?"

ANTIPODAS FABULOSAE IN HABITERE «POUNT»: "The fabulous Antipodeans lived in… Punt." The earth being round, of course, men must have had their feet turned towards us (*anti-podas*), which rather disturbed Saint Augustine and Saint Isidore.

Inhabitere means uninhabitable. The translations generally render this as *habitere*, 'live', 'inhabit', dropping the negative '*in*' which is meaningless, as we are talking about fabulous inhabitants. So this '*in*' can only mean: 'within', 'inside'. The southern continent is inhabitable, except inside grottoes and caverns and other shelters.

As for *POUNT*, i.e., 'Punt', this was the name the Egyptians gave to the land of the immortal gods, in the 'Original Mound', cradle of gods and men – paradise, hell, land of the dead, island of death. In the 7th century AD, Saint Isidore was still perfectly well aware that the cradle of humanity was near the South Pole, on the Antarctic continent, then called the 'Southern Land'.

Explorers in remote times did not, of course, have at their disposal the same means that we do. And yet we can find very old maps which are surprisingly accurate. And not only of the Mediterranean, which was considered by the Europeans to be the centre of the world.

Figure 25. *Map of the world in two hemispheres, by Johannes Schöner (1520) showing the Pacific Ocean with the southern continent shown in detail.*

Schöner

On the first globe made by the German Schöner (1515) there appears a huge *Brasilia Regio* (it has nothing to do with Brazil) separated from South America by a wide gap, a prefiguration of the Strait of Magellan.

On the same author's globe of 1520, a *Brasilia Inferior* has appeared stretching towards Antarctic latitudes, inspired by Vespucci, whereas Brazil proper is called *Papagalli Terra* (Land of Parrots).

Schöner removes the southern continent in his 1523 globe, only to bring it back again 10 years later on the Weimar globe (1533). Antarctica is represented here, doubtless on the basis of sources different from those we will see being used by Oronteus Finaeus, but the overall result is comparable.

Oronteus Finaeus

Oronteus Finaeus, professor at the Collège de France, lived in Grenoble and Paris, where he died. He published a map of France – quite a good one, though containing large deviations in longitude.

He published an amazing map of Antarctica in 1532, calling it *Terra Australis Re, center immensa, sed nondii plena cognita*, i.e., 'Region of the Southern Land, an immense centre, but not fully known to this day'. The double network of meridians and parallels is spaced out every 10°, following a cordiform projection.

If we compare this 16th century map with a present-day one, we realise with amazement that the two depictions of Antarctica are nearly identical. If we superimpose the two continents, we find that there is little variation in the proportions of the continent. The outline of the coasts is indicated with great precision. The Ross and Weddell seas are correctly situated. How was Oronteus Finaeus able, with the means at his disposal, to draw a map of the land and water systems of the gigantic block of ice that is present-day Antarctica?

The South Pole, which is also correctly situated in the middle of the continent, is located at what would today be 75° south, 45° east, i.e., some considerable distance from its current position. Certain points of the Antarctic continent – situated in the Indian Ocean – are close to reaching

Following page: Figure 26. *The Oronteus Finaeus map, the* New and Entire Description of the World *(1531).*

the Tropic of Capricorn. How can we explain the difference between this and our modern maps?

It is easy to see the strange similarity between these maps of Antarctica, with the Ross and Weddell Seas fully in evidence. Our recent information concurs with that available to 16th century cartographers. The proportions are correct, with almost 90% precision: the southern continent, not frozen at that time, must have been known well enough, all the way round, to be drawn like this, without a chronometer, and depending only on the stars to steer by!

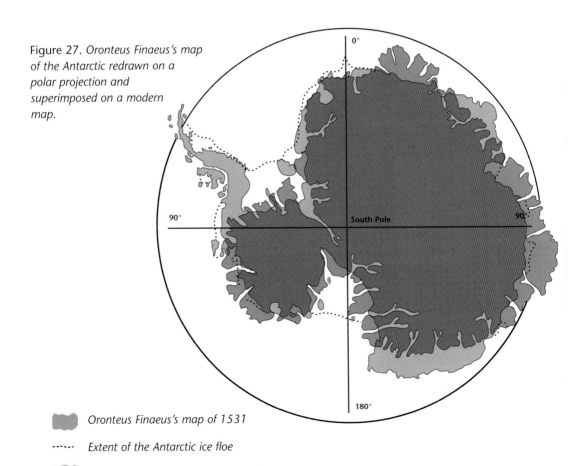

Figure 27. *Oronteus Finaeus's map of the Antarctic redrawn on a polar projection and superimposed on a modern map.*

Oronteus Finaeus's map of 1531

------ *Extent of the Antarctic ice floe*

Modern map of Antarctica

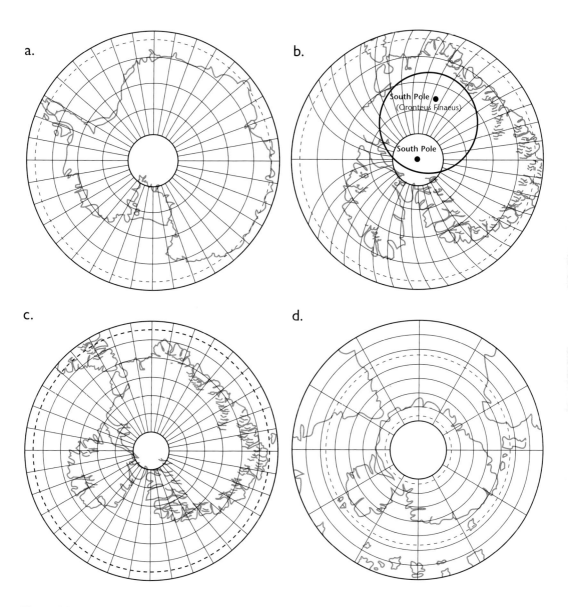

a.

b.

South Pole
(Oronteus Finaeus)

South Pole

c.

d.

Figure 28. *Four maps for comparison:*
(a.) the present-day map of Antarctica;
(b.) that of Oronteus Finaeus, from 1531–2;
(c.) the same, retranscribed in polar projection with equidistant parallels;
(d.) the globe of Schöner, from 1523–4, based on other sources.

165

Figure 29. *Piri Re'is map, 1513.*

Piri Re'is

The Turkish admiral Piri Re'is produced a map in 1513 with the help of documents seized from a Spanish pilot who had made three of Christopher Columbus's four crossings of the Atlantic and who had been captured following a sea battle in 1501. All in all, some 20 *Mappae mundi*, i.e., maps drawn in the era of Alexander and showing the inhabited parts of the world, contributed to producing it.

Conserved in the Topkapi Palace in Istanbul, and rediscovered in 1929 by Hali Edhem, one copy was presented in 1956 to the U.S. Hydrographic Office by an officer in the Turkish Navy. On recognising the reliability of this map, Charles Hapgood launched a research programme based on it at Keen Teachers' College. In this remarkable document he discovered a representation of the coast of the Antarctic continent facing the Atlantic.

Captain Lorenzo W. Burroughs, of the US Air Force Technical Squad wrote to Hapgood:

> The Princess Martha Coast of Queen Maud Land, Antarctica, appears to be truly represented on the southern sector of the Piri Reis Map. The agreement of the Piri Reis Map with the seismic profile of this area made by the Norwegian-British-Swedish Expedition of 1949, supported by your solution of the grid, places beyond a reasonable doubt the conclusion that the original source maps must have been made before the present Antarctic ice cap covered the Queen Maud Land coasts.[6]

The representation of a serpent drawn on the Antarctic continent, on the Piri Re'is map, was given an interesting explanation by Hapgood: the constellation of Hydra, between Ursa Major and Ursa Minor, was called 'Serpent' by the Greeks, and was indeed visible at southern latitudes below 70–72°, thus on Queen Maud Land.

The serpent was the symbol par excellence of this polar region, as so many texts demonstrate, as well as a great number of archaic

6   C. Hapgood, *Maps of the Ancient Sea Kings*, Chitton Books, Philadelphia / New York, 1966, p. 244.

166

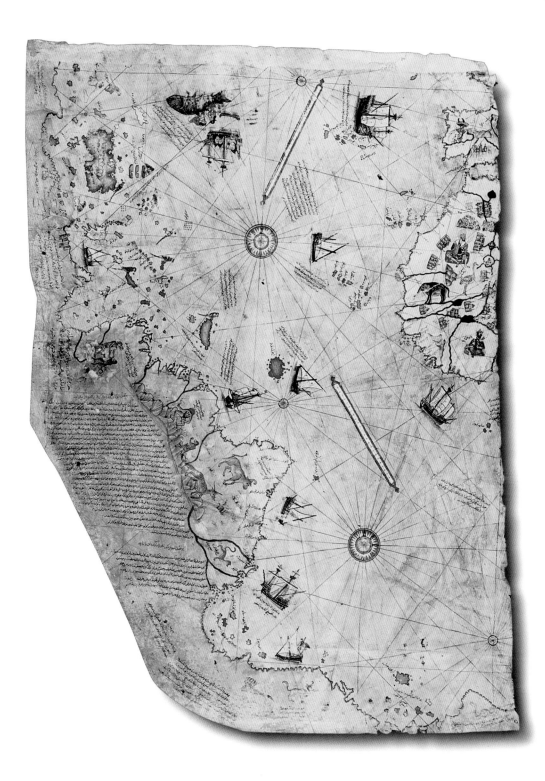

representations. The serpent hides under the ground during the winter and changes its skin – a sign of the eternal youth attributed to the gods living within the polar circle.

Mercator

Gerhard Kremer is the best-known cartographer of the 16th century: he is known by the name of Mercator. Asserting that the ancients thought the earth was flat, just because they represented it on a flat surface, is as ridiculous as believing that our own cartographers are so ignorant that they do the same!

The earth is nearly spherical, and this has long been known, despite the periods in which it was forgotten. But how can one easily represent anything at all, unless this is done in two dimensions, on papyrus, clay, stone, or paper? A sphere is not a geometrically developable surface. It is impossible to show without distortion outlines traced on a globe, or continents situated on the earth's surface.

Meridians and geographical parallels are in reality circles: it is tempting to represent them in the form of straight lines, on a plate. Mercator was not the first to trace, in two dimensions, equidistant parallels by parallel straight lines and the meridians that join at the poles by straight lines perpendicular to the former (as in reality) and thus also parallel to one another.

The problem is that, at any latitude L, the distance between two meridians is less in reality than in planar representation (multiplied by cos L). The scale would be respected if the parallels were spaced out so that the said scale were multiplied by cos L at latitude L. This was Mercator's innovation: he invented sea charts with increasing latitudes.

Figure 30. *Mercator's heart-shaped map of the world from 1538. See rear endpaper.*

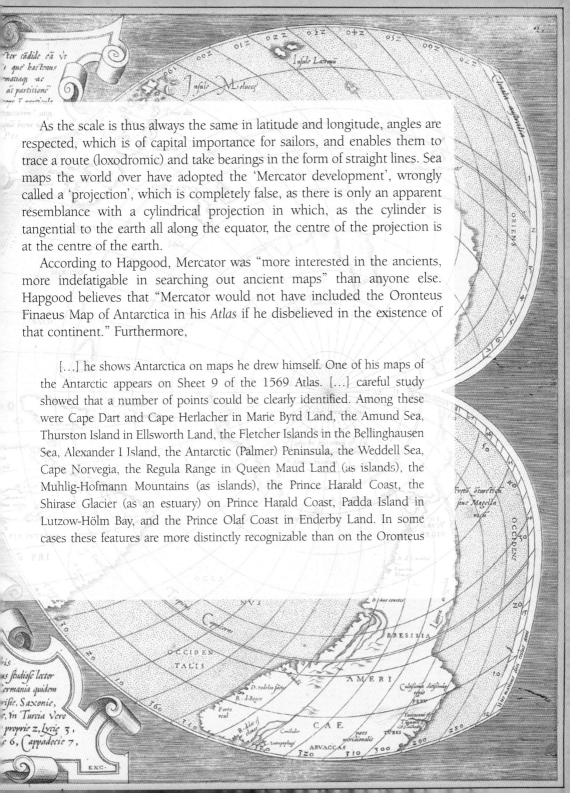

As the scale is thus always the same in latitude and longitude, angles are respected, which is of capital importance for sailors, and enables them to trace a route (loxodromic) and take bearings in the form of straight lines. Sea maps the world over have adopted the 'Mercator development', wrongly called a 'projection', which is completely false, as there is only an apparent resemblance with a cylindrical projection in which, as the cylinder is tangential to the earth all along the equator, the centre of the projection is at the centre of the earth.

According to Hapgood, Mercator was "more interested in the ancients, more indefatigable in searching out ancient maps" than anyone else. Hapgood believes that "Mercator would not have included the Oronteus Finaeus Map of Antarctica in his *Atlas* if he disbelieved in the existence of that continent." Furthermore,

[…] he shows Antarctica on maps he drew himself. One of his maps of the Antarctic appears on Sheet 9 of the 1569 Atlas. […] careful study showed that a number of points could be clearly identified. Among these were Cape Dart and Cape Herlacher in Marie Byrd Land, the Amund Sea, Thurston Island in Ellsworth Land, the Fletcher Islands in the Bellinghausen Sea, Alexander I Island, the Antarctic (Palmer) Peninsula, the Weddell Sea, Cape Norvegia, the Regula Range in Queen Maud Land (as islands), the Muhlig-Hofmann Mountains (as islands), the Prince Harald Coast, the Shirase Glacier (as an estuary) on Prince Harald Coast, Padda Island in Lutzow-Hölm Bay, and the Prince Olaf Coast in Enderby Land. In some cases these features are more distinctly recognizable than on the Oronteus

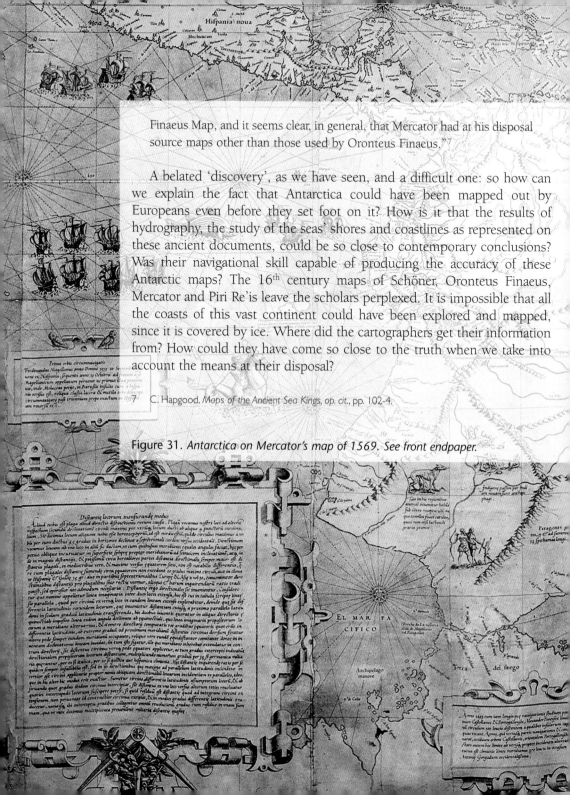

Finaeus Map, and it seems clear, in general, that Mercator had at his disposal source maps other than those used by Oronteus Finaeus."[7]

A belated 'discovery', as we have seen, and a difficult one: so how can we explain the fact that Antarctica could have been mapped out by Europeans even before they set foot on it? How is it that the results of hydrography, the study of the seas' shores and coastlines as represented on these ancient documents, could be so close to contemporary conclusions? Was their navigational skill capable of producing the accuracy of these Antarctic maps? The 16th century maps of Schöner, Oronteus Finaeus, Mercator and Piri Re'is leave the scholars perplexed. It is impossible that all the coasts of this vast continent could have been explored and mapped, since it is covered by ice. Where did the cartographers get their information from? How could they have come so close to the truth when we take into account the means at their disposal?

7   C. Hapgood, *Maps of the Ancient Sea Kings, op. cit.,* pp. 102-4.

Figure 31. *Antarctica on Mercator's map of 1569. See front endpaper.*

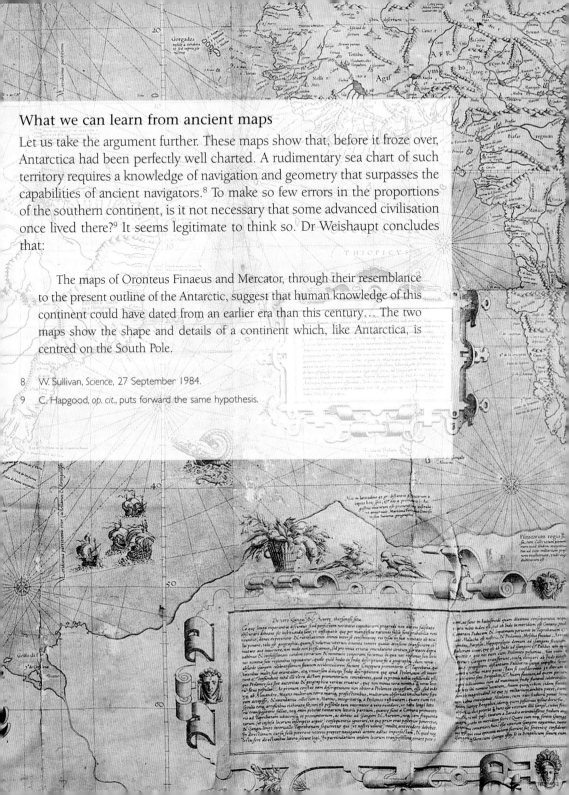

What we can learn from ancient maps

Let us take the argument further. These maps show that, before it froze over, Antarctica had been perfectly well charted. A rudimentary sea chart of such territory requires a knowledge of navigation and geometry that surpasses the capabilities of ancient navigators.[8] To make so few errors in the proportions of the southern continent, is it not necessary that some advanced civilisation once lived there?[9] It seems legitimate to think so. Dr Weishaupt concludes that:

> The maps of Oronteus Finaeus and Mercator, through their resemblance to the present outline of the Antarctic, suggest that human knowledge of this continent could have dated from an earlier era than this century… The two maps show the shape and details of a continent which, like Antarctica, is centred on the South Pole.

8   W. Sullivan, *Science*, 27 September 1984.

9   C. Hapgood, *op. cit.*, puts forward the same hypothesis.

A civilisation that lived in the Antarctic before its period of glaciation would thus have been the source of the information available to cartographers at the beginning of our era.

Now all representations of Antarctica bring out two great differences from the continent as we know it now: South America points in a straight line to Santa Marta's Land (Marie Byrd Land), at the exact place where the Antarctic Peninsula starts to jut out and fragment. So this latter phenomenon had not yet come about, curving Patagonia eastwards as far as the South Sandwich Islands and then returning south-west to join Graham's Land.

The position of Antarctica as a whole is different. It must at that time have stretched out into the Indian Ocean to around 25° south. It must have drifted some 45° south and the same distance to the west, relative to Africa – i.e., some 7,000 to 8,000 km, which agrees strangely with the conclusions of plate tectonics.

The data from the past, however distant, obviously provide us with valuable information. The great birthplaces of civilisation all refer to one and the same past on a great continent, from which they were driven away by climatic conditions that had become too harsh to sustain life, conditions which are identical to those encountered near a pole. Having embarked on seagoing vessels, the inhabitants fled in all directions.

This continent, which can only be Antarctica, has turned out to be the source of disturbing indications that it was, once upon a time, entirely free of ice. We have just found confirmation from the study of ancient cartography that a civilisation, and one that must have been advanced, came into existence on this continent when it was not situated near the pole...

How can it be, when all these extraordinary revelations speak to us of a past that is not too distant, that the dates published for the origin of rock, sediments, mountains and civilisations are in complete contradiction with our new discoveries, being much too remote in time?

2.3   Uncertainties about the length of climatic eras

Can we know, with modern dating methods, how many centuries lie between us and that epoch, unimaginable today, in which trees grew on the vast Antarctic continent? Nothing could be less certain…

At the start of the 20th century, the distinguished archaeologist Jacques de Morgan[1] revealed a number of contradictions in scientific statements. He noted: "In large numbers, geologists and prehistorians […] have exercised their wisdom researching the quaternary periods, their duration and those of post-quaternary periods; but it is clear that, in the main, these estimations, based on the most diverse chronometrical conceptions, belong to the realm of fantasy."

And Jacques de Morgan goes on to quote the dates published by a number of the acknowledged leading authorities of his period:

For the Quaternary era in total (years)

L. Pilgrim	1,620,000	G. de Mortillet	230 to 240,000
Penck	1,000,000	Warren Upham	100 to 150,000
J. Geikie	620,000	Holst	30,000
Walcott	400,000	Arcelin and Ferry	10,000

For the length of the glacial period

L. Pilgrim	1,290,000	Rutot	140,000
Penck	500,000 to 1,000,000	G. de Mortillet	100,000
Lyell	800,000	Warren Upham	20 to 30,000
Dana	720,000	Prestwich	25,000
J. Lubbock	200,000	Holst	17,000

For the post-glacial period

Forel	100,000	Rutot	16,000
Croll	80,000	Heim	16,000
Nuesch	24 to 29,000	Prestwich	8 to 10,000
Gosse	18,280	Holst	5 to 6,900
Sarauw	10 to 25,000	Arcelin and Ferry	4 to 5,000
G. de Mortillet	16,000		

1   J. de Morgan, *La Préhistoire orientale*, vol. 1, Librairie Geuthner, Paris, 1926, p. 56.

Obviously, anyone could freely express his opinion, based on his own method! In our own time it is no longer possible to parade such flimsy guesses. This subject is now taught at universities, but students do not understand that what seems to them to be the result of scientific studies is in fact little more than conjecture.

To measure different climatic periods, there are several modern dating methods including ionium dating, carbon-14 dating, or dating from the oxygen-16/oxygen-18 proportion. What do these methods consist of? Are they so certain that all doubts are removed?

Ionium dating

Three radioactive elements exist in sea water: uranium, ionium and radium, which are present in oceans in defined proportions. These three elements lose their radioactivity slowly, but at speeds that vary between each element. This decomposition occurs only when the sea water that contains them is trapped in sediments, i.e., on the ocean floor, when the water can no longer circulate. By measuring the radioactivity of the sediments, one can thus in principle determine for how long they have been trapped at the bottom of the water.

Furthermore, the character of this sediment, swept down by rivers and finally deposited in the sea, will depend on the climate of the period in which it is formed. If the sedimentary grains are fine, it is because they have made a long journey in rivers that have flowed across a land empty of glaciers. If they have been stripped from the earth's surface by the advance of the glaciers, and subsequently swept into the sea, they are much coarser. If the river is seasonal in flow, and freezes only in winter, the deposit is laid down in varves, i.e., thin alternating layers.

When we have these two types of information – the date and type of sediment – we can thus hope to date the glaciers that cover a continent such as Antarctica, for example.

In 1949, during an expedition to the Antarctic undertaken by Byrd, three core samples, called N5, N44 and N3, were taken in the Ross Sea, at a latitude of around 70° south and a longitude of 180°. The raw data give us these results, as expressed in specialist vocabulary:

- for N5: between -18,000 and -3,800 years, a matrix with fine grains and small isolated pebbles; after -3,800 years, big grains from glaciers;
- for N44: between -22,000 and -3,800 years, small eroded grains; between -3,800 and -1,200 years, medium-sized grains from glaciers; after -1,200 years, big grains from glaciers;
- for N3: between -24,000 and -1,800 years, small eroded grains; between -1,800 and +1,100 years, medium-sized grains from glaciers.

In other words, analyses reveal for each of the three core samplings a period of temperate climate in Antarctica, a period during which the Ross Sea was completely ice-free. This last 'warm' period must have come to an end between -3,800 and -1,800 years for samples N5 and N44, i.e., between -1,800 and +1,100 for N3!

This striking example shows us that this method of dating presents a significant uncertainty, even if in other respects it confirms what we already knew about the past climate in Antarctica.

Carbon-14 dating

Carbon-14 dating relies on the postulates of the American chemist Libby, as set out in 1952. Thanks to his work, we know that the level of cosmic radiation ensures that carbon-14 is produced in the upper atmosphere. According to Libby, this level has remained stable throughout at least the last 40,000 years. So the production of radiocarbon must have been constant during this period.

Furthermore, radiocarbon must be spread uniformly in air and water. Libby calls this phenomenon the 'reservoir'. Uniformly spread as it is throughout all living creatures, there is no preferential accumulation: this is his 'principle of simultaneity'.

Once it is underground and can no longer draw on the carbon-14 that comes from the upper atmosphere, the radiocarbon already stored in a living creature decomposes slowly. The 'short' life of carbon-14 means that we find it in relatively recent periods. So its quantity diminishes progressively unless, of course, it comes back into contact with the atmosphere again. The quantity of radiocarbon measured thus allows us to deduce the time that has elapsed since it was buried, or the age of a layer of sedimentation.

With such a rigorous deductive method, it would seem that there could be no possibility of error.

But there are flaws in this marvellous system. Both of this method's two basic postulates are false.

- First of all, carbon-14 is not uniformly distributed. The choice of the sample for analysis then becomes highly significant if we want to obtain a coherent result. Every organism, throughout its life, receives a quantity of carbon-14 which depends closely on its relations with its surroundings. We know for instance that water can, depending on where it is, transport a bigger or smaller quantity of carbon. One body of water that is relatively poor in this respect will, if it fosters the growth of a tree which is later used to make the plank for a ship, certainly lead to this ship being seen as much older than it is in reality.

  Sometimes we may suspect an influence of this type and endeavour to correct it. But it is obvious that the uncertainty will always remain and that this method of dating is far from definitive. Thus, each date is accompanied by a commentary which gives us an idea of its value: it is clear that the unreliable dates will be kept out of publications and the results are heavily influenced by what is expected from them.

- In addition, an independent chronometer, dated by carbon-14, has been produced: dendrochronology, i.e., the patient counting of the annual growth rings of trees. However, this method does not enable us to check carbon-14 from earlier than 7,000 years BC.

Claire Van Oosterwyck-Gastuche points out that absolutely no account is taken of the variations in the level of carbon-14 that dendrochronology has discovered. She writes:

Besides the secular variation in the levels of C14 [...], one notes, after

1500 BC, a real drift: the levels of radiocarbon increase, and the dates become systematically younger.[2]

What event could have led to such significant variations? The origin of the phenomenon, which is still not well known, has been attributed to an increase in cosmic radiation on the 'reservoirs', to a diminution in the magnetic field, or to modifications in the contents of Libby's reservoirs. If radioactivity has increased over the past 3,000 years or so, one of the most fundamental postulates in this theory thus crumbles. "Such an observation logically ought to have led to nothing less than a revolution in the dating of prehistorical eras, which in their turn have become suspect." [3]

Nothing of the kind happened. In spite of this discovery, certain scientists are still holding tight to their original position. The dates are considered by them to be correct, calibrated in accordance with archaeological ages and the statistical treatments developed by Wilson and Ward. They busy themselves with purification procedures, and eliminate unreliable material. But these judicious selections are for specialists alone and lie outside the competence of laymen.

In 1996, the problem of carbon-14 dating arose again. [4]

It was discovered that this dating took no account, in particular, of "variations in the intensity of the earth's magnetic field in the past." According to Carlo Laj,[5] the amount of carbon-14 in the atmosphere has significantly varied over time as a result of the instability of the magnetic field.

This magnetic field, indeed, stops electrically charged cosmic particles which, as they penetrate the atmosphere, preside over the formation of natural carbon-14. "The stronger the magnetic field, the more it intercepts cosmic particles, and the less carbon-14 there is," writes Laj.

2   C. van Oosterwyck-Gastuche, *Le radiocarbone, face au Linceul de Turin*, F. X. de Guibert, 1999, pp. 14-8.

3   *Ibid.*

4   "Carbone 14 : l'affaire se complique", *Science et Vie*, Jan. 1996, p. 11.

5   Director of research at the Laboratoire de modélisation du climat et de l'environnement (CNRS-CEA).

On the basis of the minute study of three core samples of marine sediment extracted from off the Azores, French researchers from the Centre des faibles radioactivités (CFR) have succeeded in retracing the history of the variations in intensity of the magnetic field over a period of 50,000 years. They have deduced significant fluctuations in the amount of carbon-14 present in the atmosphere.

In view of these results, it appears to them that the old datings, which oscillate between -20,000 years and -40,000 years, could in reality be 2,000 to 3,000 years old.

With revisions such as these, the warm periods that I have already described suddenly appear much closer to our time.

O16/O18 dating

Oxygen-18 is heavier than oxygen-16. In the oceans where both of them are present, it is thus to be expected that we will find an oxygen-16/oxygen-18 proportion that varies according to depth.

The ice contained by the poles is essentially formed by the condensation of water vapour that comes from the evaporation of the sea water. Thus we can expect that the oxygen-16/oxygen-18 proportion in the ice will be close to that measurable on the ocean surface.

Now this proportion is not constant if we study a core sample from a glacier. There are even some quite drastic changes in this proportion.

One idea has been put forward to explain this phenomenon, but it is valid only if we accept the principle of the existence of glacial and interglacial periods: namely, the idea that the volume of the polar ice must have varied significantly in the past, thereby entailing a variation in the volume of the oceans.

During these interglacial periods, the water from the melting ice returns to the sea. The oxygen-16/oxygen-18 proportion in the oceans increases because of this influx. The formation of ice then, in this theory, undergoes the same effect during the following ice age.

Some people thus imagine that they can simply read the number of alternating glacial and interglacial periods, and in this way prove the existence of the latter. But they are forgetting rather too hastily the way this theory came into being.

The elasticity of estimates

As we can see, a lot of work is still needed if we can one day assign dates with the same assurance that some are all too ready to display at present.

On the basis of consensual estimates that have been gathered from a small number of eminent authorities, certain dates are now being proposed as if they were indisputable. Until they are replaced by other dates, that is – dates that are just as certain, once they have been revised… This method allows one to quietly draw a curtain across bothersome contradictions or discoveries.

The chronologies attributed to the climatic eras of our planet are thus in general presented with a tranquil sense of certainty. The repetition, the ostensible accuracy and the self-assurance with which these figures are communicated support their official reliability and ensure that they often attract a consensus. 'We all know that…', 'we are assured that…', 'The various different methods of dating confirm that…' are typical of the phraseology that accompanies these scientific disclosures.

In reality, the dates are generally imposed without any reference to the method adopted to determine them, to their degree of consistency or to any possible margin of error. Those who 'settle dates by decree' make their assertions quite magisterially.

Thus it is that dates can easily gain or lose some thousands or millions of years. This margin of error is characteristic of the flexibility of the scientific literature when it comes to advancing dates.

In navigation, the least experienced sailor would find it odd, to say the least, to have to determine longitudes with an 'elastic' marine chronometer. A measuring instrument of this type is frequently regulated. Dead-reckoning, with logbook and chronometer, requires incessant checking, which enables any potential drift or error to be corrected. So a margin of error was sometimes allowed for. Unfortunately, certain scientists refuse to do so today when it comes to announcing dates.

For my part, the dating is not in contradiction with my idea of an advanced civilisation developing in the Antarctic, perhaps four or five millennia ago. However, it is the location of this continent some considerable distance away from its current position at the pole, not all that long ago, that leaves me perplexed.

2.4   Continental drift

Everyone today knows that the continents are not immobile. Already at the start of the 20th century this continental drift was a subject that aroused great excitement.

In particular, people based their arguments on morphological considerations. The shapes of the continents of South America and Africa, in particular, make it easy to imagine that the one continent once fitted into the other. The shapes of the two shores of the Red Sea, as well as those of Antarctica when matched with Australia, demonstrate the same phenomenon.

By complementing these deductions with the observation of zoological and palaeontological resemblances, people imagined that there was once a continent they called Gondwana, which included, in the Southern Hemisphere, Australia, Antarctica, India, Africa, Madagascar and South America. This super-continent broke up, they suggested, in the Jurassic period. As a result of the earth's rotation, it was thought, the continental blocks drifted like gigantic liners, over the ocean floors.

Palaeomagnetism

This is the study of ferro-magnetic particles deposited in sedimentary rocks or trapped in volcanic rocks. These particles allow us to find out the magnetic induction vector of a particular spot at the time it was formed.

Now this fossil magnetism shows discontinuities in the localisation of the North Pole, depending on the place it is situated. The strange routes the North Pole followed vis-à-vis Europe and America have been reconstructed: they turn out to have been divergent. To overcome this anomaly, the continents must have migrated relative to one another. Thus it was that the continents' ability to drift was confirmed.

Plate tectonics

We learn from plate tectonics that the surface of our globe is fragmented into plates almost like a jigsaw puzzle. The six biggest plates are the Pacific, Eurasian, African, American, Indo-Australian and Antarctic. Smaller plates are those of the Caribbean, Cocos, Nazca, Scotia, Philippines, and Arabia. Juan de Fuca, the Fijian Islands, the Carolinas, the Adriatic, Greece, Turkey, the south of the Caspian Sea and Tibet are eight microplates that make up the tally.

As can be seen, these plates are either terrestrial (such as the Eurasiatic plate), marine, or mixed (such as the American and African plates). They compose the lithosphere, whose thickness – which is variable – is formed by the following layers, working down from the surface:

- a crust of a thickness of 20 to 40km made essentially of granite, of a density of 2.67 to 2.77 g/cc and reduced under the oceans to a thickness of 5 to 8km of basalt, with a density of 2.9 g/cc;
- a boundary layer called the Moho discontinuity;
- around 100km of upper mantle with a density of 3.3 to 3.4 g/cc.

All of this together represents only around 1/100 of the earth's radius. These plates rest on the viscous layer of the asthenosphere, which we sometimes see emerge during a volcanic eruption.

The latter, subjected to enormous pressures, is swept by powerful convection currents, right down to the depths under discussion – perhaps 2,000 to 3,000km. These movements affect from below the rough lower surface of the lithosphere with sufficient adhesive force to move the tectonic plates. It is in this way that continental drift is produced.

When two plates come together, there are two possible configurations:

- They can slip over one another, the heavier one sliding under the lighter one. This is known as a zone of 'subduction'. For instance, a marine plate can disappear and raise the edge of a terrestrial plate to lead to mountain ranges rising, like the Cordillera of the Andes.

- They may collide without either of them gaining the upper hand. In this way, when Indo-Australia crashed into Eurasia, it created the Himalayas.

When two plates move away from each other, the magma contained in the fault separating them cools, and is incorporated into each of them individually, forming a 'dorsal'.

Here, the image of a jigsaw puzzle reveals its limits, since it implies that the pieces are not subject to deformation and are all trapped on one and the same plane.

In fact, tectonic plates can not only grow bigger to either side of a dorsal, or see their surface area diminish in the zones of subduction, but they can also become deformed under the pressure of their mutual contact.

The movement detected, in each plate, is a particularly slow movement – of the order of 1cm per year. This is much too slow to explain how the Antarctic continent might have been so far away from the pole only a few thousand years ago.

2.5 The glaciations of the Quaternary era

The Quaternary began with a strange ice age. Several glaciations then apparently followed one another in north-east Europe, covering in a layer of ice:

- the British Isles, with the exception of a narrow strip in the south, in southern Ireland and southern England between the Bristol Channel and the Thames estuary;
- Scandinavia, Denmark, Holland, North Germany and the whole of north-east Europe as far as a southern frontier extending from Belgium to the Ukraine, just to the north of the Black Sea.

But by some completely incomprehensible mystery, this glaciation stopped in the east at the Urals, sparing:

- the whole of Siberia in all its vastness, as far as the Bering Strait – even though the north-east of Siberia is a mountainous region with high ranges, in which are situated Verkhoyansk and its region which is at present the coldest in the Northern Hemisphere;
- the whole of North China.

Charles Hapgood points out that the ice covering in Europe was unusually disposed, in the form of an ice cap of a surface area comparable to the current ice caps, but with the centre of this surface occupied by the glaciers apparently and unexpectedly centred at around 71°N and 10°E.

A similar study in North America shows an ice cap of similar dimensions, but centred a dozen or so degrees further south than its European equivalent, i.e., 60°N and 83°W.

Indeed, in a similarly strange way, this Quaternary glaciation spared:

- a coastal band extending as far as Newfoundland and a territory as big as that island, to the north-west of Newfoundland;

- all the islands in the extreme north of Canada, as far as Greenland;
- the Canadian north-west as far as the Bering Strait;
- Lakes Michigan and Huron to the south;
- the south-west of Winnipeg, the entire south and west of Saskatechewan, and the whole of Alberta.

The glaciation stopped in the west at around meridian 110°W. One last, remarkable position is found in the Yukon, in Alaska, where traces of an ice cap can be found.

These glaciations of the Quaternary raise a major obstacle:

- We cannot resort to any significant continental drift, since even if we suppose that a million years elapsed, with a drift of between 1 and 3cm per year, our continents would not have moved more than 30km from their current positions.
- No hypothesis will work that relies on the intervention of a global cooling leading to circular glaciations centred on such precise positions, and not in a zone covering all the regions in the Northern Hemisphere as far as a low latitude that is practically uniform.
- No reason can be imagined that reduces these glaciations to the Northern Hemisphere alone, sparing the Southern.

The only possible explanation is perfectly logical: the geographic North Pole must have been situated at the centre of these glaciations, and these icy circular regions corresponded to the interior of a polar circle!

Corals grow in sea water to depths of between 50 and 60m. They need warm water, at temperatures between 15° and 30°C. The Chinese geologist Ying Ting Ma[1], in a study of the different varieties of coral, succeeded in determining from the examination of cells the latitude and temperature of the location at the time of formation.

The fossil coral found in terrains belonging to the Ordovician, the

---

1   Ying Ting Ma, *Research on the Past Climate and Continental Drift*, World Book Co., Taipei, 1958.

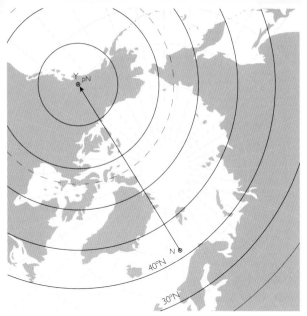

Figure 32. Circa 2000 BC, point Y, now in the Yukon, shifted to the North Pole (until circa 1250 BC). Circa 1250 BC, point N, near Norway, shifted to point Y. The lithosphere rotated 47°5' in the direction of the arrow.

Between circa 1250 and 1200 BC, point N, near Norway, was at the North Pole. Around 1200 BC, point H, in Hudson Bay, shifted to point N. The lithosphere rotated 37° in the direction of the arrow.

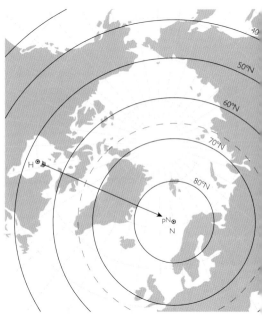

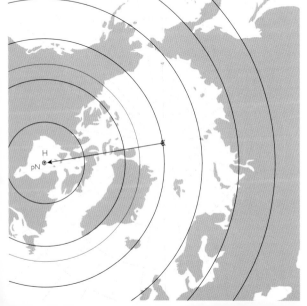

Between circa 1200 and 700 BC, point H, in Hudson Bay, was at the North Pole. Circa 700 BC, the region situated at present at the North Pole shifted towards point H. The lithosphere shifted in the direction of the arrow.

Silurian, the Devonian, the Cretacean and the Tertiary, enabled Ma to attribute the following characteristics to these terrains: altitude, latitude, and temperature at the time the coral was formed. In particular, Ma tried to situate, at each place, where the equator was situated vis-à-vis the latter – in other words, where the terrestrial poles were situated.

Ma deduced from this the successive mutations in the apparent terrestrial poles, accompanied with the relative movements of the continents. He proclaimed that the earth had thus experienced in the past:

- A "sudden and total shift of the earth's rigid exterior, that succumbed to slippages with relation to the core of the rotating earth."
- This happened at various times, separated by long periods of tranquillity.
- But these events were accompanied by intense volcanic activity, preceded and followed each time by a lesser and more local activity.
- If the latitude of the place in question then increased, the temperature decreased as did the sea level. The inverse happened if the latitude diminished.

Hapgood agreed with Ting Ying Ma in his conclusions. On the other hand, he thought that it was difficult to give credence to the deductions that had led Ma to trace the apparent zig-zag trajectory of the terrestrial North Pole with regard to the lithosphere, starting from the proximity of the present South Pole, then crossing the Indian Ocean and reaching its current position.

On the basis of numerous previous observations and sponsored by Albert Einstein, Charles Hapgood in *Earth's Shifting Crust* concluded that the North Pole must have successively occupied three geographical positions during the Quaternary period:

- 60° north and 135° west, in the Yukon;
- 71° north and 10° east, some 450km to the west of the northernmost cape of Norway;
- 60° north and 83° west, in Hudson Bay, to the north-west of Quebec in Canada.

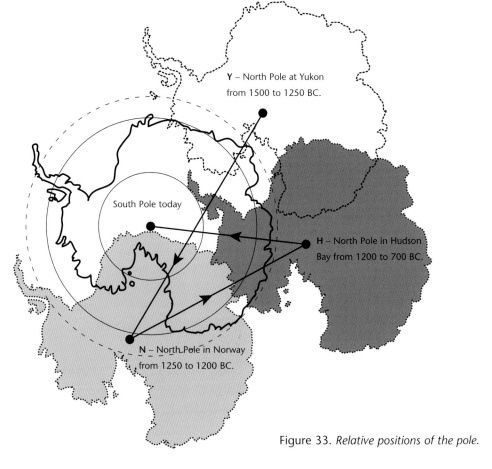

Figure 33. *Relative positions of the pole.*

In consequence, the South Pole must have been situated in regions that are at present situated:

- 60° south and 45° east;
- 71° south and 170° west;
- 60° south and 97° east.

These centres are at orthodromic distances of 48°, 36° and 30° from each other. The ice caps situated in the Southern Hemisphere were at that time essentially oceanic, each time covering only a part of the Antarctic continent. This explains the absence of Quaternary continental glaciations in South America, Africa and Australia.

These successive positions cannot be determined to a precision of one degree, but they can be located to within maybe three to five degrees. Furthermore, they remain valid for North America as far as the glaciations in the Yukon and Hudson Bay are concerned, and valid for Eurasia as far as the Norwegian glaciation goes. But they risk being somewhat different for the other continents if the plates changed position with respect to each other at the time of these changes.

This is particularly plausible for South America, and above all for Antarctica, as is suggested by the ancient maps which all show this continent lying close to Tierra del Fuego in Patagonia, with the Palmer Land Peninsula no longer separated from Coats Land. The maps of *Terra Australis* seem to have been drawn up when the western extremity of Queen Maud Land and the southernmost tip of South America met near the present Sandwich Islands, at around 57° south and 27° west. This presupposes a double drift of around 2,000km with respect to this point.

The earth's movement is extremely regular. Its annual variations are perfectly insignificant. There are only two possibilities to explain such a displacement of the poles:

- either the geographical poles suddenly migrated (the earth's axis changed inclination);
- or the continents suddenly shifted: but the tectonic plates cannot have done so over such big distances, separately, because of the obstacle presented by the neighbouring plates. In this case, it was the whole set of plates imbricated into one another that started to drift of its own motion.

The equatorial radius of the earth is 22km bigger than its polar radius, with an average figure of 6,367km. A flattening of 1/297 is very small. It is determined by the speed of rotation which, thanks to the effect of centrifugal force, reduces gravity to 9.78 m/s^2, as opposed to 9.81 m/s^2 at the poles.

The enormous inertia of the earth's mass prevents its speed of rotation from varying in any clear and perceptible way on the human scale, since the stability of its axis of rotation would be zero only if it were to stop turning. Great force is thus needed to bring about any change. We can resort to an external cause, for instance the fall of a big meteorite striking the earth's surface at a favourable angle, or an internal cause such as the rapid uplift of the Himalayas, occasioning a temporary disequilibrium. At this stage of our discoveries we cannot rule out any hypothesis.

But even massive meteorite showers can in their fall produce forces of an order of only 10 to the power 16 or 18 daN. In other terms, they are therefore incapable of causing the upheavals we have been studying. A meteorite falling onto the earth's surface corresponds, in terms of force, to a grain of dust landing on the back of a galloping mastodon!

In reality, to cause such shocks, a large asteroid would need to collide with the earth. The consequences of the collision would then be too devastating for life to survive on earth. So it seems improbable that such a collision could explain a change in the position of the poles when there would already have been human beings around to witness it!

The rigid surface of the earth, the lithosphere, whose average depth is only around 1/100 of the earth's radius, is prone to slip and slide on its fluid base, the asthenosphere. But it is difficult to be certain, when we still cannot get deep enough down below the earth's surface. Drilling enables us to penetrate only a few thousand metres or so at most. The lower levels are affected by waves and interpreting these is a matter for specialists, who work with controversial criteria.

What form – doubtless a varied one – does the surface of separation between the lithosphere and the asthenosphere take? The heat and the radioactivity prevalent in the latter doubtless create convection movements like those in a boiling liquid.

These movements affect the lithosphere from below: it is fragmented into plates. For each of these plates, these impulses set up a horizontal force tending to shift it by a few centimetres per year, in a precise direction, which has been precisely measured in our own day.

The horizontal impulse of the convection currents in the mantle thus imposes constraints on the base of the lithosphere: it is the most colossal potential energy in reserve on our whole planet. The force deployed by active volcanoes and earthquakes represents but a tiny part of that which acts on the earth's mantle, capable as it is of raising mountain ranges and shifting continents.

Each tectonic plate necessarily has a certain quantity of constraining energy proper to it, characterised by a vector torque applied at the earth's centre: its effect enables its direction and significance to be precisely determined. As for its intensity, it is impossible to know this for sure. In fact, each plate is prevented from shifting thanks to a resistant torque opposing it with an almost equal intensity.

It is the difference between the two that creates the displacement that we observe in each plate.

This resistant torque is created by the adjacent plates which have other ideas about moving to a different spot. Taken as a whole, the sum of all the vector torques applied by the asthenosphere to the plates is an aleatory and variable result, which would tend to make the lithosphere as a whole turn on the asthenosphere – which is not at all the case at present.

The only force opposing it must thus be the rubbing of the one on the other. It seems that the zones of subduction, extending far down to depths of the order of a hundred or so kilometres, act like an anchoring line on a ship and keep the whole lot immobile. Energy can thus slowly accumulate in the earth's crust, stored in the form of constraints in the compressible rocky masses. Let us imagine that one of the anchoring lines is broken: the continents could then start to drift…

The lithosphere, moved by a considerable force, would then experience an increasing angular acceleration to the point where the forces of compression disappear. These forces are gigantic, but they are stored away in a material that is not very compressible. A slight dilation leads to zero energy. Thus it is that the speed of rotation was able to grow until the angle of rotation reached about 5°, but hardly any more.

This period of angular acceleration may last for half an hour, in a non-uniform fashion, following the break-up of entire portions of the marine crust, within the subduction zones of the ocean dorsals.

If we assume a constant angular acceleration and an angle of 5° in half an hour, the continents, borne by this movement immanent to the earth, would have been shifted at up to a maximum angular speed of 20°/hour. Once the movement had begun, were billows set up by the slippage likely to appear at the asthenosphere/lithosphere limit, and to completely modify their relative adhesion? Imagine the angular deceleration then lasted for five hours, for example, and the speed would have changed from 20°/hour to 0, i.e., an average of 10°/hour over five hours. The total rotation would in this case have been 55° in five and a half hours.

This hypothesis is compatible with the distances between the centres of glaciation. We must note in passing that the rotation necessary to move a single point on a perfect sphere from one place to another is not necessarily the shortest (orthodromic). So there is little chance that this was the case for the rotations of the lithosphere and we need to envisage a shift of over 48°.

On the earth's surface, the consequences will depend on the position relative to the poles of rotation, or Eulerian poles. On these poles, there will be no shift or change in latitude. On the Eulerian equator, the ground will move with a maximum speed of 20°/hour. This is somewhat more rapid than the speed of a point situated on our equator, due to the earth's rotation, i.e., 1667 km/hour. Between these two positions, the horizontal shift will be in proportion to the distance of the Eulerian pole.

The consequences for life on the surface are quite simply catastrophic… In fact, because of their inertia and their relative thinness with regard to their extent, the oceans do not immediately change their courses. They overwhelm the mountains, causing great damage.

In the same way, the radius of curvature of the tectonic plates is not adapted to their new position. The land masses near the poles become flattened, which entails a significant compression in surface area and, in the interval, a major retreat on the part of the oceans. On the other hand, the land masses near the equator become more rounded, which entails fissures in the ground and, in the interval, a rise in water level.[2]

2   C. Hapgood, *Earth's Shifting Crust*, Museum Press Ltd, London, 1959.

On the earth as a whole, and particularly at certain points where this is startlingly obvious, we find massive deposits at unacceptable and quite unexpected altitudes, or else in estuaries. One particularly striking example is constituted by the diluvia of the Rhône and the Durance, rivers which flow into the Mediterranean in the south-east of France.

This word 'diluvium' was used in France, especially in the last century, to designate a sudden shift in continental waters, invading the interior of the continents, then immediately returning to flow out seawards, furrowing the banks of watercourses, and sweeping along sand, gravel, pebbles, blocks small and large, sometimes enormous. The water was thrown into the valley with a force which the present currents of our rivers and seas can give us no idea of.[3]

How are we to explain this enormous and brutal mass, sweeping along colossal masses of debris? Charles Hapgood imagines the sudden rise of the Alps, or the sudden collapse of a section of the earth's crust. A sudden slippage of this crust may well have been enough to produce the same result and to have created the brutal uplift of the Alps.

Without phenomenal crises in the earth's layers, the deposits of the Rhône and the Durance, among others, would not have been found so far from their estuary of origin. The same is true – and in an even more spectacular fashion – for those erratic blocks torn away from specific orogenic formations and discovered hundreds of kilometres away from their place of origin.

These innumerable rocks are found more often near the sea but sometimes far inland, in plains, on hills or the sides of mountains. They are found in completely unexpected places, in regions that are geologically quite different.

Starting out in the mountains of Scandinavia, they have been catapulted onto the Carpathians. They have also crossed the North Sea to end up in Great Britain. One of them even went and planted itself on the highest peak of the Isle of Man! In southern Sweden, in Malmö, one famous erratic block is 4,800m long, 300m wide and has a thickness of 60m. Around 280 blocks

3   C. Hapgood, *Earth's Shifting Crust, op. cit.*.

of tens of cubic metres each have come away from the Alps, crossed Lake Geneva and deposited themselves on the Jura Mountains. Others, weighing between 10,000 and 18,000 tonnes, left the granite formations of Canada and Labrador to bestrew Maine, New Jersey, Michigan, Ohio, the White Mountains, the Berkshires and the Pocono Mountains. As Charles Hapgood explains, gigantic tidal waves assaulted the continents, inundating mountains and valleys, carrying along a mass of rocks, stones and debris.[4]

All these factors enable us to conclude that the continents crashed into peaceful oceans. At great speed, they set in motion masses equivalent to those of inland seas. Several enormous swells deposited, as they rebounded, a mass of sediments at over 100m altitude, halfway up the hills and finally at 10 or 20m or so above the present level.

The British lawyer Sir Charles Lyell, considered to be the founder of geology, wrote:

> Never was there a dogma more calculated to foster indolence, and to blunt the keen edge of curiosity, than this assumption of the discordance between the ancient and existing causes of change. [...] For this reason all theories are rejected which involve the assumption of sudden and violent catastrophes and revolutions of the whole earth, and its inhabitants – theories which are restrained by no reference to existing analogies [...][5]

It is obvious that in normal periods, there are no storms, nor tidal waves, nor landslides, nor earthquakes, nor volcanic eruptions. It is also obvious that our planet has experienced, in the course of its history, long periods of stability, interrupted on rare occasions by sudden violent catastrophes, during geological upheavals, that cannot be compared to the conditions that exist now – real revolutions affecting entire regions of the earth, if not indeed the earth itself as a whole.

---

4   See the chapter 'The great extinctions' in C. Hapgood, *Earth's Shifting Crust, op. cit.*

5   C. Lyell, *Principles of geology,* John Murray, 1872, pp. 318-9.

The facts are there, readable at the surface of the earth, and we need to examine them. Lyell is forced to do so, in spite of his 'dogmatic' principles.

> when we arrange the fossiliferous formations in chronological order, they constitute a broken and defective series of monuments: we pass without any intermediate gradations from systems of strata which are horizontal, to other systems which are highly inclined – from rocks of peculiar mineral composition to others which have a character wholly distinct – from one assemblage of organic remains to another, in which frequently nearly all the species, and a large part of the genera, are different. These violations of continuity are so common as to constitute in most regions the rule rather than the exception, and they have been considered by many geologists as conclusive in favour of sudden revolutions in the inanimate and animate world.[6]

Darwin, a disciple of Lyell, wrote in his famous journal, on 9 January 1834:

> What, then, has exterminated so many species and whole genera? The mind at first is irresistibly hurried into the belief of some great catastrophe; but thus to destroy animals, both large and small, in Southern Patagonia, in Brazil, on the Cordillera of Peru, in North America up to Behring's Straits, we must shake the entire framework of the globe. [...] No one will imagine that a drought, even far severer than those which cause such losses in the provinces of La Plata, could destroy every individual of every species from Southern Patagonia to Behring's Straits. What shall we say of the extinction of the horse? Did those plains fail of pasture, which have since been overrun by thousands and hundreds of thousands of the descendants of the stock introduced by the Spaniards? [...] Certainly, no fact in the long history of the world is so startling as the wide and repeated exterminations of its inhabitants.

6   C. Lyell, *op. cit.*, p. 298.

The Equidae did indeed vanish from the Americas around the second millennium BC. Representations of the horse can be found in the civilisation that cultivated the land around Santiago del Estrero at the foot of the Cordillera of the Andes. So the horse must have walked on the New World long before the arrival of the Spaniards, only to disappear. The next year, in the course of his voyage on the *Beagle*, Darwin wrote in his journal, on 30 March 1835:

It required little geological practice to interpret the marvellous story which this scene at once unfolded; though I confess I was at first so much astonished that I could scarcely believe the plainest evidence. I saw the spot where a cluster of fine trees once waved their branches on the shores of the Atlantic, when that ocean (now driven back 700 miles) came to the foot of the Andes. I saw that they had sprung from a volcanic soil which had been raised above the level of the sea, and that subsequently this dry land, with its upright trees, had been let down into the depths of the ocean. In these depths, the formerly dry land was covered by sedimentary beds, and these again by enormous streams of submarine lava – one such mass attaining the thickness of a thousand feet; and these deluges of molten stone and aqueous deposits five times alternately had been spread out. The ocean which received such thick masses must have been profoundly deep; but again the subterranean forces exerted themselves, and I now beheld the bed of that ocean, forming a chain of mountains more than seven thousand feet in height. [...] Vast, and scarcely comprehensible as such changes must ever appear, yet they have all occurred within a period, recent when compared with the history of the Cordillera; and the Cordillera itself is absolutely modern as compared with many of the fossiliferous strata of Europe and America.[7]

7   C. Darwin, *Journal of Researches into the Natural History and Geology of the countries visited during the voyage round the world of the H.M.S Beagle*, 11th edition, John Murray, London, 1913, p. 353-4. Journal entry of 30 March 1835.

This era was recent since traces of human occupation were found by Darwin all along the elevated beaches at the foot of the Andes:

> On the west coast of South America, lines of raised terrace containing recent shells have been traced by Darwin as proofs of a great upheaval of that part of the globe in modern geological time. The terraces are not quite horizontal but rise towards the south. [...] That some of these ancient sea-margins belong to the human period was shown by Mr. Darwin's discovery of shells with bones of birds, ears of maize, plaited reeds and cotton thread, in one of the terraces opposite Callao at a height of 85 feet.[8]

The raising of the Andes Cordillera is attributed to a relative movement of the tectonic plate of South America relative to the Pacific marine plate. So this must have happened, not only in the Quaternary, but at a quite recent historical period, in which maize was grown, rushes were woven, and cotton threads were made. So we are justified in thinking that the maps of Antarctica were drawn up before the event that made South America drift some 3,000km west, between Tierra del Fuego and the Sandwich Islands, with Queen Maud Land drifting simultaneously some 1,800km south-east.

But in that case, this slippage of the South American plate, if it were rapid enough, relative to the ocean, would explain how masses of displaced water caused a series of oscillations, as well as thick flows of lava, creating those "deluges of molten stone and aqueous deposits."

Furthermore, this slippage would explain an elevation of 2,000m, as well as a difference in elevation, if South America pivoted around the Panama region, slipping much more in its southern part than in its central part. Darwin wrote:

> It is impossible to reflect on the changed state of the American continent without the deepest astonishment. Formerly it must have swarmed with great monsters: now we find mere pigmies, compared with the antecedent

---

8   A. Geikie, *Text Book of Geology,* Macmillan, London, 1893, p. 288.

allied races. [...] The greater number, if not all, of these extinct quadrupeds lived at a late period, and were the contemporaries of most of the existing sea-shells.[9]

Darwinian meditations

The changes in climate which took place, the volcanic eruptions, the movements of the earth's crust, bringing about upsurges in sea water, floods, wiped out whole peoples, and forced others to migrate.[10]

One of the most important questions in biology is indeed that of the evolution of living species. To be an evolutionist means accepting that life unfolds with variations of every sort, creating types, races or varieties, but all within the limits of its fundamental organisation. This does not really mean being a 'fixist', a creationist who believes in fixed types, since variations remain possible. It means being a 'stabilist', believer in stable types, since the species itself always preserves its own mechanism of life and its definite biological equilibria.

To be a transformist means believing that living species, animal and vegetable, proceed from one another, by means of successive transformations and genetic transmissions, whether they start out from raw matter or living matter: a materialist will view life as emanating from inert matter, by purely physico-chemical processes. Here is what Darwin wrote, in a letter of 1860, i.e., two years after *The Origin of Species*:

[...] why may I not invent the hypothesis of Natural Selection (which from the analogy of domestic productions, and from what we know of the struggle for existence and of the variability of organic beings, is, in some very slight degree, in itself probable) and try whether this hypothesis of Natural Selection does not explain (as I think it does) a large number of facts in

9   C. Darwin, *Journal, op. cit.,* 9 January 1834.

10   J. de Morgan, *op. cit.,* I, p. 46.

198

geographical distribution – geological succession, classification, morphology, embryology, etc.[11]

Teilhard writes:

I am aware of the extent to which, in itself, the exploration of the earth cannot shed any light on or offer any solution to the fundamental questions of life. I have the sense of circling a huge problem, without really getting to the heart of it. The more this problem seems to grow before my eyes, the more I see that its solution is not to be found anywhere else but in a faith, far removed from any experience. One must go against and beyond appearances…

Maurice Vernet comments:

It is very striking to see in one or other of these texts that Darwin, like Teilhard, declared himself unable to produce any scientific evidence of transformism between species. Judging by this then, the testimony of those who are best placed to know about it, transformism is pure hypothesis, and it is only through his faith that Teilhard – he himself admits it – continues to make it his own. In his case it is only a matter of a kind of mystical intuition.[12]

Slow processes of adaptation have sometimes been imagined for certain animal species. The frozen mammoths of Siberia must have adapted to the cold. Their ears must have become small enough not to freeze. Their hair must have grown to protect them from the cold, as for the woolly rhinoceros.

The limits of this theory of adaptation in cold regions lie in the fact that, for the mammoth, its sweat glands actually secrete a non-oily liquid and so in this case its hair protects it from heat alone. This same liquid is found in tropical wild animals.

11 Darwin, letter to J. S. Henslow, 8 May 1860.

12 M. Vernet, *La Grande Illusion de Teilhard de Chardin*, Éditions Gedalge, Paris, 1964.

The founder of palaeontology, Cuvier, said in 1827:

When the traveler goes through fertile plains where tranquil waters nourish with their regular flow an abundant vegetation and where the ground, trodden by numerous people and decorated with flourishing villages, rich cities, and superb monuments, is never troubled except by ravages of war or by the oppression of men in power, he is not tempted to believe that nature has also had its internal wars and that the surface of the earth has been overthrown by revolutions and catastrophes. But his ideas change as soon as he seeks to dig through this soil, today so calm. [...]

That catastrophe also left in the northern countries the cadavers of great quadrupeds locked in the ice, preserved right up to our time with their skin, hair, and flesh. If they had not been frozen as soon as they were killed, decay would have caused them to decompose. On the other hand, this permanent freezing was not a factor previously in the places where these animals were trapped. For they would not have been able to live in such a temperature.

Hence the same instant which killed the animals froze the country where they lived. This event was sudden, instantaneous, without any gradual development. What is so clearly demonstrated for this most recent catastrophe is hardly less so for the earlier ones. The rending, rearranging, and overturning of more ancient layers leave no doubt that sudden and violent causes placed them in the state in which we see them. The very force of the movements which the bodies of water experienced is still attested to by the mountain of remains and rounded pebbles interposed in many places between the solid layers. Thus, life on this earth has often been disturbed by dreadful events. Innumerable living creatures have been victims of these catastrophes. [...]

Thus, to repeat what we have said, it is vain for someone to seek in the forces which affect the surface of the earth today causes sufficient to produce the upheavals and catastrophes whose traces the earth's surface shows us.[13]

---

13 G. Cuvier, *Revolutionary Upheavals on the Surface of the Globe and on the changes which they have produced in the animal kingdom* (trans. I. C. Johnston), based on 3rd French edition 1825, http://www.mala.bc.ca/~johnstoi/cuvier/cuvier.htm.

In Africa and America, the discovery of the skeletons of dismembered and partly devoured animals, with their bones dispersed, indicates a natural death. On the other hand, it is difficult to attribute a natural death to entire buried herds when their flesh and ligaments were not yet decomposed. All their bones, even the smallest, had stayed in place.

What are we to say of the La Brea Tar Pits in California, and the giant cemeteries of fish piled up in the ground? They were buried in such a short time that the bodies of the fossils are twisted, their mouths gaping open, even the colour of their scales can sometimes be seen.

These huge burial grounds bear the manifest traces of an abnormal violence which has shifted enormous creatures so powerfully as to tear off their limbs. This violence took effect with such rapidity that these animals ended up being buried in such a way that they were sheltered from the elements and surviving predators.

Philippe Taquet has shown the necessity of "geological events," such as the raising of the Aïr desert, which would have enabled a dinosaur to be buried "in a fine sandy sediment very shortly after its death."[14]

How could human beings have forgotten to mention in their mythologies the upheavals associated with the movements of the earth's crust?

Within the texts that have long been known to us, there perhaps lies hidden a description of the gigantic cataclysms about which I have just been speculating.

14 Ph. Taquet, *L'Empreinte des dinosaures*, Éditions Odile Jacob, 1994.

202

3.1 Polynesia

In the epic known as the *Kumulipo*, a Hawaiian hymn of creation begins with these words:

> *At the time when the earth became hot*
> *At the time when the heavens turned about*
> *At the time when the sun was darkened [...]*
> *The source of the darkness that made darkness*
> *The source of the night that made night*
> *The intense darkness, the deep darkness*
> *Darkness of the sun, darkness of the night*
> *Nothing but night.*[1]

Tangaroa-the-chief sent one of his brothers "to seek a country in this world." Finding nothing, he returned to heaven and to the mountain (*rangi*). He finally spotted a "white expanse," a stretch of land or a reef. After heading towards it, he realised that he could not stand on it: "there was nowhere for him to set his foot and rest." The myths explain this fact as a result of the way Tangaroa-the-worker must have "spread over the surface of the waves an avalanche of spongy rocks." This "Earth fallen from heaven," on which you cannot set foot, where "no tree grows," is quite simply an island of pumice stone, huge examples of which can be seen near the Sunda Islands, in the Indian Ocean, following the eruption of Krakatoa.[2]

1   M. Beckwith, *The Kumulipo: a Hawaiian creation chant*, University of Chicago Press, Chicago, 1951.

2   E. Caillot, *Mythes, légendes et traditions des Polynésiens*, Leroux, 1914, p. 250.

Figure 34. *Wooden figurine from Rarotonga, dating from the end of the 18th or the beginning of the 19th century AD. It possibly represents Tangaroa, the Polynesian god of creation.*

3.2 China

The isles of the immortals

Very far to the east of the Oriental sea
Lies a bottomless Abyss: the Kouei-hiu
Where all the waters of the world mingle.
Above the Kouei-hiu
There are five magical islands
Where the Immortals reside,
Dressed in feathers and equipped with wings,
Where the plants of immortality grow on which they feed.
To start with, these islands were not fixed to the bottom of the sea,
They floated freely...
The immortals complained to the emperor of the sky.
He gave the order to Yu-kiang to fix the islands,
With fifteen big turtles, three for each island...
They should take turns... lasting sixty thousand years...
However, it happened that a giant... started to fish for the turtles.
He took away six, in one go.
The two islands, deprived of their support,
Drifted to the North pole,
And sank into the sea.[1]

If, due to its feet, the turtle can indicate the four cardinal directions, it also stands on a flat, square base, like the earth. Its back is round, like the sky, and, by its longevity, it symbolises immortality and thus the original polar world.

These islands really did travel with the Antarctic tectonic plate towards the pole. So how can we imagine that, after several centuries spent in the Northern Hemisphere, they headed not for the North Pole but the South Pole, on the other side of the world?

1   M. Granet, *La Pensée chinoise*, Albin Michel, 1950, p. 357.

204

The flood of Yao

The story of the cataclysm that brought man's happiness to an end in the seventh *ki* is related by several Chinese sages. The monster Kong-Kong is named as the cause of the flood. Niu-va then comes up behind him and re-establishes the world's order.

According to Lo-Pi, Kong-Kong summoned the flood and broke the bonds uniting heaven and earth. Niu-va fought against Kong-Kong, restored the four cardinal points, and re-established peace on earth, which was now set the right way round again.

For Yun-Tse, Kong-Kong charged with his horns into Mount Poutcheou, knocked over the pillars of heaven and broke its bonds with earth. Fortunately, Niu-va restored heaven, and fired arrows at 10 suns.

Finally, for Hoai-Nan-Tse, when Kong-Kong charged with his horns into Mount Poutcheou, the pillars of heaven were smashed and the bonds of earth broken.

These three descriptions are very similar. They refer to a major event, analogous to the upheaval described by the Polynesians.

Long ago, when Niou-koua undertook to set out the universe,
The four poles were upside down,
The nine Provinces were cracked,
The Sky did not cover everything,
Fire raged without ever being extinguished,
Waters swelled up without ever subsiding,
Ferocious beasts devoured fit and healthy men,
Birds of prey carried off the feeble.
Niou-koua, then, melted down the stones of five colours to repair the azure sky;
She cut off the legs of the turtle in order to erect the four poles;
She killed the black dragon to bring order to the land of Ki;
She piled up ashes of reed to hold back the licentious waters.
The sky was repaired,
The four poles rose up,

The licentious waters drained away,
The land of Ki was set to rights,
The ferocious beasts perished,
The fit and healthy men lived on, [...]
And union was created between Yin and Yang.[2]

Finally, Emperor Yao had the monster Kong-Kong exiled to the 'land of darkness'. Furthermore, the master of Fo-hi and Niu-va is called the first of the immortals (Sien): this is a twofold allusion to a polar region.

The waters rose up to the Sky.
Roaring, they enveloped the mountains and covered the hills.
Men perished in this sea. [...]
There was much suffering caused by this great flood
Which covered the hills from all directions, went beyond the mountains,
And seemed to reach all the way to the Heavens.[3]

The Chinese are used to floods, but you never see rivers climbing up hills and mountains. On the other hand, an extensive and rapid slippage in the earth's crust, in which the oceans and rivers do not move because of their inertia, explains such an exceptional event perfectly well.

It is accompanied by the fire of volcanoes that never become extinct, the piling up of volcanic ash, but also the sky's movement vis-à-vis its usual course:

Kong-Kong smashed the pillar of the sky and broke the moorings.
The sky tipped over, leaning toward the northeast,
So much so that the Sun, the Moon and the Constellations
Had to move towards the west,
Whereas on the earth, which, tipping in the other direction,

2   M. Granet, *La Pensée chinoise, op. cit.*, pp. 344-6.

3   R. Wilhelm, *Histoire de la civilisation chinoise*, Payot, 1931, p. 74.

Ceased to be filled to the southeast, all the rivers
Headed in the direction of this gaping space.[4]

So the ground in China suddenly slipped, which entails the corollary of an apparent fall of the stars in the opposite direction. The apparent direction of the stars' motion changed, as did the necessarily immutable laws governing the earth's rotation.

The Yin dynasty, also called Shang, succeeded the Hia.

This glorious dynasty succeeded in re-establishing order on heaven and earth: "T'ang the victorious, the founder of the Yin, ordered the course of the rivers" and "pacified the interior of the seas."[5]

4   M. Granet, *La Pensée chinoise, op. cit.*, p. 544-6.

5   M. Granet, *La Civilisation chinoise*, Albin Michel, 1948, p. 21.

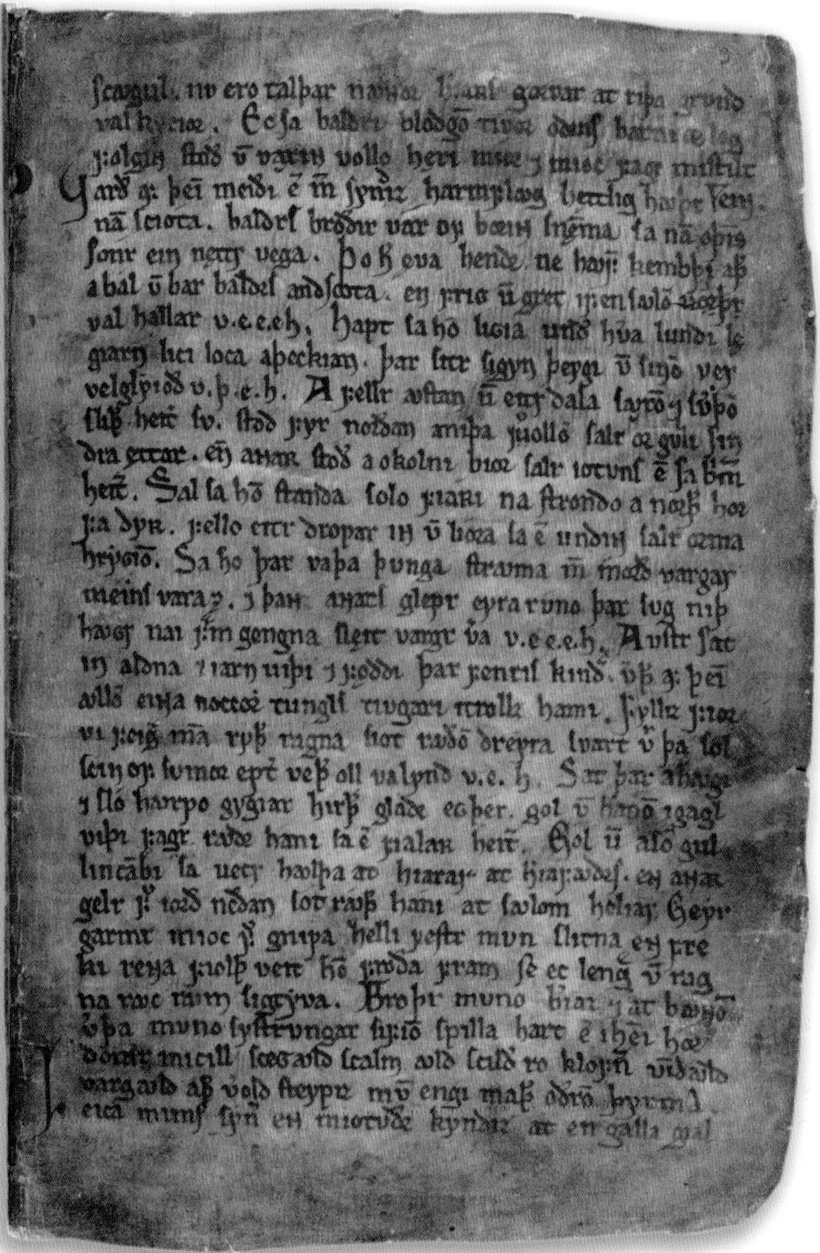

Figure 35. *Text from the* Codex Regius *of the* Edda, *a collection of ancient poems from Iceland.*

3.3 Iceland

Here, the images of the cataclysm and its repercussions become more and more precise and complement the mythologies we have previously discussed.

The great Fimbul winter

The *Edda* announces a battle that will precede the end of the world. The well ordered laws of nature will be overturned by a major event in which the forces of nature will be unleashed. To whom, or what, are we to attribute this catastrophe? To the gods' inevitable destiny, or *ragnarok*. The word *rokkr* means darkness, and the Norse poets said *ragnarokkr*, or twilight. This would also become the famous 'twilight of the gods'.

> *First, there is a winter called the Fimbul-winter, when snow drives from all quarters, the frosts are so severe, the winds so keen and piercing, that there is no joy in the sun. There are three such winters in succession, without any intervening summer. But before these there are three other winters, during which great wars rage over all the world. Brothers slay each other for the sake of gain, and no one spares his father or mother in that manslaughter and adultery.*[1]

This world could not last, as the gods themselves had shaken its foundations. The signs of the catastrophe would become increasingly numerous. Then we see a litter of wolves rising up, the sons of a giantess and Fenrir. One of these wolves would be bold enough to chase after the sun and seize it in its jaws.

Then the sun turns black, as do the summers. The sky, deprived of sunlight, was always grey and cold (as in winter), filled with gusts of snow blowing in from the four corners of the horizon. On the earth, everything totters and falls, nothing is sacred any longer, murder reigns unchecked.

---

1 Snorri Sturluson, *The younger Edda* (trans. R. B. Anderson), Scott, Foresman & Co., Chicago, 1897.

What, then, is this great winter, with its flurries, its frosts, its snows, but also its earthquakes, with the sun being driven off its usual course, turning black, and then abandoning the sky? Has Norway slipped far enough towards the North Pole for it to experience such a polar climate? Social life becomes impossible. How can these terrible years be counted? Three, and then another three? In decades?

These exceptionally harsh conditions must have produced thick snowfall, with the earth still being warm or even hot, and the upper air being icy and thus incapable of turning into water.

The *skald* (bard) sang of these terrible times in the following terms:

Brothers will fight together
And become each other's bane;
Sisters' children
Their sib shall spoil.
Hard is the world,
Sensual sins grow huge.
There are ax-ages, sword-ages –
Shields are cleft in twain, –
There are wind-ages, wolf-ages,
Ere the world falls dead.
Then happens what will seem a great miracle, that the wolf devours the
sun, and this will seem a great loss. The other wolf will devour the moon,
and this too will cause great mischief. The stars shall be hurled from
heaven.[2]

The modification of the apparent course of sun and moon, the fact that they are devoured by a wolf, shows that their course is now lower on the horizon, and thus less visible. This is to be expected, if the latitude has increased.

---

2   Snorri Sturluson, *op. cit.*

The northern stars remain unfailingly visible wherever you are in the Northern Hemisphere. Conversely, those in the Southern Hemisphere disappear as you move closer to the North Pole, until finally they disappear completely.

This astronomical observation must give us pause for thought. A sudden slippage towards the pole cannot come about without incurring colossal damage:

> Then it shall come to pass that the earth and the mountains will shake so violently that trees will be torn up by the roots, the mountains will topple down [...]
> The sea rushes over the earth, for the Midgard-serpent writhes in giant rage and seeks to gain the land. [...]
> The ship that is called Naglfar also becomes loose. [...] in this flood Naglfar gets afloat.[3]

The Arctic Sea would have been jostled by the northward rise of the Eurasian plate which includes Scandinavia. An enormous mass of water would inevitably have come pouring over the land. Would it not tend to eradicate all life? Vegetables and animals must have been swept away en masse, and deposited in an irregular fashion following the landscape's relief, with several great sea swells following after one another until the sea level finally reached equilibrium.

And what about the people there? Some human beings doubtless managed to escape.

How? Into caves, perhaps. By sea, especially: those who had taken ship, in the North Sea or the Arctic Ocean, will have been only slightly affected by the landslides, since the masses of sea water will have escaped the tremors and sudden shakings, thanks to their formidable inertia. They will have been lifted and displaced, but without any violence.

---

3   Snorri Sturluson, op. cit.

The Fenris-wolf advances with wide open mouth; the upper jaw reaches to heaven and the lower jaw is on the earth. He would open it still wider had he room. Fire flashes from his eyes and nostrils. The Midgard-serpent vomits forth venom, defiling all the air and the sea; he is very terrible, and places himself by the side of the wolf. […]

Heimdal stands up, blows with all his might in the Gjallar-horn […].
Then quivers the ash Ygdrasil, and all things in heaven and earth fear and tremble. […] Thereupon Surt flings fire over the earth and burns up all the world. Thus it is said in the Vala's Prophecy:

Loud blows Heimdal
His uplifted horn. […]
The straight-standing ash
Ygdrasil quivers,
The old tree groans,
And the giant gets loose. […]
From the east drives Hrym,
Bears his shield before him.
Jormungand welters
In giant rage
And smites the waves. […]
A ship comes from the east, […]
And Loke is steersman.
From the south comes Surt
With blazing fire-brand, […]
Mountains dash together,
Giant maids are frightened, […]
All men
Abandon their homesteads
When the warder of Midgard
In wrath slays the serpent.
The sun grows dark,
The earth sinks into the sea,
The bright stars

From heaven vanish;
Fire rages,
Heat blazes,
And high flames play
'Gainst heaven itself.[4]

The world is out of joint, the trunk of Ygdrasil is shaken by tremors: the axis of the world seems to be shifted and displaced. Then comes the great Fimbul winter, the time of axes, swords, broken shields, wolves. Horror, debauchery, incest, execution, fear – all strike at men and turn social life upside down.

People dream up names for gods, and often quite surrealistic fables: this dual reflex perhaps enables us to tame superhuman and harsh, if not intolerable, challenges. The fact remains that the *Edda* describes the brutal occurrence, happening within a few hours, whereby Scandinavia drifted to the North Pole, in a certain historical period. The description is unique, showing the arrival of the ice age! Nothing enables us to say precisely when it happened, nor how many years or decades it lasted.

The end of winter

The earth rises again from the sea, and is green and fair. The fields unsown produce their harvests. Vidar and Vale live. Neither the sea nor Surt's fire has harmed them, and they dwell on the plains of Ida, where Asgard was before. Thither come also the sons of Thor, Mode and Magne, and they have Mjolner. Then come Balder and Hoder from Hel. They all sit together and talk about the things that happened aforetime, – about the Midgard-serpent and the Fenris-wolf. They find in the grass those golden tables which the asas once had.[5]

4   Snorri Sturluson, *op. cit.*

5   *Ibid.*

A second change in latitude occurred in the other direction.

In fact, after a new unleashing of the forces of nature, equal in magnitude to the first, the great winter comes to an end, and for a second time the earth emerges from the floods. This time, the earth is fresh and green. This fact is clearly attested. The climate in Scandinavia then underwent what has been called a 'climatic optimum', noticeably warmer than the present climate.

The cataclysm narrated from age to age

If we are to believe different legends, two brutal upheavals in nature thus occurred successively, several years or decades apart. The memories of these two events became confused, mixed up, and embroidered. We find them in the stories of the pilot Nagifar, the giant Hrym, the wolf Fenrir, Loki, Beli, Frigg, Surt, and the god Odin.

The latter doubtless really existed. The prologue of the prose *Edda* presents him as the grandson of Priam, King of Troy. Furthermore, this name is attributed to a chieftain of the Asas, who are supposed to have crossed Russia via the Don and the Dniepr to reach Denmark in the 4th century BC.

The Asas – warriors, hunters, and pig-breeders – came up against the Vanes of Njord, who were sailors, farmers, traders, jurists and artists, peaceful by nature, rich from the wealth they gained from mines and metalworking. After a long war between the two peoples, they finally fused together and became the Vikings.

The fjords of Norway have long, deep jagged inlets, of great interest to geologists. According to Jacques de Morgan, they are:

> eroded valleys which could only have been formed in the open air, by rivers [...] These cracks in the earth, so exactly extended beneath the sea, existed in their continental state until a change in sea level determined their partial submersion under the expanse of sea water. This change seems to have been very abrupt, otherwise the fjords would not have retained their similarity to valleys [...]. But the current sea level in the fjords has not

remained the same since their original subsidence, the glacial terraces are proof of that. The two Christiana terraces are 75m and 163m above sea level, and these terraces are ancient marine beaches.[6]

6   J. de Morgan, *La Préhistoire orientale*, Librairie Geuthner, 1926, pp. 66-7.

3.4 Mexico and Guatemala

Situated between the Pacific and Atlantic Oceans, Mexico and Guatemala present tangible traces of civilisations from both oceans, despite the fact that a properly Mexican culture had developed before the Aztecs and the Mayas.

On the Atlantic side, there is nothing to suggest that maritime visits were impossible in very ancient times, even if they were doubtless the exception. In the second millennium AD, visits by Normans or Basques certainly did take place, but they had no significant influence on Mexican civilisations. The most recent transformations evidently occurred right at the end of the 15th century with and after Christopher Columbus.

Mexico's most significant cultural influences doubtless came from the Pacific side, since we can find ancient similarities between the Mexican Olmecs and the Pre-Inca Peruvians – for instance, tens of thousands of truncated step pyramids. The *teocallis* of Mexico have their analogues in the *wakas* of Peru. In Peru, we must remember that various advanced civilisations prospered: Chavin, Tiahuanaco, Chimu-Mochica and, right at the end, the Incas.

On the other hand, their gods – with names like Mammacocha, Viracocha, Pariakaka, Wallalo or Wampu – have no Mexican equivalent. Caught between the high range of the Andes and the Pacific, Peru may have looked out on to the Pacific, but it had been evolving in isolation for millennia. The essential similarity between the Olmecs and the ancient peoples of Peru, the similarity that we are interested in here, is thus the common memory of an original country situated south of the Pacific.

In particular, we find a memory of the disappearance of the constellation called the Pleiades. The land that stayed in people's memories was thus at a latitude greater than 76° south. Now it is highly unlikely that this common memory was communicated from one people to another, in particular by the Olmecs. In Peru, before the arrival of Pizarro, the civilisations which coexisted or (most probably) succeeded one another after the second millennium BC underwent no further major influence from outside, and flourished autonomously. Thus, even as far as architectural or religious

Figure 36. Drawing of Quetzalcóatl, after a depiction in the Codex Borbonicus.

similarities are concerned, it is difficult to understand how this information could have circulated, since the Peruvian peoples lived largely separate from the rest of the great Olmec and Mayan civilisations.

The traditions described by the famous *Popol-Vuh* equally show that the high Mexican cultures owed absolutely nothing to Peru for millennia.

This mysterious document seems absolutely devoid of any influence from the civilisations of the Atlantic or the Pacific. It owes nothing to China, nor to the other great civilisations that people the shores of the two oceans. And yet, the original land of the Mexican people is referred to at length in it.

The *Popol-Vuh* seems to have been written by a Quiché sage, i.e., a Guatemalan sage speaking a Mayan language. Centuries-old traditions are recorded in it. At the beginning of the 18th century, Father Francisco Ximenes discovered it and translated it. "The *Popol-Vuh*," he wrote, "has been preserved among the Indians under the seal of such great secrecy that, among the ancient priests, it was not even mentioned."

This document is divided into four ages that represent the same number of historical sequences. The first three ages correspond to bygone ages. The fourth narrates the present.

The different ages are separated by a destructive cataclysm which on each occasion wipes out the preceding state. Each age is brought to a close by a sudden and total transformation.[1]

---

[1]   All of the following passages are taken from R. Girard, *Esotericism of the Popol-Vuh* (trans. B. A Moffett), Theosophical University Press, 1987.

The First Age: polar memories

After an enumeration of the gods, the *Popol-Vuh* describes the formation of the world. "Grandiose were the description and the story of the creation of Heaven and Earth, of how everything was formed and shared out in four parts, of how the Heaven was marked out and measured."

The cardinal directions, and the height of the celestial pole, need to be redefined. Observation and measurement were needed, to seek "the angles of the firmament, [and measure] what was there [...] establishing the points of what is in heaven and earth." The sides, the angles, the distances and the base points were determined once and for all, for the whole duration of an age. The new calendar was to fix the "works of the *milpa*," the maize and the crops. Each of the extreme positions of the sun is taken into consideration: the directions of the rising and setting of the sun at the summer and winter solstices.

Tzakol, Bitol, Alom and Cajolom were the first four gods.

On One Chuen, [Divinity] took out from itself its divinity and made heaven and earth. [...]
All was created by our Father God, and by his Word, there, where before there was no heaven or earth, was his Divinity, which through itself made itself into a cloud, and created the universe. [...]

In earlier paragraphs Tzakol, Bitol, Alom, and Cajolom were identified as the Regent-gods of the four cosmic corners. These, on coming together in heaven in union with Tepeü and Gucumatz, form god-Seven or Heart of Heaven, an entity that is distinct from each one of its components but which embraces them all, agreeable to the Quiché-Maya's monotheist conception. [...] It should be noted that the general name Gucumatz, the counterpart of Quetzalcoatl, is applied as much to a particular god – one of the septemvirate – as to the creative gods in general, which radiate light and are called Gucumatz "because they were covered with a green mantle like the quetzal bird." Gucumatz literally means "serpent-quetzal" or "serpent-bird." It can be translated also as "serpent with quetzal plumes," since the voice guc or q'uc means both quetzal (*Pharomachrus mocino*) as well as the long and beautiful green tail feathers of that bird; and cumatz means serpent. There is a synonymy between the solar ray as a symbol and the divine feathers or hairs of the plant-life mantle, whose magical properties are held to be equivalent.

Monotheism underlies an apparent polytheism: "Both the *Popol Vuh* and the *Chilam Balam* of Chumayel agree on the progressive order of creation carried out by a creator, which is an uncreated Divinity and the first cause of all that exists."

One theme is fundamental – that of the gods or serpents covered with a coat of feathers: "Gucumatz, the counterpart of Quetzalcoatl [...] serpent with quetzal plumes [...]. The voice of Heart of Heaven is made objective in the trinomial – Lightning Bolt: its Brilliant Flash: Thunder."

Among the Chortís, the stone axe is a symbol of the lightning bolt, the drum that of thunder, and the wooden sword that of a lightning flash. The formation of mountains, coasts and valleys was seen as something supernatural and wonderful.

> It was a miraculous thing, says the *Popol Vuh*, strange and marvelous, how the mountains, the coasts, and the valleys of the earth were formed; how at the same time populated forests appeared on its surface. Then was formed "the roadway of the waters" and these began to flow forth at the foot of and among the mountains. Before the formation of the earth, the waters had vacated the place where it was to appear. Such picturesque description of the earth, "flat like a plate," and of the formation of the coasts and water courses speaks to us of a maritime landscape of broad coasts, limited by mountains and cut by rivers. [They believe that] the earth is surrounded by water and built upon the sea.

The darkness, the cold that forces the gods to cover themselves with coats of feathers, and an island origin – these are all elements which point us once again towards the Antarctic continent.

The creation of the universe resembles a continental drift which brought the Mexican people to a region near the South Pole. Thus the rivers which appear can be the route which the waters of the ocean, rising up to assail the mountains, had to open for themselves before they could flow out to sea.

In the course of the First Age, "man was condemned to live in caves and hollows like the animals," "men lived in caves and among the rocks, and fought against the wild beasts."

The polar cold explains the striking contrast between the 'great scholars' and 'thinkers' with their 'lofty feelings', monotheistic in belief, and a wretched life where people had to find shelter in caves, covering themselves with feathers during the harsh polar night, on the land of the gods, mountainous and flowing with rivers, isolated in the midst of the southern waters.

The so-called Gucup Cakix is the father of two terrible sons, the first of which, the giant Zipacná, fashions mountains and volcanoes, and the second, Caprakán, "busied himself moving the large and small hills and volcanoes." He frightens heaven by making the earth move. On this earth, there were thus many active volcanoes and earthquakes were frequent.

The legend of the 400 boys recounts how the hero-gods Hunahpú and Ixbalamqué destroy Zipacná. The 400 boys dig a hole to plant a mast for the *palo volador* (flying pole) with which they want to build their house. This scene is imitated in a traditional game which survives in parts of Mexico, recalling the most ancient times when the axis of the world was vertical. Nacelles rotate around it horizontally, like the stars at the pole. Zipacná avoids being buried in the hole, and brings about the death of the young men by causing the house in which they had gathered to collapse.

In order to avenge the deaths of the 400 boys, Hunahpú – the sun – and Ixbalamqué – the new moon – then draw the giant into a cave and "let fall on him the mountain that they had bored into through the middle, crushing the giant who became transformed into stone." The Maya traditions also mentioned that men turned to stone, i.e., to ice.

"That divine Word tells the twins that they should now do away with Caprakán, the last of the giants." They "find him busy moving the mountains" and "see to it that he goes toward the place where the sun comes up." The twins tied him up, "with hands behind, the collar tied to the feet, and then they buried him in the earth. Thus finished the First Age."

Certain clues in this passage from the *Popol-Vuh* thus come together, quite unexpectedly, to situate the first land inhabited by the Mexicans near a pole.

The Second Age

"A kind of foggy cloud enwrapped the seven Ahpú." The Chortís evoke this dark age in the dance of the giants, when the actors who personify the sun and the moon cover their faces with veils. They illustrate the period when "the earth had not become lit." According to Girard, "The same idea is repeated when it is said that the seven Ahpú 'were born during the night,' i.e., when neither the sun nor moon nor Maya culture had yet been produced."

The Ahpú are seven civilising heroes. Sons of one of the Ahpú, the brothers Hun Batz and Hun Chouen are "great sages," of "divine nature". They possess the gift of the arts, are good jewellers, writers, chisellers and cutters of stone. Thus they sing and pray, are soothsayers, flute players and experts on the blowpipe. They teach men science and the arts of life.

Every day, the seven Ahpú gather to play the ball game. "During the ball game they wear their resplendent ceremonial gear – that is, they exhibit their insignia as solar deities." They play on a cosmic court: the two zones of the court were separated by a line symbolising the clear sky and the cloudy sky, day and night, light and darkness. "We find six stone carvings of the macaw, aligned three on the east and three on the west side of the court, in accordance with the astronomical positions of the respective hypostases of god-Seven. The line of the parallel, i.e., of the passage of the daystar through the zenith, crosses the center of the court from east to west, symbolizing the 'road of the sun', according to Chortí expression. The ball, together with the six macaws, completes the symbol of the god-Seven."

The seven Ahpú are invited to take the road to the world below, in order to play tennis. A messenger bird from Hunrakán, the god of thunder and thunderbolts, shows them the way. They have to follow the road to Xibalbá, which is none other than the underworld. If the lords of this place wish to play with the Ahpú, it is apparently because they intend "to take away from the Ahpú their accoutrements of splendor." Before journeying to the underworld, the Ahpú ask Hun Batz and Hun Chouen to keep the sacred fire permanently alight in their memory, establishing the god of the hearth as their representative.

There is a ritual commemorating this harsh period: the trial of the black cave. This consists of staying "in that hellish cavern that is filled with smoke from torch pine and cigars [...] that converts the cave into a hot, stinking and suffocating oven." This description of the cave cannot fail to remind us of the one in which ancient peoples lived while they awaited the return of the sun within the polar circle, or at least its immediate vicinity.

"Following the agony of the black cave, there followed that of the freezing cave, where 'it was cold and an icy wind blew.' Then the victims passed on to the cave of jaguars, 'which roared and killed each other with their claws, both male and female.'"

Eventually the priests invoked the return of life – germination, dawn and the resplendent lord with his penetrating rays.

An annual period of darkness alternates with an interminable dawn, then with a sun that rises to an apex of some 40° above the horizon... at a latitude of 70°, you do indeed have to keep a regular fire going to keep yourself warm, but also to give yourself sufficient light in the caves during the dark period. This did not prevent the inhabitants and the Ahpú of this age from singing, praying, playing the flute, chiselling jewels, cutting stones, and studying the arts and sciences. The Second Chortí Age finishes with a dawn which has long been awaited.

Third Age: the men of wood

In the Third Age, human beings "multiplied like the sands of the sea and overran the land". Beans and maize were cultivated. These strange men wandered aimlessly around, and had neither feet, nor hands, nor blood. "Their fingers did not protrude from their bodies."

"An inundation, a great flood, came to wipe out the beings of the third creation":

There fell torrents of resin from the heavens (a probable allusion to a volcanic cataclysm, a frequent occurrence in the original territory of Maya culture). Finally strong winds from the sea concluded the destruction of the wooden beings, whose eyes were torn out, heads lopped off, their flesh and bowels devoured and nerves and bones eaten by the agents of the god of Death [...]. Even the animals and household implements are shown in the Popol-Vuh as helping to destroy the "men of wood," contributing to the heavenly punishment.

The wooden people started running two by two, like ears of corn, and went up on top of the houses. But when they got to the gutters, they all fell down. They tried to climb up into the trees, but these collapsed under their weight. They wanted to take refuge in caves, but these repelled them as soon as they approached. "In this manner the people were destroyed, thus was their end." There were few survivors and so the dismal Third Age came to an end.

It is clear that at every transformation which marks the passage from one age to another, a clean division between two epochs when the apparent motion of the stars is perfectly well regulated, major events occur. The change always takes the shape of a ravaging cataclysm.

The Fourth Age

Only one of the dancers was now visible: Ixbalamqué. "Get up!" she commanded Hunahpú, who instantly revived. [...] Immediately [they] raised themselves to heaven: one to the sun and the other to the moon; instantly the celestial vault and the face of the earth were illumined.

The Mexican people left their ancestral home to reach the American continent. At the same time, the twins, the sun Hunahpú and the new moon Ixbalamqué, would be again visible every day, all year round.

"Then there also rose up the 400 boys whom Zipacná had killed, and these became the companions of the twins and were transformed into stars in the heaven. Once they had become stars, the four hundred were invited by the moon and the sun to "illumine the Dawn of the Fourth Creation". They "are transformed into the souls of the stars and enter into partnership with the sun," and become the constellation of the Pleiades which will be the eternal companion of the sun and the moon.

This precise stellar reference opens some exciting possibilities. For the Mexicans, the stars, numerous and dense, number 400 in the constellation of the Pleiades. Prior to that, they were brave young men, before they were slain by the shaper of volcanoes, Zipacná. They then ceased to be visible above the horizon.

From this we can deduce that the land inhabited by the Mexicans in Antarctica drifted to a latitude of more than 76° to 78° south. The rising of the Pleiades, after the major event that inaugurated the fourth and final Age, necessarily presupposes that their land moved to a latitude below 76° south.

As in the Polynesian myths, the Pleiades were to become eternally visible. It would be necessary for the sun and the moon to leave the Antarctic Circle. The 'rising up towards the light' would be in proportion to the distance from the pole, extending as far as the tropical regions. This great departure, this migration that brought salvation, was decided on after much deliberation. "The divine council once more came together to form a new humanity [...] they sent their prayers amidst the darkness of the night." Now that they were warmed by the fiery heat of the sun, the people gave expression to their joy: "they found what would form the flesh of the new humans," the maize that was so delicious for starving people. They were:

> filled with joy, having found that place full of good and delicious things where the yellow and white maize ears abounded, where were abundant also the *pataxte* [*Theobroma bicolor*, a variety of cacao] and cacao, and groves of zapotes, *annonas* [custard apples], apples, cherries, and honey. Full of succulent foods were the places called Paxil and Cavalá.

Beans and maize were in any case to be the basis of the diet of the new men of the Fourth Age. The Mexicans are aware that their mythical paradise, the homeland of maize, the gods and cultivation, was located in the south.

Figure 37. *Hippopotami on a fresco from the Bovidian, Tin Tazarift, Algeria. Silhouettes based on a photograph by András Zboray.*

3.5 The Sahara

The Sahara – a Mediterranean climate in recent times

Covering some 8 million km², stretching from Mauretania to Egypt, from the Mediterranean to Chad, the Sahara is the largest desert in the world. Regardless of whether it is covered with sand or with stone, it is also one of the most arid. In certain regions, precipitation does not exceed 100mm per year.

And yet the Sahara had a period of very mild, fresh and damp weather, of a Mediterranean type. Lakes and huge rivers occupied territories that today are dry and infertile.

In ancient times, Chad was a vast inland sea. On the Tunisian coast, Chott-el-Djerid and Chott-el-Melghir were united as a vast lake – Lake Triton – in touch with the ocean.

Between the basins of Lake Chad and Lake Triton, the mountainous region enjoyed a cool climate. Forests covered the slopes, grasslands and cultivated fields stretched out over the Tripoli region, and the beneficent waters of the small Cynips river irrigated the Great Leptis area. Rivers, like the Ger from Tassili and Hoggar, flowed freely across the plain.

On the coast there were many people, of many races – Mediterraneans, Anou, Nasamones, Gindanes, Lotophagi, Machlyans, Zygantes, Maxyans and Numides. To the west, the Moors had links with the Atlantans and lived as sailors and fishermen. At the foot of the Atlas mountains, the Getulians inhabited the high grasslands of the savannah with buffalo and elephants. The nomadic Garamantes roamed the steppes further south. The ancient Nile irrigated the region of Bahr-bala-mâ, and the great oases, in whose waters hippopotami swam, were ringed with prairies.

In Carthaginian times, the Getulian savannah could still feed the elephants of Hannibal's army. The expeditions of Suetonius Paulinus and Cornelius Balbus give evidence that in the first centuries AD, the country of the Garamantes was dotted with flourishing towns such as Cydamus and Garama. Suetonius Paulinus reached as far as the River Ger and Cornelius

Balbus reached Tibesti-tou, without apparent suffering to their troops in the course of their Saharan expeditions.

In the central ranges, around Lake Triton in Chad, nature is still verdant and productive. There is the tale of the three young Nasamons, who, leaving Cyrenaica, ventured south to distant Agisymba where they found the steppes luxuriant with flowers. A little later, the centurions Julius Maternus and Septimus Flaceus headed into the interior of the continent and made it to Chad.

It was in the third century AD that the advance of the desert increased with a startling rapidity. Sands invaded the whole of Libya, as far as Bornu and Fezzan. To the west, it reached the Niger and the Mauritanian coast. It was at this time that the emperor Septimus Severus introduced the camel into the region. The elephant disappeared completely from the Getulian. Horses became confined to the coastal regions and the plateau, where esparto grass replaced the cereals which used to grow there.[1]

[…] in former times, the Sahara was fairly thickly populated […] it contained a fauna similar to that still to be found in the savanna country […]. The aquatic character of the predominant fauna indicates surroundings which were damp and the existence of numerous rivers in full flood.

[…] After all, just what is the Tassili? Its name in the Tuareg language means 'plateau of the rivers'.[2]

On various estimates, generally accepted by the scientific community, a climate of this type must have been prevalent some 10,000 years ago.

But at Tassili in Algeria, caves have been discovered on the walls of which there are great rock-paintings that shed a quite different light on this chronology. The Tassili rock-paintings are wonderful artworks, painted in a realistic style, comparable to those of Lascaux.

1   E. Le Danois, *Le Rythme des climats dans l'histoire de la terre et de l'humanité*, Payot, 1950, pp. 189-91.

2   H. Lhote, *Search for the Tassili Frescoes* (trans. A. Houghton Brodrick), Hutchinson, London, 1973, pp. 18, 40.

They bear witness to the rearing of different animal varieties and abundant harvests, but also rivers on which navigation was possible – in other words, indisputable traces of a climate that was altogether favourable and propitious to the development of agriculture and human life.

Bovids in the Sahara

Another discovery in the Sahara, that of stone millstones, pottery fragments, stone axes, awls made of bone, small discs cut into ostrich eggshells, necklaces, pendants, and schist enamels, indicates that there was a significant population of herdsmen tending bovids, and thus reveals a climate favourable to the rearing of such grazing animals.

Figure 38. *Cattle-rearing in a rock-painting from Jabbaren, Algeria.*

We can even speculate that the climate was damp: Lhote writes, "In five different places we found on the rock-paintings representations of Egyptian-type Nile barges," and at an altitude of 2,000m, at Tassili, canoes made of rushes that seem to be circling round three hippopotami.

An Egyptian influence appears at Aouanrhet, Jabbaren and Timenzouzine, where one can see "little goddesses with the birds' heads [which] must belong to an historical period, maybe that of the 18th or 19th Dynasties, and so, approximately, to 1200 BC."

Henri Lhote thinks he can distinguish several periods: that of the hunters, or the hartebeest; that of shepherds and bovids; that of shepherds with chariots and cavalry; and finally that of the camel, introduced only at the beginning of our era.[3]

3   H. Lhote, *op. cit.*, pp. 63, 72, 244.

Figure 39. *A herd of cattle depicted at Tin Tazarift, Algeria.*

Climatic upheaval

Hugot recognises that the present desert became such only after a profound climatic change.

> Between 2000 and 1000 BC, a sudden worsening of conditions occurred. We find no warning sign of a decline in Aterian trade. On the contrary, it was to be found in all its purity, in all the richness of its forms – and then, nothing! Its authors seem to have disappeared as if by magic.
>
> If the Aterians disappeared so abruptly and with no transitional period, it was possibly quite simply due to a sudden climatic change which turned the Saharaian ecology on its head.
>
> Water became scarce after a serious change in climate, that which had been paradise was transformed into hell [...] From this time, exodus was unavoidable.
>
> [We have] proof of great migrations dictated by modifications to climate [...] If Europe, almost simultaneously, was passing from a glacial to a temperate period, the Sahara, following a parallel route, progressed inexorably from temperate to desert.

This climate change was so brutal that the inhabitants completely abandoned the Saharan region. They fled as though afraid of something even worse than the heat of the desert:

> In certain areas of the Sahara, researchers often have the impression that the last occupants of the country left fleeing a sudden and terrifying cataclysm, because they find, as if they had been abandoned only the day before, and in the greatest haste, moveable objects so fine and beautiful that they are a joy to behold and become the pride of museums.[4]

The Yukon was at the Pole, at the start of the Quaternary, and the equator passed through Dakar, Tamanrasset, and Sinai, at the head of the Red Sea.

---

4   H.-J. Hugot, *Le Sahara avant le désert*, Éditions des Hespérides, 1974, pp. 20, 28, 74, 84.

Figure 40. *Rock-paintings of chariots at Tassili in Algeria.*

The climate was equatorial, and suitable for the period of the hunters, or the wildebeest. The heavy rainfall and tropical heat favoured a style of dress reduced to a loincloth, hunting and fishing, lions, rhinoceroses, elephants, hippopotami and giraffes. This period was that of the Old Empire in Egypt. The inhabitants of the Sahara in the Neolithic period had no need of stone dwellings; but possessed a sophisticated culture capable of producing highly refined art, as demonstrated by their elegant drawings and jewellery.

The sudden climatic change occurred, and a new climate, fresh and damp, set in, when the European region to the west of the northernmost cape of Norway suddenly started to drift towards the North Pole, decimating the population who abandoned their dwellings. From then on, Tamanresset, in the heart of the Hoggar, was at around 40° north.

The neolithic inhabitants, influenced by the Sudanese, gave way to a polymorphous type similar to the Ethiopians,

who were slim and supple with a slender profile. Oxen, sheep, goats, dogs, broad-brimmed hats, a kind of Phrygian cap, feathered hats, and a diverse range of hair styles and colours appeared.

The art of the herdsman is dynamic, lively, with such fineness of features, the beauty of colour and an inimitable style.[5]

---

5   H.-J. Hugot, *op. cit.*, p. 269.

The Canadian south-east moved in its turn to the North Pole, at which point Tamanresset was at 20° north, and the eastern – but not the western – Sahara started to dry up.

The horse appeared. It is known to have been domesticated only quite late on,

> at the beginning of the second millennium in Asia, and first introduced into Egypt at the time of the Hyksos invasions, during the period between the Middle and the New Empires.[6]

Horses succeeded cattle. There are many depictions of chariots, drawn by between one and four horses, whose slender wheels have four to six spokes, with light nacelles for between one and three drivers. The classic style is the 'flying gallop', that is reminiscent of the Mycenaean period and, at a greater distance, the art of the steppes.

> The building of a chariot involves the use of metal, and this was a problem for our Saharan chariots, which appeared in the neolithic period. A chariot requires tyres, pins, washers, rivets or nails, metal for harnesses, at a pinch made of bronze but above all of iron.[7]

6   H.-J. Hugot, *op. cit.*, p. 291.

7   *Ibid.*, pp. 280-3.

These chariots are very frequently reproduced in engravings or paintings on the rocky slabs of the Hoggar, the Tassili, and other mountainous regions, and they are shown being pulled at a gallop: "they are not made to travel slowly" like ox-carts. "The origin of the chariots must be sought elsewhere than in the Sahara [...] They arrived suddenly in the place where they were depicted." The Sea Peoples were defeated circa 1230 BC by the Pharaoh Merneptah. The "first chariots had a short-lived existence in the Sahara." Their "depiction would thus be merely the commemoration of a major event whose origin lies, of course, outside the Sahara."[8]

We can thus situate the end of the period of the bovids quite precisely, as well as the short-lived intrusion of chariots into the Sahara – to the 13th century BC.

The desert was at this time sufficiently fertile for cattle, and then horses, to roam and graze at a crucial epoch corresponding to the explosion of the island of Santorini and the Trojan War.

---

8   H.-J. Hugot, *op. cit.*, pp. 280-3.

3.6 Egypt

In temples, the absent sun was still worshipped

A great variety of stories refer to the major event that caused the sun suddenly to cease circulating normally in the sky. According to one of these stories:

> a drop of spittle dribbled from his [Ra's] mouth and fell to the ground. Unbeknownst to everyone, Isis mixed the saliva with the earth that clung to it, fashioning this mass into a snake. [which bit Re] [...] this incident brought on a cataclysm similar to the end of the world; the earth was plunged into darkness, shards of pottery began walking about, stones began to talk, and mountains took to wandering hither and thither.[1]

This is a fascinating description of what must have happened if the earth shuddered and slipped violently and rapidly: everything not attached to the earth assumed a rapid relative movement. Objects of all kinds were overturned. The stones made a noise as they moved, and thus seemed to speak. And the mountains, as they were subjected to the slippages that contemporary geologists can observe, went walkabout.

The golden age in this divine continent is often described – before it was brutally transformed into a hell:

> *The world saw a period of abundance, bellies were full; there were no famines. In the days of the primeval gods, walls did not fall, nor did thorns prick. Perversion did not exist on earth, the crocodile did not carry off his prey, the snake did not bite.*[2]

Nostalgia for the most ancient of times, which were well blessed both

---

1   D. Meeks and C. Favard-Meeks, *Daily Life of the Egyptian God* (trans. G. M. Goshgarian), John Murray, London, 1997, p. 98.

2   *Ibid.*, p. 112.

materially and spiritually, leads to the observation that the natural dangers represented by plants and animals were assuaged by a state of goodness that also disappeared with the transformation in climate and outlook.

The worship celebrated in the temples was an attempt to venerate the power of the sun, and the cosmic combat that brought it to an end in the ancestral land: the heavenly powers had to be begged to ensure that the same thing would not happen in Egypt.

The temple, standing solid on its foundations, symbolised the desired stability in the natural order of the cosmos, despite its violent mutations that extinguished light and heat:

> For as long as the sky rests on its four supports, for as long as the earth remains firm on its foundations, for as long as Re shines by day, and the moon shimmers at night [...] and the stars remain in their places, the temple... will endure, firm like the sky... without end, like Re, eternally.[3]

The best-known material embodiment of the cult of Ra was the obelisk, the gold-plated pyramidion of which was meant to capture the sun's rays. Its stability was apparently an image of the stability desired for the world's axis, and its vertical direction was that eventually assumed by this axis in the land of the gods, in other words, the vertical (at the pole). The observation of the precise shadow of the pyramidion at its top enabled its length to be measured at midday, on perfectly horizontal ground, so that the inclination of the world axis, and hence the latitude, could be deduced. The periods when the length of the shadow was shortest or longest enabled the solstices to be determined.

"The principal statue of a cult [...] was shut up in the temple's deepest recesses, in a shrine called the *naos*. A text describes its seclusion: "It is more inaccessible than what happens in the heavens, more veiled than the state of the other world, more revered than the inhabitants of the Primeval Ocean."[4]

3   D. Meeks and C. Favard-Meeks, *op. cit.*, p. 122.

4   *Ibid.*, p. 126.

The obscurity that was the combined result of the night, the depth of the temple, and the narrow and sacred enclosure of the *naos*, was an image of the sun's absence during the terrible polar night. The priests would fast and keep vigil as they awaited the coming of day, and the statue of the sun-god was brought out for all to see when the sun itself emerged above the horizon: "The god's face was unveiled the instant the Sun peeked over the horizon", and, in the words of the prayer:

> rise over the earth, just as you emerge from Nun! May your rays illuminate the earth! [...] (while) your bark remains steady in the sky![5]

This cult shows that the daily sunrise, the stability of the apparent course of the sun in the sky, was no longer something that could be inevitably counted on, ever since the laws of the cosmic order had on one occasion undergone profound transformations.

The *Book of the Dead*

This papyrus from Ancient Egypt is full of invocations seeking a return to life. These prayers are recited by the dead who wish, like Osiris, to come back to life. They seek to be reborn from the long night of the underworld – that icy night that precedes the awaited dawn. The night of the dead recalls that of the original polar island, overwhelmed by chaos.

Thus a description starts to emerge of a distant memory of chaos that pulled the primordial continent to the pole, with the appearance of the first long period of terrifying darkness.

This unprecedented night took place at the same time as the "great flowing away of the worlds," when the destruction happened. Conflicts or catastrophes took place "in the midst of the Darkness." Tempests and floods occurred, culminating in "the collapse of the worlds."[6]

---

5   *Ibid.*, p. 127.

6   All extracts taken from G. Kolpaktchy, *Livre des morts des anciens Égyptiens*, Dervy, 1991.

This was at the time of a fateful night of judgement.

The night is also described as succeeding the "day of massacres and confusion." The night massacres mortals amidst violence and the unleashing of brutal forces in which "the voice roars like a peal of thunder in the vast regions of the dead."

This was during "the chaos of the earliest times," an 'original' moment.

In this "region where darkness reigns [...] the paths are immersed in an eternal night."

On his arrival in the valley of darkness, the dead man asks himself:

What is this place that I have now reached?
Alas, there is no clean air to breathe. There is no water here!
Everywhere, in the midst of these Shadows, I can make out nothing but chasms and precipices!
What impenetrable darkness!
My hesitant steps explore the terrain, I feel my way along.
All around, one can sense the roaming of souls in distress.
In truth it is not possible to live at peace here,
Nor to know the sensual pleasures of love.

The chaos that accompanied the polar night also awoke many volcanoes. Thus the volcanic activity of the original continent is evoked at length in many different images. The volcano is present in the shape of a lion, Rehu. It is described thus: "Flames belch forth from your mouth, your head is surrounded by fire [...] He grinds the dead in his jaws, while his eyes dart forth flashes of lightning."

A serpent lives in the flames of the lion. This is the serpent Rerek who, like some creeping spirit, lives in the mountains and revives the fire. We can recognise this as the lava flows that stream down the sides of the volcano. "Stretched out on the mountainside, the great serpent lies. Behold him: He-who-lives-amidst-the-flames."

Streams of incandescent lava or rivers of oil that sometimes gather into pools are mentioned: "a lake of fire," "fields of fire," the "lake of the double fire," or "the city whose entrance is surrounded by flames."

"In truth, your torrents are a devouring liquid fire. Gods and spirits gaze at these torrents of fire, and recoil without quenching their thirst."

However, there is also a description of harvests which contrasts with the devastation caused by the fire: they made it possible to make offerings to the gods, on the "flowery edges of the lake" and on the "fields of peace."

The god "standing on the deck of the boat, at the tiller [...] steers over the limpid surface of the waters." He navigates in this boat and sails along the heavenly routes that lead to the fields of the heavenly Hermopolis, "in peace, in peace – furling and unfurling the rigging."

In the land of the gods, in those "regions of peace," on the lake and in the cities, are the "blessed souls" who dwell in "the beautiful land of Amenti," the "sacred land of the lord of truth and justice [...] lord of the written law."

Thus a single divinity was already reigning in heaven, at a time when the earth with its mountains did not yet exist. "Creator of all that exists [...] at the dawn of time," he "fashioned the language of the divine hierarchies," "wrested beings from the primal ocean" and saved them, setting them on an island in the lake of Horus.

This divine country suddenly drifted towards the vicinity of the pole. All the stars in the opposite hemisphere ceased to be visible: "In that cursed zone into which the stars fell, cast down into the abyss, they were unable to reassume their previous orbits."

The axis of the world is more or less markedly inclined on the horizon, depending on the latitude. At the pole, it is vertical: Djed, "the vertebral column of Osiris" is in fact the axis of the world.

One commemorative ceremony was that of the "setting the Djed that lay flat upright again."

A legend at Heliopolis

"The real creator is Ra, the sun, the great god of Heliopolis and of most of the cities of Egypt." This god-king, after a centuries-long reign, is considerably weakened:

> His bones were now of silver, his flesh was gold, his mouth lapis-lazuli [a stone which resembles ice] [...] Taking advantage of his decrepitude [Isis] uses the most disloyal means to tear away from him the most precious talisman he has left, the secret of his magic name, with which she intends to acquire a greater power than the other gods.
>
> Ra decided to make an example, [...] men themselves having joined in the conspiracy [...] After having consulted [...] the assembly of the gods, he dispatched Sekhmet, the goddess with the head of a lioness, with orders to massacre them without mercy.

Only night could halt him in his murderous course, and Ra, seized with pity, resolved to spare the rest of mankind. To appease Sekhmet, who was intoxicated with the carnage, he mixed beer and mandragora juice with the blood of humans, and had a considerable quantity of this liquid poured out around her.

> When she awoke, the goddess saw this potion, drank it, became calm and then intoxicated, and forgot her victims. Ra pardonned the men who had repented, but, tired of reigning, he abdicated and chose an inaccessible retreat upon the body of Nut, goddess of the sky, his daughter.
>
> It is easy to detect in this legend the memory of one of the cataclysms which shook a whole section of the earth, like the flood recounted in the Chaldean texts, as well as the Bible, which devasted Mesopotamia and its neighbouring countries.[7]

Here, one ancient period seems to be attached to the name of Ra, the

---

7   G. Jéquier, *Histoire de la civilisation égyptienne*, Payot, 1913, pp. 37-8.

sun, whose apparent course changes rapidly. A hurricane (or an ocean?) rushes forward like a lioness intoxicated with carnage, massacring huge numbers of human beings in its murderous course, and then quickly comes to a halt, sparing the remainder. The sun, Ra, suddenly disappears into an inaccessible retreat. It is the start of a new era.

A descendent of Ra is Osiris, elder sun of Qeb, the earth-god, and Nut, the sky-goddess, "Osiris personifies at the same time vegetation, the fertile nature of Egypt, and the vivifying water of the Nile." With Isis, his wife – or sister – he organises society, agriculture, the growing of cereals and vines, and "sets out to conquer the world, an entirely pacific conquest in which he makes men yield to him by persuasion and gentleness."

Osiris is thus the sun that has returned, benevolent, but never as powerful as his father. "The god Seth, Osiris' own brother, forms the most absolute contrast with him. We can even say he is his exact counterpart": he represents the burning desert, the lightning stroke and the tempest.

Seth dreams up a perfidious trap, he shuts Osiris into a wooden coffer, and throws him into the sea where he is devoured by fish. We can interpret this as the coming of the polar night, personified by Seth.

Isis undertakes long and patient searches to find the remains of her husband and finally gathers all the fragments except for one, the phallus that had been devoured by the fish of Oxyrhynchus, but she could not restore him to life.

The moon, Isis, continues to manifest herself during the long polar night. She thus bears within herself the seed that gives hope that the light has not been definitively extinguished, and that it will return again to this world. Horus is the realisation of this hope. But this sun-child is Harakté, illuminating the horizons, north and south. He is the scarab beetle rolling his ball to the horizon, the bringer of life.

Mummification, and the ceremonies that Horus dedicated to his father, enabled Osiris to "enjoy a new life in the dwelling of the dead,"[8] and he becomes king of the underworld.

8   G. Jéquier, *op. cit.*, pp. 41-3.

Every religious centre in Egypt – Hermopolis, Memphis, Heliopolis – interpreted the past in its own way: not in contradiction with the others, but, rather, so as to complement them.

At Heliopolis, two distinct periods followed each other, both in the southern continent. This vast region appeared at some ancient period, when governed by the course of the sun Ra, to enjoy a stable and mild climate.

Another period followed, under the sun, Osiris: this followed a terrible tempest that annihilated a portion of mankind and constituted a major event. A new era permitted agriculture to flourish, as well as social and religious organisations.

A new upheaval brought an end to the era of Osiris, now relegated to the underworld. Horus is a reference to the polar day, in everlasting competition with the polar night, Seth.

The sun changes course

Several pieces of evidence suggest that in Egypt, the apparent course of the sun was modified several times. One papyrus refers to a major event of this kind:

> I am Shu, under the face of Ra
> Sat in the middle of his father's eye.
> I will make the earth fall into the expanse of water,
> Putting south in the place of north throughout the whole world!
> Let my voice be heard
> As the voice of the great goose Nakak was heard in the night!
> I am Ba, the great![9]

This expression is often encountered: if the sun's apparent course was, for several hours, in overall terms directed eastwards, towards the place of its rising, then north and south have been switched, as the sun seems temporarily to have been trying to set in the east. This could not have

9   Fr. Lenormant, *Histoire ancienne de L'Orient*, vol. 3, A. Lévy, 1882, p. 135.

occurred without the speed of the ground westwards being higher than 2,000 to 3,000 km/hour, or slightly more. This would have needed an apparent wind of the same magnitude that made a noise like a voice, or the cry of a goose. There was a flood in Egypt at the time of Osorkon III in the 8th century BC.

"Nun is the Great Ocean that surrounds the Earth and extends into the lower world [...] The Nun climbed on to this earth in its entirety," i.e., an invasion of the sea on to land comparable to that which occurred in the primeval ocean. This Nun "came battering against the two mountainsides, as at the time of origins. This Earth was handed over into its power, as into that of a sea."[10]

The destruction was total, but civilisation was affected less than elsewhere. Egypt was in a relatively fortunate position, relatively far from the oceans. But such events can serve as an explanation for the end of the Old Empire and subsequently that of the Middle Empire.

The end of the Old Empire

The period of the so-called Old Empire is often dated to circa 2140 BC. In a papyrus discovered by W. Golenischeff, the tragic story of the disappearance of that glorious period is told in the literary form of the prophetic story.

Following a generally accepted convention, this literary genre, "highly favoured by the Egyptians," according to Gustave Lefebvre, consisted in narrating, "as if they were still to come, events [...] that already belonged to the past."[11] We will shortly be encountering a similar genre in Roman literature and in the prophecies of the Bible.

The Egyptian prophetic story in question presents us with a dramatic depiction of the end of the Old Empire: an invasion of the Delta, chaos, violence, ruin, misery, a shortage of goods, an increase in selfishness and an insensitivity to death, all accompanied by a natural upheaval:

10 P. Garelli and M. Leibovici, *La Naissance du monde*, Éditions du Seuil, 1959, p. 22, 24.

11 G. Lefebvre, *Romans et Contes égyptiens de l'époque pharaonique*, Adrien Maisonneuve, 1988, pp. 92-4.

The solar disc being hidden, it no longer shone so that men could see [it].
We will no longer be able to live, for clouds [cover it up].
And men will be stunned by the fact of its absence.[12]

And, further on, "the sun will go far away from men. It will indeed rise at the right time, [but] nobody will know it is midday, its shadow will be indistinguishable." In other words, on the sundial, the shadow of the sun will be too far from the foot of the gnomon to be measurable, even at midday.

"Your face will not be dazzled when you gaze on [the sun], and your eyes will not water: it will be in the sky like the moon." However, its normal circular course will not be disturbed, "its rays will be before your face as in olden times."

A sudden increase in latitude is the only thing that can explain a solar trajectory apparently lying lower on the horizon, as the sun gives off both less heat and less light.

During this time, on earth, other irreversible upheavals occurred:

The rivers of Egypt having dried up, the water could be crossed on foot.
Water will be sought so that ships can sail,
The river bed [where it flowed] having become the bank; the bank [in its turn will become] water,
and the water will take the place [once again] of the bank.
The south wind will face the north wind: the sky will no longer belong to one single wind.[13]

---

12 *Papyrus 1116 B* at the Library of St Petersburg.

13 *Ibid.*

Only an unexpected and rapid movement of the ground could have been able to empty the Nile so suddenly, as well as diverting the other rivers in Egypt from their beds. The modification of the climate that followed the change in latitude was extremely brutal. It brought with it a south wind, as opposed to the north wind that had been the prevailing wind until that time.

3.7 Greece

Many archaeologists and Hellenists now agree that several exceptional seismic upheavals occurred in Greece and Crete around the second millennium BC. They describe the effects of the successive catastrophes, certain of which had a general worldwide impact. These events had nothing to do with human factors, but were linked to "violent geological upheavals, such as earthquakes, volcanic eruptions and subsidence."[1]

The discoveries of the archaeologist Nicolas Platon enable us to corroborate these observations. On the island of Santorini, to the north of Crete, under metres of hardened ash, an Aegean town from the 13th century BC has been uncovered.

Frescoes depicting palaces of several storeys, elegant square-sailed boats fitted with oars, with passengers in fine costumes sitting down under cover and lotus-eaters, all indicate a happy and refined lifestyle.

The interest of this discovery resides, as far as the present study is concerned, in the fact that the vegetation and animals depicted do not fit the Mediterranean climate of this region. The palm trees, lions, monkeys, certain fish and crustaceans are of tropical origin, and yet here they are in the middle of the Mediterranean! Starting from this remarkable site, Nicolas Platon has sought the causes of the total catastrophes which "radically renewed the forms of civilisation, [...] the destruction from top to bottom of the first palaces." He has endeavoured to show that the end of these original civilisations "seems to have been sudden, radical and general."

Later on, the new palaces experienced a similar fate. They were not destroyed by Achaean invaders who settled in Knossos and elsewhere in Crete, but by a new and terrible natural catastrophe.

The texts of antiquity that have been preserved limit themselves to drawing up inventories of men and provisions. We have to wait until the 8th

---

1   H. van Effenterre, *La seconde fin du monde*, Éditions des Hespérides, 1974; A. G. Gallanopoulos and E. Bacon, *L'Atlantide, la vérité derrière la légende*, Albin Michel, 1969.

century BC, with Hesiod and Homer, to find traces of the memory of survivors of these great natural disasters. The 6th century saw an abundance of literature on the catastrophes of old that had devastated the first Greek civilisations – witness Pericles, Euripides and Aeschylus. On the other hand, the desire for historical and chronological veracity was not the most important thing: the main catastrophes had already been embellished and distorted after several centuries of oral transmission.

Hesiod

You will remember that the battle that set the Titans against Zeus and his sons was terribly violent. Fiery colours, deafening noises, juddering earthquakes – all the ingredients of a natural cataclysm are combined in this passage from the *Theogony* of Hesiod. All the great powers of the earth take part in this combat.

> For the Titan gods and as many as sprang from Cronos had long been fighting together in stubborn war with heart-grieving toil, the lordly Titans from high Othrys, but the gods, givers of good, whom rich-haired Rhea bore in union with Cronos, from Olympus [...] and their spirit longed for war even more than before, and they all, both male and female, stirred up hated battle that day, the Titan gods, and all that were born of Cronos together with those dread, mighty ones of overwhelming strength whom Zeus brought up to the light from Erebus beneath the earth. A hundred arms sprang from the shoulders of all alike, and each had fifty heads growing from his shoulders upon stout limbs. These, then, stood against the Titans in grim strife, holding huge rocks in their strong hands. And on the other part the Titans eagerly strengthened their ranks, and both sides at one time showed the work of their hands and their might. The boundless sea rang terribly around, and the earth crashed loudly: wide Heaven was shaken and groaned.[2]

2 Hesiod, *Theogony*, in *The Homeric Hymns and Homerica*, (trans. H. G. Evelyn-White), William Heinemann Ltd, London, 1914, lines 630-80.

The combatants are enormously powerful, more so than any army of men could ever be. Their force is truly supernatural. This can only be a war between higher powers.

As well as the Titans, the divinities of the earth, the seas and the sky join in and take part in the violence of the combat. This is a total war in which the greatest powers on earth confront each other:

> high Olympus reeled from its foundation under the charge of the undying gods, and a heavy quaking reached dim Tartarus […] the bolts flew thick and fast from his [Zeus's] strong hand together with thunder and lightning, whirling an awesome flame. The life-giving earth crashed around in burning […][3]

The earth is in uproar. The sea is unleashed. The cataclysm is at the height of its powers of devastation:

> the vast wood crackled loud with fire all about. All the land seethed, and Ocean's streams and the unfruitful sea. The hot vapor lapped round the earthborn Titans: flame unspeakable rose to the bright upper air […] Astounding heat seized Chaos: and to see with eyes and to hear the sound with ears it seemed even as if Earth and wide Heaven above came together; for such a mighty crash would have arisen if Earth were being hurled to ruin, and Heaven from on high were hurling her down; […] Also the winds brought rumbling earthquake and duststorm, thunder and lightning and the lurid thunderbolt, […] A horrible uproar of terrible strife arose: mighty deeds were shown and the battle inclined.[4]

This must have been a major event. At the same time that the sky is shaken and Olympus totters, the stars, considered to be fixed to the celestial vault, change their trajectory.

3   Hesiod, *Theogony, op. cit.*, lines 680-95.
4   *Ibid.*, lines 695-710.

François Le Normant describes the cataclysm in the light of Hesiod's account:

> The setting and epic form of Hesiod's account were influenced by the memory of a large-scale geological event produced by subterranean forces, which took place in the Greek regions and which was witnessed by man; doubtless that event which geologists call the Taenarus upheaval, the last of the plutonic cataclysms which shook the ancient world, making its effects felt from central France to the coast of Syria.
>
> Italy was effectively broken down its length, Tuscany burst forth volcanoes, the Phlegrean Fields went up in flames, and Stromboli and Etna erupted for the first time.
>
> In Greece, the Taygetos mountains emerged in the centre of the Peloponnese. New islands (Thera, Delos, Melos, Kithnos) rose from the boiling waves of the Aegean. Those who witnessed these terrible convulsions of nature naturally believed themselves caught up in a battle of titans [...] against the forces of heaven, who were aided by the hecatoncheires [hundred-handed monsters, sons of heaven and earth]. In their imagination, these adversaries were all powerful, the one side making a stand on the summit of Olympus, the other on Mount Othrys, from where they hurled flaming boulders at each other.[5]

---

5   Fr. Lenormant, *Histoire ancienne de l'Orient*, vol. I, A. Lévy, 1882, p. 51.

Homer

I begin to sing of Pallas Athena, the glorious goddess, bright-eyed [...]
Athena sprang quickly from the immortal head and stood before Zeus who
holds the aegis, shaking a sharp spear: great Olympus began to reel
horribly at the might of the bright-eyed goddess, and earth round about
cried fearfully, and the sea was moved and tossed with dark waves, while
foam burst forth suddenly: the bright Son of Hyperion stopped his swift-
footed horses a long while, until the maiden Pallas Athena had stripped
the heavenly armour from her immortal shoulders.[6]

Homer is clearly alluding to a major upheaval, with the seas being hurled
against the land, as well as the sun being halted in its normal course.

The *Odyssey* also narrates this event that was so powerful that "vast
Olympus was shaken by it." Homer situates a major event of this kind at the
time of the Trojan War, around the 13th century BC.

Dazzling flames make "the lovely waters" of the river start to "bubble and
boil [...] as does the fat of a carefully reared pig. [...] The Xanthus refused
to flow any more [...] suspended its course," laid low by the "the fire's
violence."

There is no doubt that, in Hesiod as in Homer, a cataclysmic event of this
kind occurred very suddenly, even if it seemed to last an eternity to those
who lived through it.

The action starts very abruptly and violently with "this day," and
everything ends just as suddenly with the words "Then, the combat waned."

In the *Odyssey*, it is Hephaistos, the god of fire, who puts an end to the
conflagrations. "He extinguished the fire that the gods had caused to flame
up." The surge of the Xanthus was tamed. "The rivers calmed down," for
Hera restrained them.

To date this cataclysm, we need to know that time was measured in lunar
months, as in Egypt.

6   *Hymn 28 to Athena* in *Homeric Hymns and Homerica, op. cit.,* lines 1-15.

[...] tell of the long-winged Moon. [...] bright Selene having bathed her
lovely body in the waters of Ocean, and donned her far-gleaming raiment,
and yoked her strong-necked, shining team, drives on her long-maned
horses at full speed, at eventime in the mid-month: then her great orbit is
full and then her beams shine brightest as she increases. So she is a sure
token and a sign to mortal men.[7]

Aeschylus

The order of the sky, apparently immutable for centuries, was suddenly transformed. The changes in the sky allowed several historical epochs to be distinguished, under the successive reigns of Ouranos and Chronos, and finally Zeus.

Aeschylus thought that the third epoch, in which we still live, would soon be driven away by a new sky. This order, he says, "which rules at present, is one which I will soon see being ignominiously driven away too."

Therefore let the lightning's forked curl be cast upon my head and let the
sky be convulsed with thunder and the wrack of savage winds; let the
hurricane shake the earth from its rooted base, and let the waves of the sea
mingle with their savage surge the courses of the stars in heaven [...] the
earth rocks, the echoing thunder-peal from the depths rolls roaring past
me; the fiery wreathed lightning-flashes flare forth, and whirlwinds toss the
swirling dust; the blasts of all the winds leap forth and set in hostile array
their embattled strife; the sky is confounded with the deep. Behold, this
stormy turmoil advances against me visibly, sent by Zeus to frighten me.[8]

Aeschylus's choice of words is astonishing. A simple earthquake makes the whole earth rock and vibrate. But during a major event of the kind

---

7   *Hymn to Selene* in *Homeric Hymns and Homerica,* op. cit.

8   Aeschylus, *Prometheus Bound* in *Aeschylus* (trans. H. Weir Smyth), HUP, 1926, lines 1040-91.

apparently being described here, the earth is "shaken from its rooted base," uprooted. Could this be an ancient way of describing the brutal displacement of the tectonic plates? Confusion overcomes the orbits of the stars, the sky is different. But it must be the earth itself, rather, that starts to move, amid the din of the "echoing thunder-peal" emerging from its depths.

Euripides

In Euripides' tragedy, *Hippolytus*, a tidal wave submerges the lands at the mouth of the Saronic Gulf.

> *There a great noise in the earth, like Zeus's thunder, roared heavily – it made one shudder to hear it. The horses pricked up their heads and ears to heaven, while we servants were taken with a violent fear at the thought where this voice came from. When we turned our eyes to the sea-beaten beach, we saw a wave, immense and uncanny, set fast in the sky, so great that my eye was robbed of the sight of Sciron's coast, and the Isthmus and Asclepius' cliff were hid from view. And then as the sea-surge made it swell and seeth up much foam all about, it came toward the shore where the chariot was. With its very swell and surge the wave put forth a bull, fierce and heaven-sent. With its bellowing the whole land was filled and gave back unearthly echoes, and as we looked on it the sight was too great for our eyes to bear.*[9]

The noise made by the earth as it comes away from its base is like a subterranean thunder, a "great noise" which "roared heavily." Its brutal movements relative to the sea, whose inertia is immense, obliges the latter to surge up against the land. The marvel of this wave rising skywards, as well as its irresistible momentum and its roar, must quite justifiably have made everyone tremble.

We can thus understand more easily why the Cretans took the bull as

---

9   Euripides, *Hippolytus*, in *Euripdes* (trans. D. Kovacs), HUP, 1995, lines 1200-20.

their emblem, and used it as the figurehead on their powerful sailing boats that ploughed through the seas.

Another work by Euripides, *Iphigenia in Tauris*, depicts an earthquake conjointly with a change in the course of the stars:

I dreamed that I had left this land to live in Argos, and to sleep in the midst of the maidens' rooms; but the earth's back was shaken by a tossing swell. When I escaped and stood outside, I saw the cornice of the house fall, and the whole roof hurled in ruins on the ground, from the highest pillars. […] troubles dart out from troubles: Pelops, on his horses swiftly whirling, made his cast; the sun changed from its seat the holy beam of its rays.

Orestes says to his sister Iphigenia, so that she will recognise him:

[…] Ask me something about our ancestral home.
Iphigenia (cautious): Shouldn't it be you that tells, and me that learns?
Orestes: I'll tell this first, by hearsay from Electra: you know there was strife between Atreus and Thyestes?
Iphigenia: I've heard; there was quarrelling over a golden lamb.
Orestes: Well you know you wove it in a piece of fine weaving?
Iphigenia: O dearest one, you are brushing close to my memory!
Orestes: And wove on the loom a picture of the sun's shifting?[10]

It is clear that, in the same way as when we are in a train at a station, we have the impression that the train on the neighbouring track is advancing whereas in fact it is our train which is starting to move, the witnesses of these cataclysms had the impression that the sun was moving away, while it was the earth beneath their feet that was shifting.

While it is difficult to imagine how the continents could detach

---

10 Euripides, *Iphigenia in Tauris* (trans. M. J. Cropp), Aris & Phillips, Warminster, 2000.

themselves from their roots, well anchored in the depths of the earth, it is even more difficult to believe that the sun could have deviated from its course.

Plato

This Greek philosopher, the heir of Socrates in the 4th century BC, narrated his story of Atlantis in the *Critias* and *Timaeus*. This story, which was supposedly related to Solon by Egyptian priests, speaks of 8,000 years, which are certainly in fact moons – for this was how the Egyptians counted. This dates the story reasonably accurately to the 13th century BC, at the memorable period of the battles between Rameses II and Rameses III against the Sea Peoples.

The end of the Middle Empire, the geological upheavals at the time of the Trojan War and the period of Thyestes and Atreus, the alliances of the Egyptians with the Libyans and the Greeks, and their subsequent turning against them, correspond to the time at which the island of Santorini exploded, when Moses also brought the Hebrew people out of Egypt.

"There have been and there will be," said Plato, "many and diverse destructions of mankind, of which the greatest are by fire and water, and lesser ones by countless other means." And Plato continues by drawing on the Greek legend of Phaethon:

> Phaethon, son of Helios, yoked his father's chariot, and, because he was unable to drive it along the course taken by his father, burnt up all that was upon the earth and himself perished by a thunderbolt – that story, as it is told, has the fashion of a legend, but the truth of it lies in the occurrence of a shifting of the bodies in the heavens which move round the earth, and a destruction of the things on the earth by fierce fire, which recurs at long intervals. At such times all they that dwell on the mountains and in high and dry places suffer destruction more than those who dwell near to rivers or the sea [...] And when, on the other hand, the Gods purge the earth with a flood of waters, all the herdsmen and shepherds that are in the mountains are saved but those in the cities of your land are

swept into the sea by the streams [...] the truth being that in every place where there is no excessive heat or cold to prevent it there always exists some human stock, now more, now less in number.[11]

The record of these great events has been preserved in Egypt "which we know by report, all such events are recorded from of old and preserved here in our temples."

While the Greeks and other peoples "are but newly equipped, every time, with letters and all such arts as civilised States require and when, after the usual interval of years, like a plague, the flood from heaven comes sweeping down afresh upon your people, it leaves none of you but the unlettered and uncultured." The Greeks "remember but one deluge, though many had occurred previously."

The Pythagorean school tried to systematise and rationalise, imagining astronomical cycles that regularly brought different floods with them. But in fact these great events were a matter of chance.

Depending on the abrupt and significant drift of the tectonic plates in the Mediterranean, and depending on their direction, certain seashores were overwhelmed by deep tides, while others were less affected.

Volcanoes started to erupt. Crevasses appeared, as did orogenic uplifts that affected certain regions more than others. Plato simplifies when he talks essentially about shores or mountains, and the action of water or fire. He is right, however, to note that a deviation sometimes, if rarely, occurs in the apparent course of the stars.

11 Plato, *Timaeus* in *Plato in Twelve Volumes*, vol. IX (trans. W. R. M. Lamb), Loeb Classical Library, Harvard University Press, 1969.

3.8 Rome

Deucalion's flood in Ovid

Jupiter, the god of lightning, thunder and light, decides to annihilate the human race. He unleashes a cataclysm in which all the elements take part. Jupiter's anger is phenomenal and courses throughout his body, which is like a desolate polar earth.[1]

> *the Southwind flies abroad with dripping wings,*
> *concealing in the gloom his awful face:*
> *the drenching rain descends from his wet beard*
> *and hoary locks; dark clouds are on his brows*
> *and from his wings and garments drip the dews:*
> *his great hands press the overhanging clouds.*

The mighty god wields the clouds, squeezing them in his hand, causing a terrible din. The repercussions on the earth are catastrophic.

> *loudly the thunders roll; the torrents pour;*
> *Iris, the messenger of Juno, clad*
> *in many coloured raiment, upward draws*
> *the steaming moisture to renew the clouds.*
> *The standing grain is beaten to the ground.*

Jupiter orders the waters to join in the task of destroying both land and human beings.

> *Neptune, their ancient ruler, thus began;*
> *"A long appeal is needless; pour ye forth*
> *in rage of power; open up your fountains;*
> *rush over obstacles; let every stream*

1 Ovid, *Metamorphoses*, Book I (trans. Brookes More), Cornhill Publishing Co., Boston, 1922.

pour forth in boundless floods."
And Neptune with his trident smote the Earth,
which trembling with unwonted throes heaved up
the sources of her waters bare; and through
her open plains the rapid rivers rushed
resistless, onward bearing the waving grain,
the budding groves, the houses, sheep and men,–
and holy temples, and their sacred urns.
The mansions that remained, resisting vast
and total ruin, deepening waves concealed
and whelmed their tottering turrets in the flood
and whirling gulf. And now one vast expanse,
the land and sea were mingled in the waste
of endless waves – a sea without a shore. […]
the surging waves
float tigers and lions […]
The waves increasing surge above the hills,
and rising waters dash on mountain tops.

The flood of Deucalion is different from an ordinary flood. Some extraordinary tidal wave would be needed to "surge above the hills" and "dash on mountain tops." There is also a great jolt which makes the earth tremble, as if from the blow of a trident, and which is responsible for a great uproar. The brutal way the ground is set in motion, as described by Ovid, is extensive enough to affect the rivers which leap out of their riverbeds, and Neptune, the ocean which sweeps in and covers the plains, the harvests, the flocks, the humans, the houses. Deucalion and his sister Pyrrha are, in this account, the only ones to escape this redoubtable deluge. Zeus's anger wanes,

he scattered all the clouds; he blew away
the great storms by the cold northwind.
Once more

the earth appeared to heaven and the skies
appeared to earth. The fury of the main
abated, for the Ocean ruler laid
his trident down and pacified the waves,
and called on azure Triton [...]
[to] blow in his sounding shell, the wandering streams
and rivers to recall with signal known [...]
and all the waters of the land and sea
obeyed. Their fountains heard and ceased to flow;
their waves subsided; hidden hills uprose;
emerged the shores of ocean; channels filled
with flowing streams; the soil appeared; the land
increased its surface as the waves decreased:
and after length of days the trees put forth,
with ooze on bending boughs, their naked tops.

The catastrophe is thus limited in time. The elements resume their places, leaving the lands devastated. It is noteworthy that, quite logically, the rivers are flowing at full strength so they can drain off the water that has built up on the land as a result of the rising of the oceans.

The myth of Phaethon in Ovid

Phaethon is the son of the sun-god and a mortal woman. The Sun rashly authorises his presumptuous son to drive his chariot of fire for a day. Unable to master the horses, Phaethon's chariot swerves, "the car leaped lightly in the air, and in the heights was tossed unsteady as an empty shell." Finally, "tossed by raging Boreas," the north wind, the chariot's horses fling themselves into an unknown region of the air. The sun has "left the beaten track," i.e., its usual course, and no longer follows the same direction as previously.[2]

The stars and the constellations that they constitute follow one and the

2   Ovid, *Metamorphoses*, Book II, *op. cit.*

same trajectory at a given place, and at a constant speed. The same is almost true of the sun, which goes noticeably more slowly, and passes through the 12 signs of the zodiac in a year in the opposite direction to that of their apparent rotation. Ovid explains this by resorting to the image of the Empyrean, or the Great Olympus, to designate the heavenly sphere linked to the stars, and the chariot of the sun which follows the well worn and habitual track, until Phaethon indulges his whim, which threatens the entire earth with destruction.

The horses of the chariot deviate from their course, rushing haphazardly forward and charging up into the heights of the ether, towards the abyss with the same wild momentum.

Phaethon can no longer steer his course, nor does he know "where the way might be." Should he steer westwards or eastwards? "At first his gaze is fixed upon the west, which fate has destined he shall never reach, and then his eyes turn backward to the east." He is left "stupefied and dazed."

The stars are panic-stricken in their turn, Ursa Major and Ursa Minor as well as Draco, "Warmed in the sunshine, never felt before, the gelid Triones [septentriones, seven stars of the Plough] attempted vain to bathe in seas forbid." As if they were being jolted and shaken, they seem to have changed position as a result of various chaotic movements. This image corresponds to the fact that the ground in Greece has undergone movements of an extent incommensurable with a mere earthquake.

Ovid gives two important details here. First of all, the apparent anarchic drift of the sun took place in broad daylight and could clearly be seen. Then, Callisto, Ursa Major, and his son, Arcas, Ursa Minor, were lifted to the highest part of the sky, which argues for a sudden increase in latitude.

This must without a doubt have been a major event. Many different consequences inevitably ensued from it. "The highest altitudes are caught in flames, and as their moistures dry they crack in chasms." The earth gapes, "great cities perish with their walls," entire territories as well as whole populations are reduced to ashes by the fire. The forests burn. "The huge mountain tops, once covered by the ocean's waves, reared up, by which the scattered Cyclades increased." The number of the Cyclades increases. The

Ebro and the Stymon in Spain, the Rhine, the Rhone, the Po and the Tiber all dry up.

"The Nile affrighted fled to parts remote, and hid his head forever from the world, now empty are his seven mouths, and dry without or wave or stream." The sea shrinks, "The sea contracted and his level waste became a sandy desert."

The myth of Phaethon, as related by Ovid, does not enable us to give specific details or to date a major event that certainly happened, albeit a very long time ago. Several sets of memories have become superimposed and melded, being compiled with erudition but without any real attention to chronology.

The prophecy comes true

In his tragedy, *Hercules Oetaeus*, Seneca says of Hercules, that this formidable creature could not be conceived in a single night.

Seneca prophecies that one day all the gods will perish, and a day will come for the universe when all its laws will be turned topsy-turvy:

> *Soon, soon, when to the universe shall come the day that law shall be o'erwhelmed, the southern skies shall fall upon Libya's plains and all that the scattered Garamantians possess; the northern heavens shall overwhelm all that lies beneath the pole and that Boreas smites with withering blasts. Then from the lost sky the affrighted sun shall fall and banish day. The palace of heaven shall sink, dragging down East and West, and death in some form and chaos shall o'erwhelm all gods in one destruction; and death shall at last bring doom upon itself.[3]*

This poetic technique, consisting of prophesying *a posteriori*, is a classic device frequently used by Roman authors.

---

3   Seneca, *Hercules Oetaeus* in *Seneca's Tragedies*, vol. 2 (trans. F. J. Miller), Heinemann, 1917, p. 275.

At the end of his life, Hercules is immolated on a pyre. He implores Jupiter, his father, the supreme god:

> *Turn back, O shining Sun, thy panting steeds, and let loose the night; let this day wherein I die perish for the world, and let heaven shudder in the pitchy dark [...]. Now, father, were it fitting to restore blind chaos; now this side and that should heaven's frame be burst and both poles rent assunder.*[4]

This is what actually happened. Upheavals affected the laws of the universe, modifying the apparent course of the sun. "And behold, the sun stops at the end of its course. For you, Hercules, the sky stopped in its revolution."

For the Romans and the Greeks, the death of such a hero could not be signalled by any homage less than the arrival of the sun itself, and the overthrow of its laws.

The flood in Seneca

The floods and the retreat of the sun are described in different texts of Latin mythology. The gods and heroes change their identity, and the events described are not always the same. From this we may deduce that there were perhaps several major events at different periods, always with the same ingredients: a spectacular overflow of the seas and rivers, orogenic uplifts, and the withdrawal of the sun, accompanied by a disturbance in the apparent direction of the stars' courses.

For Latin literature, the myth of Phaethon and Deucalion's flood constituted two major upheavals in the course of the world's history. Seneca, the 1st century AD Latin writer, in turn tells the story of a cataclysm. How does it come about that the sun's disappearance is mentioned in this account too?

---

4   Seneca, *Hercules Oetaeus, op. cit.*, p. 277.

Let us remember that, before the Trojan War, Atreus, the father of Agamemnon, was involved in a contest for the throne of Mycenae with his brother Thyestes. It was on this occasion, according to Apollodorus, that Atreus stipulated to Thyestes that he would become king if the sun were to go backwards. Atreus had little chance of becoming king, given the bizarre nature of the agreement and the high degree of improbability of such an event. Thyestes accepted the conditions, whereupon the sun set in the east.

Seneca is here following Euripides, for whom, as we have seen, the sun reversed its course. In his tragedy *Thyestes*, Seneca describes another major event just as strange. The chorus addresses the sun in these terms:

> *Whither, O father of the lands and skies, before whose rising thick night with all her glories flees, whither dost turn thy course and why dost blot out the day in mid-Olympus? Why, O Phoebus, dost snatch away thy face? Not yet does Vesper, twilight's messenger, summon the fires of night; not yet does thy wheel, turning its western goal, bid free thy steeds from their completed task; not yet as day fades into night has the third trump sounded; the ploughman with oxen yet unwearied stands amazed at his supper-hour's quick coming. What has driven thee from thy heavenly course? What cause from their fixed track has turned aside thy horses?*

> *Heaven's accustomed alternations are no more; no setting, no rising shall there be again. The dewy mother of the early dawn, wont to hand o'er to the god his morning reins, looks in amaze upon the disordered threshold of her kingdom; she is not willed to bathe his weary chariot, nor to plunge his steeds, reeking with sweat, beneath the sea. Startled himself at such unwonted welcoming, the sinking sun beholds Aurora, and bids the shadows arise, though night is not yet ready. No stars come out; the heavens gleam not with any fires: no moon dispels the darkness' heavy pall.*

> *[…] the Wain, which was ne'er bathed by the sea, shall be plunged beneath the all-engulfing waves; the slippery Serpent which, sliding like a river, separates the Bears, shall fall, and icy Cynosura, the Lesser Bear,*

together with the Dragon vast, congealed with cold; and that slow-moving driver of his wain, Arctophylax, no longer fixed in place, shall fall.

Have we of all mankind been deemed deserving that heaven, its poles uptorn, should overwhelm us? In our time has the last day come?[5]

Seneca is clearly describing a major event, which is for once precisely characterised. The sky detaches from its axes, its poles are wrenched away. The regular alternation of heavenly phenomena is destroyed, and the sun suddenly changes route. This disaster intervenes around the middle of the afternoon, when the farmers' animals have not yet finished their day's ploughing. As the day is about to end, the sun, declining in the west, hesitates and finally disappears while night is not yet ready to appear. The sun forces the darkness to rise up. Furthermore, Ursa Major and Ursa Minor as well as Draco, that twists between the two of them and was thus called the 'Serpent', plunge to their lowest level in their course beneath the horizon, fall into the sea and are swallowed up.

From this we may deduce that the declinations of these three constellations were more than 70°. The latitude of Greece must then necessarily have been less than 20°. This position presupposes a climate that was, if not equatorial, at least tropical – a hypothesis that is unexpectedly confirmed by the famous myth of Tantalus.

Seest thou how the water, driven far within, deserts the springs, how river banks are empty, how the fiery wind drives away the scattered clouds? Every tree grows pale, and from the bare branches the fruit has fled; and where this side and that the Isthmus is wont to roar with neighbouring waves, dividing near seas with narrow neck of land, the shore but faintly hears the far off sound. Now Lerna has shrunk back, the Phoronean stream has disappeared, the sacred Alpheus no longer bears his waters on, Cithaeron's heights have lost their snows and nowhere stand hoary now,

5   Seneca, *Thyestes* in *Seneca's Tragedies*, vol. 2 (trans. F. J. Miller), Heinemann, 1917, pp. 157-63.

and the lordly Argos fears its ancient drought. [...].

Weary, with empty throat, stands Tantalus; above his guilty head hangs food in plenty, than Phineus' birds more elusive; on either side, with laden boughs, a tree leans over him and, bending and trembling 'neath its weight of fruit, make sport with his wide-straining jaws. The prize, though he is eager and impatient of delay, deceived so oft, he tries no more to touch, turns away his eyes, shuts tight his lips, and behind clenched teeth he bars his hunger [...]. Then comes a raging thirst, harder to bear than hunger; when by this his blood has grown hot and glowed as with fiery torches, the poor wretch stands catching at waves that seem to approach his lips; but these the elusive water turns aside, failing in meagre shallows, and leaves him utterly, striving to pursue; then deep from the whirling stream he drinks – but dust.[6]

This long quotation expresses it well: the water springs withdraw into the ground, the clouds are dried up by a wind of fire, the rivers stop flowing, the banks are desiccated and the trees turn yellow, as are their fruits, since the branches can no longer support their weight. As is perfectly logical, "no layer of snow" comes to "whiten the surface of the mountains" any more, since Greece has slipped southwards. The average level of the Mediterranean is lowered, since the Isthmus of Corinth (between the Ionian and the Aegean Seas) grows wider.

Continental drift in *Medea*

There will come an age in the far-off years when Ocean shall loose the bonds of things, when the whole broad earth shall be revealed, when Tethys shall disclose new worlds and Thule not be the limit of the lands.[7]

An American military base, situated in the north of Greenland and long

6   Seneca, *Thyestes, op. cit.,* pp. 101-3.

7   Seneca, *Medea,* in *Seneca's Tragedies,* vol. 1 (trans. F. J. Miller), Heinemann, 1917, p. 261.

kept secret, has been given the name Thule, in memory of an island, perhaps Iceland, which the ancients considered to be the northernmost in the North Sea.

How can we fail to be intrigued by this single fact – that the successive changes of the latitude occupied by different lands, in particular the Scandinavian regions, allowed Seneca to foresee an apparent change in the pole?

Such a change would have the effect of making the ice set free one of the continents that are today imprisoned in the ice floe.

3.9 India

Demons of the night

The Vedic hymns give us a good description of the violent and dazzling apparitions that lit up the polar night:

> Owing to the presence of demons, the heavenly community lead a difficult existence [...] the Rudra complement the Marut, young warriors of the atmosphere, whose battles take the form of storms [...] the Marut, customary companions of Indra, are said to be the sons of the Rudra.[1]

The Maruts are described as:

"shining like snakes," "blazing in their strength," "brilliant like fires."
"O Indra [...] terrible with the terrible ones [...]
Your march, o Maruts, appears brilliant [...]
Like the dawn, they uncover the dark nights
with red rays [...]
with their brilliant light [...]
they have assumed their bright and brilliant colour.[...]
You have caused men to tremble,
You have caused mountains to tremble [...]
The terrible train of untiring Maruts...
Full of terrible design, like giants. [...]
You shake the sky.
[...] even what is firm and unshakeable
is being shaken.
When they whose march is terrible have caused the rocks to tremble,
or when the manly Maruts have shaken the back of heaven.
Hide the hideous darkness,
make the light we long for![...]

---

1 G. Dumézil, *Les dieux souverains indo-européens*, Gallimard, 1977, pp. 35-6.

These Maruts are men brilliant with lightning,
they shoot with thunderbolts,
they blaze with the wind,
they shake the mountains.[2]

We can see that terrible jolts shook the mountains during the hours when the ground of the ancestral land suddenly slipped and moved to the vicinity of the South Pole, while the apparent course of the stars in the sky was severely affected.

A radical climate change

Ahura Mazda spake unto most beneficent Zarathustra, saying:
I have made every land dear to its dwellers, even though it had no charms whatever in it: had I not made every land dear to its dwellers, even though it had no charms whatever in it, then the whole living world would have invaded the Airyana Vaêgô.

The first of the good lands and countries which I, Ahura Mazda, created, was the Airyana Vaêgô, by the good river Dâitya

Thereupon came Angra Mainyu, who is all death, and he counter-created by his witchcraft the serpent in the river and winter, a work of the Daêvas.

There are ten winter months there, two summer months; and those are cold for the waters, cold for the earth, cold for the trees. Winter falls there, with the worst of its plagues.[3]

The supreme deity, Ahura Mazda continues:

2   Extract from the *Vedic hymns* cited in I. Velikovsky, *Worlds in Collision*, Abacus, London, 1972, pp. 270-6.

3   *The Vendidad*, I, 1-5 (trans. J. Darmesteter) in *Sacred Books of the East*, vol. 4, Oxford University Press, Oxford, 1880.

O fair Yima, son of Vivanghat! Upon the material
world the fatal winters are going to fall, that shall bring the fierce, foul
frost; upon the material world the fatal winters are going to fall, that shall
make snow-flakes fall thick, even an aredvî *deep on the highest tops of*
mountains.

And all the three sorts of beasts shall perish, those that live in the
wilderness, and those that live on the tops of the mountains, and those
that live in the bosom of the dale, under the shelter of stables.

Before that winter, those fields would bear plenty of grass for cattle: now
with floods that stream, with snows that melt, it will seem a happy land in
the world, the land wherein footprints even of sheep may still be seen.[4]

The dramatic arrival of this winter – a highly unusual winter, since it is
accompanied by floods, excessive snowfall and an almost total destruction
of fauna – is sudden and unexpected. Indeed, before the coming of the night
and the cold, the lands were fertile and had thus never known such climatic
conditions.

The original mountain

In 1898, Dr William F. Warren wrote a book whose title could not fail to
attract my attention: *The Cradle of the Human Race at the North Pole. A Study
of the Prehistoric World.* As the work's name indicates, the author claimed
that mankind had originated at the North Pole.

A Vedic scholar, Lokamanya Bal Gangâdhar Tilak, continued Warren's
work and published a book in 1903 with the title *The Arctic home of the
Vedas.* These works are excellent, apart from one detail, and a major one at
that: the cradle of mankind cannot have been at the North Pole.

On top of all the evidence that we have gleaned from the texts of the
earliest civilisations, one proof has been highlighted by Charles Hapgood: all

4   *The Vendidad, op. cit.*

the texts, whether of Indian, Mexican, Polynesian or Icelandic origin, mention a lofty mountain. But there is no such mountain on the Arctic Ocean. Nor has any significant trace of civilisation been found in the Arctic seas.

And how indeed could we imagine a migration starting out from the vicinity of the North Pole, and crossing the immensity of the Asiatic steppes without leaving any trace? How could men have crossed the highest mountain range in the world, the Himalayas, to reach the high plateaux of Iran and arrive in the Indus? On the other hand, there is no logical or material obstacle to their having left the Antarctic continent on sail boats and disembarked in the Persian Gulf, reaching the Nile by the Red Sea or the mouth of the Indus. This represents a month's voyage at an average (and modest) speed of five knots with a favourable crosswind.

A great number of Indian, Persian, Greek and Mesopotamian texts situate the origin of mankind at the pole. There was, it must be granted, a certain logic in these inhabitants of the northern hemisphere locating it at the North Pole. This was still how it was commonly imagined in the 19th century, before the great modern expeditions set out. The Germanophiles, who invented the myth of the Indo-Europeans as the ones who had civilised the world, located mankind's origins in the Arctic, as did Dr Warren. René Guénon and Julius Evola were also supporters of this idea.

The swastika (originally the *svastika*), outrageously appropriated by the Nazis, is found on every continent in the world. It is found in China, in Central America, even on Easter Island, and from the remotest periods. Could its origins be polar, the symbol's four arms representing the four cardinal points or the stars comprising the constellation of the Southern Cross? Near the poles the point of reference in relation to the stars is close to the vertical. The Southern Cross thus appears to rotate about its own axis.

For more than 3,000 years, people would continue to remember an axis of the world close to the vertical, seen from the land of their ancestors. Now in India as in Persia, only the celestial North Pole is visible, at 20° or 30° above the horizon, with Ursa Major and Ursa Minor turning around it. Thus the ancient texts went on to transpose to the north what was in the south.

The 'Seven Shining Ones' were mentioned in the texts under the name of Rishis. A play of words turned 'Rishis' into 'Rickshaw', a four-wheeled chariot drawn by three horses.

The flood of Manu

Manu or Vaivaswata was a holy monarch. He was the witness and the survivor of an infernal flood, thanks to the protection of Brahma, the lord of creatures, who had assumed the shape of a mysterious fish. This flood is recounted in the *Brâhmanas* and the *Mahâbhârata*.

Brahma appears first of all in the shape of a little fish who craves the protection of Manu. For fear of being swallowed by bigger fish than himself, he asks him to pull him out of the river and put him in a vessel filled with water.

Manu obeys. The fish grows spectacularly, and keeps needing a bigger and bigger habitat. Soon, not even a whole lake or the River Ganges are large enough. He ends up in the sea. To reward the sage Manu for his kindly treatment, the fish, now gigantic in size, tells him that a terrible flood is about to devastate the entire earth.

> In a little while all things on earth shall be destroyed.
> The time has come for whole worlds to be submerged.
> The terrible moment of dissolution is at hand for all living things.

He recommends that he construct a solid boat and place every type of grain on board with him. Manu obeys.

Soon, the fish reappears. Manu attaches the ropes of his vessel to his powerful horn. Then the fish "made the boat sail across the sea with the greatest speed, despite the impetuous waves and the violent storm, which meant one could no longer make out either the earth, or the Heavenly Regions." After many long years, they strike land, at the summit of Mount

---

4   «Lois de Manou» cited in G. Pauthier, *Livres sacrés de l'Orient*, Firmin Didot, 1840, p. 337.

Figure 41. *Fragment of a statue of Brahma, from the 11th–12th centuries. Blue schist, from the region of Gwalior in India.*

Himavat (doubtless in the Himalayas). Then the fish makes himself known under his true identity:

> *I am Brahma, Lord of Creation [...] No being is my equal.*
> *Taking the form of a fish I saved you from danger.*
> *Manu, go now and oversee the creation.*[4]

Then Manu can start to create all beings.

The Indian race is disinclined to seafaring. Its whole tradition reflects its fear and hatred of the ocean. To leave the original continent, Manu is helped by a great sailor, one of the founders of the first cities at the head of the Persian Gulf.

This is why the Indus Valley was populated at around the same time as Egypt and Sumer.

When a world cycle comes to an end

> *When a world cycle is destroyed by wind... there arises in the beginning a cycle-destroying great cloud... There arises a wind to destroy the world cycle, and first it raises a fine dust, and then coarse dust, and then fine sand, and then coarse sand, and then grit, stones, up to boulders as large... as mighty trees on the hilltops. [The wind] turns the ground upside down, [large areas] crack and are thrown upwards... all the mansions on earth [are destroyed in a catastrophe when] worlds clash with worlds.*[5]

5   Extract from the *Visuddhi-Magga* cited in I. Velikovsky, *Worlds in Collision*, Abacus, London, 1972, p. 64.

3.10 Mesopotamia

Chronology

Sumerian tablets have been found in Mesopotamia, in the city of Larsa. On them we can read the list of the kings who reigned before the flood, *lam abubi*.

Some 10 or so kings apparently governed five or six cities. Nothing enables us to say whether these cities succeeded one another or coexisted. But the respective reigns of the kings, if we are to believe these remains, must have lasted between 241,200 and 456,000 long years! This excessive number of years can be explained logically if we bear in mind the extent of the Mesopotamians' knowledge of astronomy.

The Mesopotamian astronomers knew, among other things, how to foretell eclipses precisely. Around 325 BC, Berosus, the priest of Bel-Marduk, wrote a history of Babylonia. His contempt for Greek culture was so great that we find no trace of it in his history. The sources he used have been found in the monumental libraries in Nineveh, Babylon, Alexandria, Byzantium and Carthage.

The Mesopotamians had rounded the year to 360 days, the number of moons being approximately 12 per year, and the year being constituted of 12 months with 30 days each. This number was a very effective multiple divisor for finding out the years of the kings' reigns.

The priest Berosus attributed 3,600 human years to a *sar*, a divine year. Three hundred and sixty years would have been a more logical number: in the vicinity of the pole, the year does indeed last for a day and a night.

In order to confer on the gods the prestige due to them, and to belittle the Greek gods, who were far from attaining such longevity, Berosus had the idea of multiplying by 10 these 360 human days. Thus, if we simply divide the number of years of the kings' reigns by 3,600, they do not exceed 150 years. Should we deduce that men really lived longer then than they do now? Or, more reasonably, that the reigns in fact included a whole line of kings bearing the same name?

If we study the royal lineages described by Mesopotamian scholars, we can locate a period of three centuries at most between a flood that devastated the land, and the appearance of the Sumerians who disembarked mysteriously in Mesopotamia.

Vulcanism

The voyage of Enki across a tumultuous ocean is narrated in these terms:

> *After he had set sail, after he had set sail,*
> *After the father had set sail against Kur,*
> *After Enki had set sail against Kur,*
> *Against the king, the small ones it [Kur] hurled;*
> *Against Enki, the large ones it hurled.*
> *Its small ones, stones of the hand,*
> *Its large ones, stones of "dancing" reeds,*
> *The keel of the boat of Enki*
> *In battle, like the attacking storm, overwhelm.*
> *Against the king, the water at the head of the boat*
> *Like a wolf devours,*
> *Against Enki, the water at the rear of the boat*
> *Like a lion strikes down.*[1]

This crossing of the tempestuous ocean starts out from the holy mountain Kur. We can recognise once more the erupting volcanoes spitting out blocks of hardened lava and hurling them far into the stormy sea.

Heaven and earth are separated

After a period of wealth and abundance, heaven and earth were separated from one another, which is another way of referring to the anarchic movement of the stars:

> *After heaven had been moved away from earth,*

1   S. N. Kramer, *History begins at Sumer*, Thames and Hudson, London, 1958, pp. 227-8.

After earth had been separated from heaven,
After the name of man had been fixed,
After (the heaven-god) An carried off the heaven,
After (the air-god) Enlil carried off the earth…[2]

The ambition of Gilgamesh

Uruk, founded by Enki, the civilising king, was ravaged, as we know, by a great flood called Abubi. The other holy cities in the region suffered the same fate. Abubi caused the death of a multitude of men and women, and destroyed the crops. The sea, having risen from its bed at the head of the Persian Gulf, went crashing into the Zagros Mountains in the east, those of Armenia to the north and those of the Lebanon to the west. The ocean finally returned to its bed, leaving such a mass of sedimentary deposits that the shore withdrew some 130km. The Tigris and the Euphrates, instead of flowing separately into the Gulf, then joined together in one single river mouth to form the Shatt-al-'Arab.

Gilgamesh, the King of Uruk, was the fifth king of the first dynasty after the flood. In his epic, mention is made of the death of the demon Asaq who is killed by Ninurta, the south wind. The demon's death causes a disaster in Sumer, that leads to the waves overflowing:

> As a result of their violence no fresh waters can reach the fields and gardens […]. The Tigris does not rise; it has no 'good' water in its channel.[3]

The famine that ensued was terrible. It was accompanied by major crises in the climate and the population of the country. In Claude Schaeffer's view:

> These successive crises which punctuated the principle periods of the second and third millennia were not caused by human acts. Quite the contrary, compared with the magnitude of these general crises and their

2   S. N. Kramer, *op. cit.*, p. 133.

3   *Ibid.*, p. 228.

profound effects, the exploits of conquerors and the machinations of a few statesmen seem trifling.[4]

Suspecting nothing, Gilgamesh tries to work for the restoration of Uruk, his ravaged city. He also aspires to make sure his name passes down to posterity. This is what he will say to the sun, Utu, after he has lamented the devastation visited on his people:

> O Utu, a word I would speak to you, to my word your ear,
> I would have it reach you, give ear to it.
> In my city man dies, oppressed is the heart,
> Man perishes, heavy is the heart,
> I peered over the wall,
> Saw the dead bodies… floating in the river;
> As for me, I too will be served thus; verily 'tis so.
> Man, the tallest, cannot reach to heaven,
> Man, the widest, cannot cover the earth.
> Not (yet) have brick and stamp brought forth the fated end,
> I would enter the 'land', I would set up my name;
> In its places where the names have been raised up, I would raise up my name,
> In its places where the names have not been raised up, I would raise up the names of the gods.[5]

This is how the *Epic of Gilgamesh* begins. Having experienced the death of his people, he sets off to tame a nature that transcends him, and his quest for immortality begins.

While he is looking for wood on the original continent, he encounters Humbaba, a terrible monster, who was then guarding the forest of cedar:

---

4   C. Schaeffer, *Stratigraphie comparée et chronologie de l'Asie occidentale*, Oxford University Press, 1948, p. 567.

5   S. N. Kramer, *op. cit.*, pp. 234-5.

Figure 42. *Section of the* Epic of Gilgamesh *on a tablet from the collection of Yale University.*

Figure 43. *Ritual vase from Uruk, circa 3000 BC, depicting Gilgamesh with a bull and a bird.*

In the forest terrible Humbaba lives
[…] his roaring is the Great Flood,
His mouth is fire,
His breath is death![6]

The return to Sumer was doubtless a triumphant occasion. Gilgamesh and Enkidu had beaten Humbaba and the monsters of the underworld. They were also credited with victory over the flood Abubi which had ravaged Uruk with the force of a charging bull: "With the snort of the Bull of Heaven, pits were opened and a hundred men of Uruk fell into them."[7]

Various sculptures were to immortalise the image of the two heroes overcoming the bull, and examples are found as late as in our own medieval art.

The flood survivor

In the course of his travels, Gilgamesh meets Utanapisti. This is his ancestor from the time of the flood, who still lives on the original continent, having acquired the immortality proper to that place. Utanapisti reveals a great secret to Gilgamesh.

The text then refers to a well-known Biblical episode: that of Noah. Utanapisti has survived the flood thanks to the ark which he built on the advice of Ea (or Enki), the god of Waters. Utanapisti has, in the past, already been wise enough to heed the advice proffered by this all-powerful god:

O man of Shuruppak, o you son of Ubara-Tutu,
Tear down your hut of reeds,
Build of them a reed boat
Abandon things
Seek life
Give up possessions

---

6   R. Temple, *He Who Saw Everything: a verse version of the Epic of Gilgamesh*, Rider, London, 1991.

7   *Ibid.*

Keep your soul alive!
And into the boat take the seed of all living creatures. […]
But he [Enlil] will shower down upon you.[8]

Everything which the god ordered him to do, Utanapisti did:

Whatever I had I loaded aboard,
Whatever I had of silver I loaded aboard,
Whatever I had of gold I loaded aboard
Whatever I had of seed of all living creatures
I loaded aboard.
I caused all my family and kinsfolk to go aboard.
The beasts of the field,
The wild creatures of the plain,
All the craftsmen –
All these I made to go aboard.[9]

Utanapisti makes provision for seven decks and nine compartments in the ship. He brings on board oxen, sheep, barley beer, fine beer, oil and wine. When the hull has slipped into the water and is two-thirds immersed, the flood arrives with sudden violence:

A black cloud rose from the horizon
Inside it Adad the storm thundered,
While Shullat and Hanish, the storm-heralds, rose ahead,
As advance messengers over hill and plain. […]
Astonishment at Adad the Storm reached to the very heavens.
He turned to blackness all that had been visible.
He broke the land like a pot.
For a whole day the South Storm blew,

8   R. Temple, *op. cit.*
9   *Ibid.*

Gathering speed as it blew, drowning the mountains,
Overcoming the people as in battle.
Brother saw not brother.
From heaven no mortal could any longer be seen. [10]

The unfortunate gods try to take refuge in the celestial heights, in the mountains, using torches to light their way.

The Anunnaki – the Great Gods – raised their torches,
Lighting up the land with their brightness. [...]
Even the gods were struck by terror at the deluge,
And, fleeing, they ascended to the celestial band of An.
The gods cowered like dogs,
Crouching by the outer wall of that celestial band. [11]

Ishtar laments:

Oh, how could I command havoc for the destruction of my people
When I myself gave birth to my people?
Now the spawn of fishes, the sea is glutted with their bodies!
The Anunnaki – the Great Gods – wept with her,
Their lips were shut tight in distress in the Assembly, one and all.
For six days and seven nights
The flood wind blew as the South Storm swept the land. [12]

After seven days, the wind and the waves are calmed:

At sunrise in the seventh day
The South Storm, bringer of the flood, and

10   R. Temple, *op. cit.*
11   *Ibid.*
12   *Ibid.*

Which had fought like an army, abated its attack.
The sea grew quieter,
The storm subsided,
The flood ceased.
I looked at the weather;
It had gone quiet.
All men had returned to clay.[13]

Then Utanapisti offers a sacrifice at the summit of the mountain, setting out seven hearths on which to burn incense. He crushes reeds, cedar wood and myrtle. He makes a wish to cook the meat after the offering rites. "The gods smelled the savour, the gods smelled the fine odour!" The survivors, among the Anunnaki, starving after a week of fasting, rejoiced that they could eat at last.

13   R. Temple, *op. cit.*

3.11 The Bible

The Bible owes its uniqueness to several factors:

- The genealogical lines of descent are very detailed and exceptionally rich, thus presenting us with quite an accurate historical chronology, as opposed to the imprecision and uncertainties revealed by the writings of the great civilisations: the oral tradition of the Hebrews is more reliable than the most ancient writings.
- The Hebrew people remained cut off and separated from the developed cultures of the Near East, and this fundamental segregation prevented any contamination from Egypt or Mesopotamia from occurring: no gods were invented to personalise the major events that happened at several crucial historical moments. Everything is attributed to a single God, Yahweh, who protects or chastises Israel, and who always punishes the hostile peoples that surround Israel.
- The Hebrews were nomads or farmers by vocation, and were neither builders nor artists nor seafarers: living in tents or in natural shelters, they were able to observe nature and its upheavals with great exactitude, without resorting to myth. They succeeded more effectively in surviving than did the inhabitants of the great cities that were subject to destruction.
- Practical rather than philosophical in nature, they did not seek to explain rationally and symbolically the exceptional phenomena that turned their lives upside down, as their neighbours did: they viewed them as the simple expression of Yahweh's will.

The Exodus: Moses leads the Hebrews out of Egypt

Abraham lived circa 1800 BC and the Exodus occurred circa 1240 BC. Abraham lived for 175 years, Isaac his son 180 years, and the son of the latter (Israel or Jacob), 147 years. Twelve children – 12 tribes – sprang from Israel, including Joseph.

Seven years of drought followed seven years of plenty: this was the prophecy of Joseph, who managed to interpret the Pharaoh's dream vision of seven fat cows followed by seven lean ones. Having become the Pharaoh's overseer, Joseph brought the members of his family to come and live in Egypt – a situation which the Egyptians disliked.

Moses, the grandson of Israel, was angry at seeing his people mistreated and Yahweh visited Pharaoh with 10 plagues. The waters of the Nile ran with blood so that the fish died; there was an invasion of frogs; people were inflicted with lice; swarms of flies appeared; murrain struck down the cattle of the Egyptians; boils appeared; there was a terrible hail mixed with fire which battered the plants and in the fields – the barley in the ear and the bolled flax were lost, but the wheat and the rye were not affected, since they had not yet grown ripe; there was an invasion of locusts destroying all the greenery; thick darkness for three days; and the death of the firstborn. "And there shall be a great cry throughout all the land of Egypt, such as there was none like it, nor shall be like it any more" (Exod. 11: 6).

On 14 Nisan, the first month of the year, in the middle of the night, Yahweh passed "through the land of Egypt" (Exod. 12: 12). All the houses of Egypt collapsed. "All the hosts of the Lord went out from the land of Egypt" (Exod. 12: 41): "about six hundred thousand on foot that were men, beside children. And a mixed multitude sent up also with them; and flocks, and herds, even very much cattle" (Exod. 12: 37–8). "Six hundred chosen chariots, and all the chariots of Egypt" (Exod. 14: 7), set out in pursuit of the Hebrews, and could not catch up with them because of a "cloud" that shone at night time.

The Hebrews encamped "before Pi-hahiroth, between Migdol and the sea, over against Baal-zephon" (Exod. 14: 2). "The Lord caused the sea to go back by a strong east wind": he "made the sea dry land" (Exod. 14: 21). The Hebrews went across. "In the morning watch," the Egyptian cavalry "took off their chariot wheels, that they drave them heavily" (Exod. 14: 24–5). At dawn, "the waters returned, and covered the chariots, and the horsemen, and all the host of Pharaoh that came into the sea after them" (Exod. 14: 28).

Some two and a half centuries later, circa 1000 BC, David described the Exodus: "Then the earth shook and trembled; the foundations also of the hills moved and were shaken" (Ps. 18: 7).

There went up a smoke out of his nostrils, and fire out of his mouth
devoured: coals were kindled by it.
He bowed the heavens also, and came down: and darkness was under his
feet.[…]
He made darkness his secret place; his pavilion round about him were
dark waters and thick clouds of the skies
At the brightness that was before him his thick clouds passed, hail stones
and coals of fire.
The Lord also thundered in the heavens, and the Highest gave his voice;
hail stones and coals of fire.
Yea, he sent out his arrows, and scattered them; and he shot out
lightnings, and discomfited them.
Then the channels of waters were seen, and the foundations of the world
were discovered.
(Ps. 18: 8–15)

His going forth is from the end of the heaven, and his circuit unto the ends
of it.
(Ps. 19: 6)

The voice of the Lord is upon the waters: the God of glory thundereth: the
Lord is upon many waters.
The voice of the Lord is powerful; the voice of the Lord is full of majesty.
The voice of the Lord breaketh the cedars; yea, the Lord breaketh the
cedars of Lebanon.
He maketh them also to skip like a calf; Lebanon and Sirion [Mount
Hermon] like a young unicorn.
The voice of the Lord divideth the flames of fire.
The voice of the Lord shaketh the wilderness; the Lord shaketh the
wilderness of Qadesh.
The voice of the Lord maketh the hinds to calve, and discovereth the
Forests […].
(Ps. 29: 3–9)

This event took place in the middle of the night, with flames of fire spurting up from the ground: there are no details about any change in the apparent course of the stars, which are much more difficult to observe than the sun is, in daytime.

The sudden rapid shifting of the Egyptian ground, relative to motionless sky, explains the powerful and majestic sound, of which the thunder gives us a small idea, as well as the flaming rocks belched out by the volcanoes, which become projectiles comparable to arrows. It is easy to understand how the oaks are shaken and the forests stripped, at the same time as the harvests are devastated.

Compression and depressions of varying intensities occur underground, so that the mountains of Lebanon and Hermon are shaken, skipping "like a calf" or "like a young unicorn" (Ps. 29: 6). Yahweh "gathereth the waters of the sea together as an heap: he layeth up the depth in storehouses" (Ps. 33: 7). "All thy waves and thy billows are gone over me" (Ps. 42: 7).

The motion of the ground, relative to the still ocean, results in the latter being shaken and building up inside the land in basins like great reservoirs or storehouses.

"Therefore will not we fear, though the earth be removed, and though the mountains be carried into the midst of the sea; Though the waters thereof roar and be troubled, though the mountains shake with the swelling thereof. [...] The heathen raged, the kingdoms were moved: he uttered his voice, the earth melted" (Ps. 46: 2–6). "God is gone up with a shout, the Lord with the sound of a trumpet" (Ps. 47: 5).

Thou waterest the ridges thereof abundantly: thou settlest the furrows thereof: thou makest it soft with showers: thou blessest the springing thereof.
Thou crownest the year with thy goodness; and thy paths drop fatness. [...]
The pastures are clothed with flocks; the valleys also are covered over with corn; they shout for joy, they also sing.
(Ps. 65: 9–13)

A climatic change means that damp weather follows drought, and rich crops follow meagre pastures. And cooler temperatures follow the heat:

The earth shook, the heavens also dropped at the presence of God […]
Thou, O God, didst send a plentiful rain, whereby thou didst confirm thine
inheritance, when it was weary. […]
When the Almighty scattered kings in it, it was white as snow in Salmon.
(Ps. 68: 8–9, 14)

He clave the rocks in the wilderness, and gave them drink as out of the
great depths.
He brought streams also out of the rock, and caused waters to run down
like rivers. […]
Behold, he smote the rock, that the waters gushed out, and the streams
overflowed.
(Ps. 78: 15–6, 20)

The waters stood above the mountains.
At thy rebuke, they fled; at the voice of thy thunder they hasted away.
They go up by the mountains; they go down by the valleys unto the place
which thou hast founded for them.
Thou hast set a bound that they may not pass over; that they turn not
again to cover the earth.
(Ps. 104: 6–9)

Out in the open sea, during a short, rapid rotation of the lithosphere, for a short while everything must have remained calm. But immediately after the event occurred, there will have been huge oscillations.

Deep-sea sailors seem to have escaped these dangers, as David tells us:

They that go down to the sea in ships, that do business in great waters;
These see the works of the Lord, and his wonders in the deep.
For he commandeth, and raiseth the stormy wind, which lifteth up the waves.

They mount up to the heaven, they go down again to the depths: their soul
is melted because of trouble.
They reel to and fro, and stagger like a drunken man, and are at their
wits' end.
(Ps. 107: 23–7)

The masses of sea-water which were trapped inland all dried up, depositing great masses of salt. Then, in apparent contradiction to this, dampness prevailed.

Yahweh "turneth rivers into a wilderness, and the watersprings into dry ground; a fruitful land into barrenness [...] He turneth the wilderness into a standing water, and dry ground into watersprings" (Ps. 107: 33–5).

David sings tirelessly of the mighty deeds of Yahweh, before which man with all his pride, and great civilisations with their marvellous treasures, find themselves stripped bare and reduced to almost nothing.

The sea saw it, and fled: Jordan was driven back.
The mountains skipped like rams, and the little hills like lambs.
What ailed thee, O thou sea, that thou fleddest? thou Jordan, that thou
wast driven back?
Ye mountains, that ye skipped like rams; and ye little hills, like lambs?
Tremble, thou earth, at the presence of the Lord.
(Ps. 114: 3–7)

If it had not been the Lord who was on our side, when men rose up
against us:
Then the waters had overwhelmed us, the stream had gone over our soul:
Then the proud waters had gone over our soul.
(Ps. 124: 2–5)

The Book of the Wisdom of Solomon says: "For when unrighteous men thought to oppress the holy nation," when the Hebrews fled from Egypt under Moses, "they were scattered under a dark veil of forgetfulness, being

horribly astonished, and troubled with strange apparitions. And neither
might the corner that held them keep them from fear" (Wis. 17: 3–4).

*For while all things were in quiet silence, and that night was in the midst
of her swift course,*
Thine Almighty word leaped down from heaven out of thy royal throne, as
a fierce man of war into the midst of a land of destruction [...] but the
wrath endured not long [...]
For when the dead were now fallen down by heaps one upon another,
standing between, he stayed the wrath [...]
Unto these the destroyer gave place, and was afraid of them: for it was
enough that they only tasted of the wrath.
(Wis. 17: 14–25)

For the whole creature in his proper kind was fashioned again anew,
serving the peculiar commandments that were given unto them.
(Wis. 19: 6)

The sun and moon stand still

As the Amorites "fled from before Israel, and were in the going down to
Beth-horon, that the Lord cast down great stones from heaven upon them
unto Azekah, and they died; they were more which died with hailstones
than they whom the children of Israel slew with the sword" (Josh. 10: 11).

Then Joshua spoke to Yahweh, on the day that Yahweh delivered the
Amorites to the children of Israel, and said in the sight of Israel:

Sun, stand thou still upon Gibeon; and thou, Moon, in the valley of Ajalon.
And the sun stood still, and the moon stayed, until the people had avenged
themselves upon their enemies. Is not this written in the book of Jasher?
So the sun stood still in the midst of heaven, and hasted not to go down
about a whole day.
(Josh. 10: 12–13)

The duration of such an exceptional event, so sudden and violent, with flaming stones being hurled down like a burning hail towards the south-east, as a result of the great velocity assumed by the ground in a north-westerly direction, was impossible for the survivors to estimate. The time it took became necessarily exaggerated: rather than "a whole day," it probably just lasted a few hours.

The force of inertia meant that the waters of the rivers left their riverbeds, as in the case of the Jordan:

> *And as they that bare the ark were come unto Jordan, and the feet of the priests that bare the ark were dipped in the brim of the water, (for Jordan overfloweth all his banks all the time of harvest,)*
> *That the waters which came down from above stood and rose up upon an heap very far from the city Adam, that is beside Zaretan: and those that came down toward the sea of the plain, even the salt sea, failed, and were cut off.*
> (Josh. 3: 15–6)

After several hours, when the whole nation – 4,000 men – had crossed the Jordan, "the waters of the Jordan returned unto their place, and flowed over all his banks, as they did before" (Josh. 4: 18).

The slippage of the earth's crust must have partly been directed southwards if the waters of the Jordan were to accumulate upstream. The major event that happened under Joshua, circa 1200 BC, was thus experienced in Palestine as a movement of the ground in a southwesterly direction. The cold, damp climate then came to an end.

So two rotations of the lithosphere followed in succession, 50 or so years apart, in the second half of the 13th century BC.

Ecclesiasticus

Here we find two descriptions, not in themselves contradictory but opposed, of two sudden transformations to the apparent direction of the sun (and thus observable in the daytime) that occurred in the past. "Did not

290

the sun go back by his means? And was not one day as long as two?" (Ecclus. 46: 4).

This happened in Joshua's day, circa 1200 BC, and the Greeks and Romans based the myth of Phaethon on it. "Great is the Lord that made it; and at his commandment it runneth hastily" (Ecclus. 43: 5).

This corresponds to the story told by Seneca in *Thyestes*, where the sun suddenly stopped in its course and set in the early afternoon. This phenomenon occurred in the time of Phoebus, 'father' of Phaethon, and thus at some previous epoch which needs to be determined.

Isaiah

During the reign of Hezekiah, in the 8th century BC, Isaiah announced a major event.

> For the day of the Lord of hosts shall be upon everyone that is proud and
> lofty, and upon everyone that is lifted up; and he shall be brought low;
> And upon all the cedars of Lebanon, that are high and lifted up, and upon
> all the oaks of Bashan,
> And upon all the high mountains, and upon all the hills that are lifted up,
> And upon every high tower, and upon every fenced wall,
> And upon all the ships of Tarshish, and upon all pleasant pictures.
> (Isa. 2: 12–6)

> And the loftiness of man shall be bowed down, and the haughtiness of men
> shall be made low; and the Lord alone shall be exalted in that day.
> (Isa. 2: 17)

> And now go to; I will tell you what I will do to my vineyard: I will take
> away the hedge thereof, and it shall be eaten up; and break down the wall
> thereof, and it shall be trodden down:
> And I will lay it waste: it shall not be pruned, nor digged; [...]
> I will also command the clouds that they rain no rain upon it. [...]
> Yea, ten acres of vineyard shall yield one bath, and the seed of an homer

shall yield an ephah.
(Isa. 5: 5–6, 10)

*Therefore my people are gone into captivity, because they have no
knowledge: and their honourable men are famished, and their multitude
dried up with thirst.*
(Isa. 5: 13)

The climate, previously damp, will thus become dry, as at present.

*Then I said, Lord, how long? And he answered, until the cities be wasted
without inhabitant, and the houses without man, and the land be utterly
desolate,
And the Lord have removed men far away, and there be a great forsaking
in the midst of the land.*
(Isa. 6: 10–2)

*And the Lord shall utterly destroy the tongue of the Egyptian sea; and with
his mighty wind shall he shake his hand over the river, and shall smite it in
the seven streams, and make men go over dryshod.*
(Isa. 11: 15)

The Nile, like all rivers, will thus be emptied of its water, with the seven
mouths of the delta remaining dry so that people can pass across while still
wearing their sandals.

*Howl ye; for the day of the Lord is at hand [...]
Behold, the day of the Lord cometh, cruel both with wrath and fierce
anger, to lay the land desolate: and he shall destroy the sinners thereof out
of it.
For the stars of heaven and the constellations thereof shall not give their
light: the sun shall be darkened in his going forth, and the moon shall not
cause her light to shine [...]*

Therefore I will shake the heavens, and the earth shall remove out of her place, in the wrath of the Lord of hosts, and in the day of his fierce anger.
(Isa. 13: 6, 9–10, 13)

And Babylon, the glory of kingdoms, the beauty of the Chaldees' excellency, shall be as when God overthrew Sodom and Gomorrah.
It shall never be inhabited.
(Isa. 13: 19–20)

And the waters shall fail from the sea, and the river be wasted and dry up. And they shall turn the rivers far away; and the brooks of defence shall be emptied and dried up: the reeds and flags shall wither.
The paper reeds by the brooks, by the mouth of the brooks, and every thing sown by the brooks, shall wither, be driven away, and be no more.
(Isa. 19: 5–7)

Be still, ye inhabitants of the isle; thou whom the merchants of Zidon, that pass over the sea, have replenished [...]
Be thou ashamed, O Zidon: for the sea hath spoken, even the strength of the sea [...]
Pass through thy land as a river, O daughter of Tarshish: there is no more strength.
He stretched out his hand over the sea, he shook the kingdoms: the Lord hath given a commandment against the merchant city, to destroy the strong holds thereof.
(Isa. 23: 2–3, 10–1)

It would be difficult to describe the situation more precisely. The latitude has suddenly increased, and the climate has become drier. In its northward movement, the earth raised masses of water that then covered it.

In those days was Hezekiah sick unto death. And the prophet Isaiah the son of Amoz came to him, and said unto him, Thus saith the Lord, Set thine house in order; for thou shalt die, and not live.

Then he turned his face to the wall, and prayed unto the Lord, saying,
I beseech thee, O Lord, remember now how I have walked before thee in
truth and with a perfect heart, and have done that which is good in thy
sight. And Hezekiah wept sore.

And it came to pass, afore Isaiah was gone out into the middle court, that
the word of the Lord came to him, saying,

Turn again, and tell Hezekiah the captain of my people, Thus saith the
Lord, the God of David thy father, I have heard thy prayer, I have seen thy
tears; behold, I will heal thee: on the third day thou shalt go up unto the
house of the Lord.

And I will add unto thy days fifteen years; and I will deliver thee and this
city out of the hand of the king of Assyria; and I will defend this city for
mine own sake, and for my servant David's sake.

And Isaiah said, Take a lump of figs. And they took and laid it on the boil,
and he recovered.

And Hezekiah said unto Isaiah, What shall be the sign that the Lord will
heal me, and that I shall go up into the house of the Lord the third day?

And Isaiah said, This sign shalt thou have of the Lord, that the Lord will
do the thing that he hath spoken; shall the shadow go forward ten degrees,
or go back ten degrees?

And Hezekiah answered, It is a light thing for the shadow to go down ten
degrees: nay, but let the shadow return backward ten degrees.

And Isaiah the prophet cried unto the Lord: and he brought the shadow
ten degrees backward, by which it had gone down in the dial of Ahaz.
(2 Kgs. 20: 1–11)

Isaiah says exactly the same:

Behold, I will bring again the shadow of the degrees, which is gone down
in the sun dial of Ahaz, ten degrees backward. So the sun returned ten
degrees, by which degrees it was gone down.
(Isa. 38: 8)

294

The sun's shadow was carefully observed every day at true noon, when it was cast towards the true north by the gnomon on a sundial. The length of the shadow was at its maximum at the winter solstice, and at its minimum at the summer solstice.

This shadow had started to go back, so the month indicated was July and August. The increase of 10 degrees means an increase in latitude of ten degrees.

Hudson's Bay, now situated at 30° south of its previous position at the North Pole, indicates – subject to the relative drift of America vis-à-vis Europe – that the latitude of Jerusalem must have then increased by 18°. The imprecision is very small, if we take into account the inexactitude both of the Hebrew text, and especially of the estimated position of Hudson's Bay once it left the North Pole.

July or August, in the course of a night in Jerusalem circa 700 BC, is thus the date of the last rotation of the lithosphere.

The Book of Isaiah is full of precise and logical details that can only indicate a sudden and rapid slippage of the earth's crust, relative to the sea and the atmosphere that inertia left behind, with great masses of seawater assuming a relative motion to the earth, and exceptional winds. The rivers were emptied of their water, the earth tottered on its base, the ground split and allowed a burning, sulphurous lava to well up, a hurricane struck, as deadly as hail, flattening everything and making a sound like a trumpet or a voice of thunder. Many human beings died all at once.

The event must have taken place at night, otherwise Hesiod and all the Greek or Latin authors would have described the apparent behaviour of both the sun and the moon, given that those authors reported with such care the earlier memories of various abnormal and dramatic perturbations in the apparent course of the stars. "The Lord shall go forth as a mighty man, he shall stir up jealousy like a man of war: he shall cry, yea, roar; he shall prevail against his enemies. [...] I will make waste mountains and hills, and dry up all their herbs; and I will make the rivers islands, and I will dry up the pools" (Isa. 42: 13–15).

The "war cry," the "trumpet," the "roar," the "majestic voice," the "great noise," the "roaring of a lion," the "din," the "rumble," the "hubbub," the "almighty word," the "thunder," were all the noise of an apparent wind 10 times more powerful than that of a tempest or a hurricane, with an effect 100 times greater.

The Greeks gave this phenomenon a significant name: Io, or Ia, and the Romans turned Io-pitar into their Jupiter. For the Hebrews, this terrifying name would be unpronounceable: IAHWEH or IEOUAH, which then became Yahweh, or Jehovah.

Amos

Human actions were responsible for the major event that occurred at the time of Isaiah, in the 8th century BC:

> *Shall not the land tremble for this, and every one mourn that dwelleth therein? and it shall rise up wholly as a flood; and it shall be cast out and drowned, as by the flood of Egypt.*
> *And it shall come to pass in that day, saith the Lord God, that I will cause the sun to go down at noon, and I will darken the earth in the clear day.*
> (Amos 8: 8–9)

There are two possible solutions to the problem of dating chronologically, in Hebrew and Greek history, the day when the sun appeared to set when it had already arrived at its zenith, i.e., at the beginning of the afternoon.

Then the day was shortened and the night fell much earlier than anticipated. This would have required, in the eastern Mediterranean, a sudden and rapid shift in the ground, with one part going eastward, and an increase in its habitual movement.

- Either this could date from the middle of the 13th century BC, when the Jewish Passover, 14 Nisan, a date which changes in the evening, would have occurred on a night that fell prematurely. It could have to do with the flood of Deucalion, whose memory the Greeks commemorated with

the feast of the Anthesteria, on the 13th of the month of Anthesterion –
the same month, but the date of the 13th did not change before the
morning that followed this memorable night. The Egyptians placed this
same event on the 13th of the month of Tut, for the same reasons. Seneca
alluded to this event in Thyestes, at the time of Phoebus.
- Or this unexpected apparent movement of the sun westwards, this
  sudden and rapid eastwards drift of the land, in the eastern
  Mediterranean, must have occurred circa 700 BC.

Since the night fell all of a sudden, few contemporaries will have had the
chance to see the sun disappearing in the west so quickly. Only on the
following day, after the cataclysm, will they have noted that the shadow of
the sun at midday on the sundial of Ahaz had gone back 10 or 14 degrees,
that the army of Sennacherib had lost 185,000 men, and that the climate
was losing its precious dampness and drying up.

Amos, like Isaiah, describes the upheavals that then happened.

And the Lord God of hosts is he that toucheth the land, and it shall melt,
and all that dwell therein shall mourn: and it shall rise up wholly like a
flood; and shall be drowned, as by the flood of Egypt.
It is he […] that calleth for the waters of the sea, and poureth them out
upon the face of the earth: The Lord is his name.
(Amos 9: 5–6)

For, lo, I will command, and I will sift the house of Israel among all
nations, like as corn is sifted in a sieve.
(Amos 9: 9)

3.12 New chronology

It is now established that in the Quaternary era there were three centres of glaciation in the vicinity of the North Pole. But the great civilisations preserve the stigmata and the memories of at least four major events called chaos, flood, or the anger of the gods.

The memory of the Hebrews is a veritable mine of information on the chronology of the events that occurred before our era. With its continuous series of chronicles, it is possible to establish a relatively reliable chronology at least up to Abraham. From Adam to Noah, people's lives are strangely long, sometimes lasting as many as 900 years. Was age then calculated in lunar, rather than annual, units, following solar cycles? According to this reading of the Bible, mankind as a whole would have dated from around 4,000 years BC. So we can perhaps situate the more recent events circa 1250, 1200 and 700 BC.

In the light of the Biblical revelations, but also of the numerous correspondences between the texts of ancient literature across the world and the most ancient maps, we can thus propose a new chronology for mankind.

This sheds a new and surprising light on the geographical positions assumed by the continents. It gives added weight to the hypothesis that these continents successively shifted following at least four major events.

The original continent, situated at the ends of the earth and surrounded by the ocean-river, was indeed the Antarctic continent, the *Terra Australis* which, as the ancient maps show, was situated just south of the Tropic of Capricorn. It left several scattered memories of a happy time when the climate was warm and damp enough to allow agriculture and animal rearing.

The Sumerian Enki set sail to found the first holy cities at the mouth of the Euphrates and the Tigris. He reached the Red Sea and sailed up the Nile to settle in the Indus Valley.

The poles must then have been situated somewhere in what are now the tropics. This probably happened in the 13th century BC.

Cities came into being, with many sorts of craftsmen and temples in the shape of truncated step pyramids, or ziggurats – a memory of the original mountain. The Persian Gulf was linked to the Indus, the Nile, and Crete, by experienced sailors who came and went between there and the Island of Dilmun, or Punt.

Some major event occurred which ravaged the shores of the Indian Ocean when Ziusudra was Prince of Uruk. At the time he had put into Dilmun, where he settled. The flood Abubi destroyed cities and plantations in Sumer, and deposited Noah's Ark on Ararat, drowning the whole Adamic land or Adamah. It placed Dilmun near the South Pole.

The land of the Anunnaki gods was then inside the polar circle: there was a long, hard night with a glacial cold that froze up rivers and ocean, forests torn up and buried underground, together with many human beings.

As the ancient maps show, South America was then in the immediate vicinity of Queen Maud Land; the Weddell Sea was closed by the land that now forms Graham Land and the string of islands that extends to Patagonia; and the South Sandwich Islands must have constituted a point at which the three plates – South America, Africa, and Antarctica – met.

After this flood, the Yukon was at the North Pole, the mouth of the Hoang-ho in North China was at 25° north in the vicinity of the tropics, in a warm climate, just like the south of Japan. Mexico was some 42° north and Yucatan was 15° or so further north than at present, and so cooler.

The equatorial climate of North Egypt, Sumer and the Sahara is explicable by the fact that the equator passed through the Nile Delta, and the head of the Persian Gulf. The survivors of the southern continent had to reach the shores of the polar circle, and live on fishing, since agriculture and animal breeding were now impossible.

Expeditions that set out from the southern continent were then able to reach China, during the period of the Hia, and Japan at the time of Jomon art. Others managed to sail along the coasts of America and create the first Nazca and Olmec civilisations.

The tropic passed through Paris and Warsaw. Europe was invaded by tropical animals. Lions, tigers, hippopotami, rhinoceroses, monkeys and humans lived in the region between the Aegean islands and Provence. Crete, the Troad, and Greece had reached the Bronze Age. There was intensive

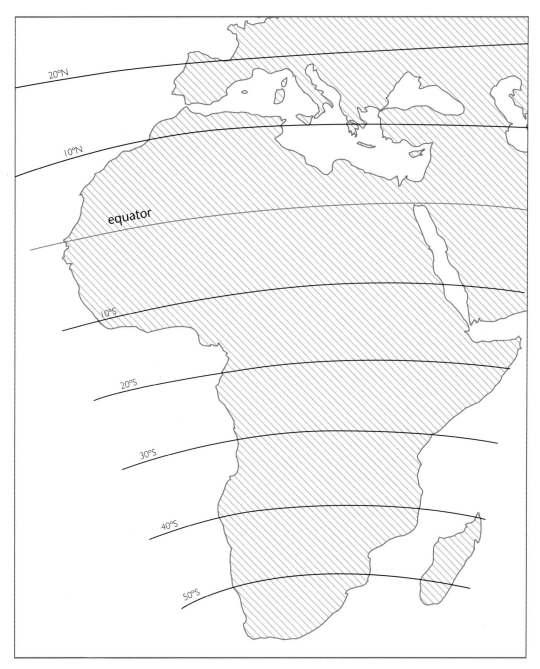

Figure 44. *Africa, 1500–1250 BC.*

navigation as far as the Baltic. Egypt was flourishing under the Old Empire. Superb temples were constructed in Sumer, Elam, and in the Indus. Navigation was highly developed.

Caravans set out and countries came into being in the interior. Migrants from Europe abandoned agriculture for building, rearing and fishing. They also became horse riders. The melding of all these peoples gave rise to related languages, known as Indo-European languages.

Then an event put an end to this era of development. It most probably took place circa 1250 BC, on 14th Nisan for the Hebrews, the 13th day of the month of Tut for the Egyptians, and during the Anthesteria according to the Greeks. All the dates put forward situate the cataclysm during the month of the spring solstice. In this period a major event led to northern Europe being covered by a sheet of ice. In China, the climate remained warmer than it is today, and the Zhou, less refined and more violent, replaced the Shang.

All the coasts were ravaged, there were no more great navigations across the oceans, the oar replaced the sail, coastal shipping became commercial and aggressive, as different races all competed for their place in the sun.

The Hebrews shook off the Egyptian yoke during that Jewish Passover that fell from the sky: they wandered for 40 years across ancient deserts that had now become damp and cold.

The Sahara was covered with lakes, rivers and forests.

Life resumed in the Indus Valley, in Mesopotamia and in Egypt during the Middle Empire. On the periphery of Europe, Achaeans, Ionians and Dorians invaded the Aegean. They formed an aristocracy of horsemen, rough and rustic.

In Crete and Greece, it was the Mycenaean period. The palaces of Tiryns, Mycenae and Argos were built as protection against the cold. The megalithic constructions in the Mediterranean were built for the same purpose. Life in the Mediterranean flourished, especially in Africa.

In the Black Sea, at the foot of the Caucasus, the inhabitants were captive to cold and storms – hence the allegorical legend of Prometheus, bound to a pillar, his liver gnawed by an eagle.

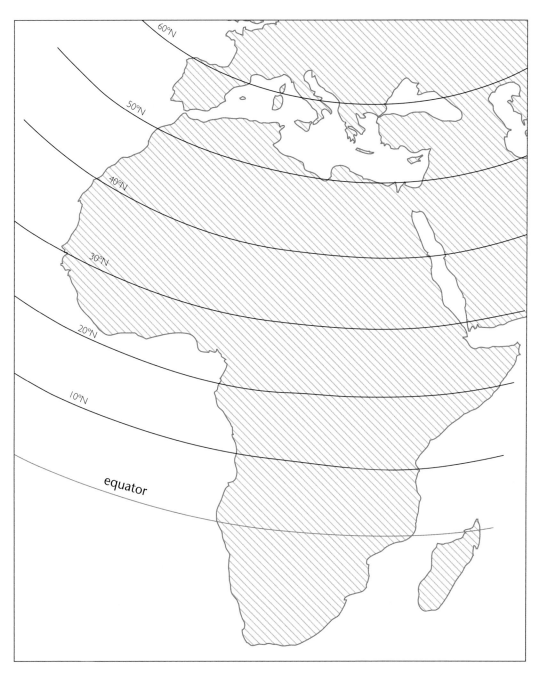

Figure 45. *Africa, 1250–1200 BC.*

The Scandinavians succumbed to the dreadful Fimbul winter. The survivors holed up in terrible conditions.

Niniveh, Cairo, and Tamanrasset were at 50° north, and Athens, Naples and Barcelona at 60° north. Only the southern Mediterranean continued to be active and populous. Ursa Major and Ursa Minor dipped into the sea.

The Middle Empire was to be short-lived – a violent age, with several barbarian invasions.

Around 1200 BC, at the time of Joshua, the ground of Palestine slipped suddenly south-west. The latitude of Jerusalem shifted from 48° north to 14° north. A major event again demolished cities and empires. This was the flood of Phaethon, following which Ursa Major and Ursa Minor reached their zenith in the sky.

The west of Norway slipped to the extreme east of Hudson Bay, on the frontier between Canada and the United States.

Northern China, at the mouth of the Hoang-ho, moved from a latitude of 30° to 7° north. China's climate remained warm, tropical or equatorial, given its geographical position. Unlike most other regions in the world, the Middle Kingdom did not really undergo a climatic revolution properly speaking. The animals indigenous to torrid climes stayed faithfully at their posts.

Mexico and Guatemala had practically reached their current position, at 15° north. Spain, France and the Baltic experienced a climatic optimum and were situated at 40° north. The temperatures of northern Europe were noticeably warmer than today.

The north was oriented to the present-day north-west. At Gibraltar, the west passed through the Canaries and near Cape Verde. The islands in this archipelago were to receive the name Hesperides, 'nymphs of the setting sun'. Greek and Roman stories identified them with the direction of sunset, in the direction of Antarctica, at the foot of Atlas.

The terraces of Scandinavian and British agriculture were oriented towards the present-day south-east. Navigation resumed slowly towards England and the Baltic: the winter climate was less harsh than it is today. The English Channel was open. It was no longer necessary to sail round Ireland and Scotland to seek amber in the Baltic, which was experiencing a mild climate.

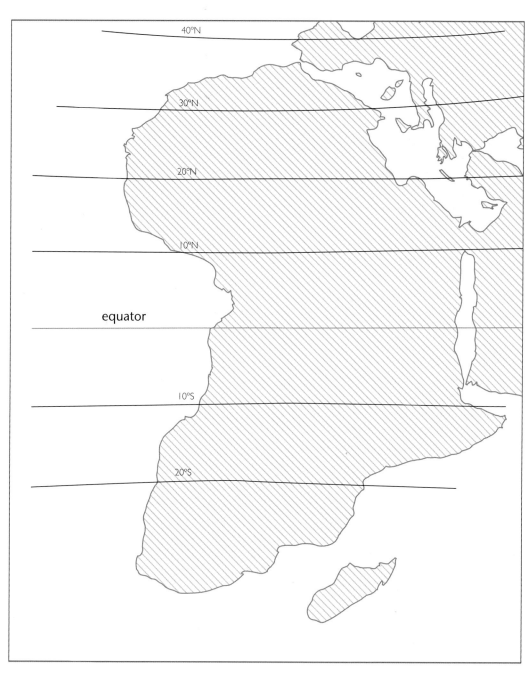

Figure 46. *Africa, 1200–700 BC.*

The 30th parallel then passed through Mauretania, Tunisia and the Ukraine. The Sahara turned into a desert in its eastern parts, but not in the west, where it remained damp.

The tropic passed through Tamanrasset and Tripoli, between Greece and the Aegean, and near Byzantium. The tenth parallel passed through Aswan and Babylon.

The climate was equatorial in Egypt and in Mesopotamia, and tropical in Greece. Lions flourished again in south-east Europe.

The upheavals due to the last cataclysm were so great that people were plunged into a dark age. The Phoenicians, travelling to the Azores, were more traders than craftsmen and sailors.

Maps were copied and recopied. In the Middle Ages, they were to serve as models for portulans. According to Charles Hapgood these very ancient maps do not show North America, which was frozen at that time. The British Isles and Scandinavia were surrounded by glaciers. But the cartographers did have available documents showing Greenland and Antarctica without their ice cap. One historical period rapidly gave way to another, with sudden climate changes.

Around 700 BC, under Hezekiah, in the time of Isaiah, there was another sudden shift in the position of the continents. The centre of glaciation was in Hudson Bay. This region drifted to its present position, having started out at the North Pole.

In Jerusalem, the shadow of the sun at midday started to go back. It would in reality go back 18°, and not 10° as the Biblical text tells us. Jerusalem moved from a latitude of 14° to one of 32°.

As a result of this cataclysm, the earth started to experience its present-day climatic conditions. In Siberia, the latitudes suddenly increased by 30°.

The Siberian mammoths froze, after being trapped in hills of muckite with many beasts and trees. They were preserved by the sudden cold. Alaska underwent the same fate.

Europe and China grew slightly chillier, with the current climate. The western Sahara became a desert.

In Antarctica, the Polynesians were taken by surprise when this cold descended, and when a polar night fell in the month of July. They were only a few degrees from the South Pole. They were doubtless among the last to leave the original continent, which until then had remained partly habitable.

Greece and Italy were reborn to enjoy a period that would be of historic importance; chronology finally becomes reliable, and there was an amazing host of objective historians, well-documented and sometimes very accurate. Civilisations flourished again after one or two centuries of darkness, combat and chaos.

More than two millennia would elapse before transoceanic exchanges again became possible across the vast Pacific Ocean and the Antarctic continent – *Terra Australis* became *Inhabitabilis, Nondum Cognita*, the Punt to which no one had ever been.

These are the most consistent results of this new chronology.

A close look at the foundational texts of ancient civilisations has turned out to be of great value for our investigation into the origin of the Polynesian peoples. We already knew, through the study of anthropomorphic kinships, blood relations and genetic similarities between the inhabitants of the continents that surround the Pacific Ocean, that the Polynesians came neither from Asia, nor Africa, nor America, nor even Australia. Polynesian culture seems to have 'forgotten' to take a sufficient number of basic cultural elements from the continents from which it might have sprung.

By examining the texts that deal with the origins of Polynesian culture, we have discovered that their land of origin was a continent, which, even today with all the powerful technical means at our disposal, is difficult to approach and impossible to live in: Antarctica.

The polar origin of the Polynesians is described in these primordial texts. Again and again we hear of the memory of an endless night and a capricious sun that never returns. Men live in dark caves and shelter from the cold.

This mythology, which one would not have expected from a region today in the tropics, tells of the difficulties that travellers encountered when they wanted to leave their original land.

As our investigation of the texts of the greatest civilisations has progressed we have come across striking similarities. These do not allow us to attribute any sort of primacy to one original cultural centre other than the Antarctic continent. Indeed, each civilisation, in its own way, points to this extraordinary continent.

The Polynesian *marae*, that truncated step pyramid, can be found everywhere in the architecture of the sacred places of the Mesopotamians, with their ziggurats – and also in the temples of China and the *teocalli* of South America. This construction depicts the original mountain, the world axis, which is also a recurrent theme in the earliest world literature.

The continent that all those starving men were forced to leave was called Hawaiki by the Polynesians, Punt by the Egyptians, Ogygia by the Greeks, Airyana-Vaêjo by the Indians, and Xibalbá by the Mexicans.

The Antarctic was, given sturdy sails, one month's navigation away from all the great seedbeds of future civilisations. Numerous pots, and an equal number of drawings and engravings show great ships, such as the marvellous barque of Cheops. The exchange of seals and various refined objects, and maps of the world that show its coasts in great detail, attest to the existence of large vessels, constructed by fine sailors and able to sail across the three oceans as early as the second millennium BC – in other words, after the war of the gods and the tragic cataclysms mentioned in all those revealing foundational texts.

The apparent course of the stars changed several times, in particular circa 700 BC, 1200 BC and 1250 BC. Different races bequeathed to us eye-witness accounts of stars and entire constellations suddenly disappearing for good. As Albert de Lapparent put it so well, "we should not believe that the axis of the poles was necessarily obliged to keeping a fixed position relative to the earth's surface."[1]

The relative position of the poles did indeed change, at some period that, as we have seen, can only have been quite recent. The maps of Antarctica available from the 16th century onwards and showing this continent clear of any ice, as well as the discovery of a habitat not found in polar regions, prove as much, beyond any shadow of a doubt.

The upheavals that ensued from such an event are described in ancient accounts from all civilisations. After a crisis of this type, climates changed, as did the altitude of the land.

Geological faults appeared as a result of powerful orogenic uplifts. After a brief period of violence, with exceptional winds and, above all, several floods caused by a tempestuous and overflowing sea that rose up over the coasts and mountains, equilibrium was restored. The continents had changed axis, and the previous astronomical reference points were now obsolete. The apparent course of the stars seemed to be perturbed.

The contrasts to be found within the great southern land go on forever.

---

1   A. de Lapparent, *Traité de géologie*, Masson, 1906, vol. I.

All knowledge comes perhaps from that land where, once upon a time, the climate was pleasant. Plantations, orchards, industry, craftsmanship, writing and metallurgy developed, but those who came ashore were as starving as wild beasts. What had been Eden and Paradise had been transformed into Hades, Tartarus, Erebus and Sheol. What had been the origin of life was henceforth associated with disease, suffering, struggle, despair, hunger, dereliction, solitude and death.

This continent is a marvellous illustration of the laws of nature and the precariousness of man's existence. Sudden crises on the earth's surface completely changed the existing order and radically altered the lives of different races. It seems improbable that, even if we were able one day to demonstrate these mechanisms, we would be able to foresee the event that would trigger them. Man finds himself powerless, recognises how fragile is his power over the world, and how laughable his strength. Is this enough to make us feel a bit more modest? The face of the Godea, the meditative silence of the Polynesian *tiki*, the figurines with their dilated pupils gazing on a night that is quite out of the ordinary – are these not emblematic of man's awareness of his own weakness in the face of the gigantic forces of nature?

Men seek society as well as solitude. Are they not in this respect similar to all natural phenomena, that are both attracted and repulsed? The sea and the air spontaneously arrange themselves into distinct levels. Homogeneous masses suddenly separate out from their neighbours.

So do different land masses, as well as the intermediate layer of magma in the earth's depths. Is there not an irreducible similarity in all the elements of the earth? Each of them affirms its identity with those of its kind, and nonetheless seeks the company of others, showing both its originality and its incompatibility, its solidarity and its individuality, its conformism and its singularity. Societies, nations and individuals, just like matter, are based on attractions and repulsions, in other words on vital contradictions.

The vegetable domain is full of inventiveness: we cannot get enough of the marvellous intelligence shown by plants. But what about matter? Its ways are just as fabulous, even if its aims remain inaccessible to mankind. Most of the time, we content ourselves with admiring the harmony and beauty of its phenomena. This is true of the southern dawns, the glinting hues of the glaciers and the spectacle of the waves on the sea.

Man does however have the great merit of having invented the sailing boat. For the sailor, this magnificent instrument proves the humility of which we are capable in the face of natural elements. My dear departed friend Éric de Bisschop used to say, "Sailing? It is a way of honouring the sea."

At the end of these pages, so much still remains to be discovered and understood. Archaeological excavations should, one day, enable us to reveal the earliest appearance of different civilisations on earth. Will these traces be found on a high mountain, near the world axis of the Ancients? Will the archaeologists find a richly decorated temple, with a series of terraces surrounding it? Will they succeed in unearthing cities, other engraved rocks, ports, writings that open up the gates of knowledge and truth, and provide us with the answer to the riddle of the great south land?

I fervently hope so.

Aeschylus (trans. H. Weir Smyth), Harvard University Press, Cambridge (Mass), 1926.

Africanus (Julius), *The Anti-Nicene Fathers* (eds A. Roberts and J. Donaldon), Hendrickson, Peabody (Mass), 1994.

Argod R., *Nouveau regard sur les migrations polynésiennes*, Éditions Haere po no Tahiti, Papeete, 1997.

Aubert de la Rue E., *Terres françaises inconnues*, Société Parisienne d'Édition, 1930.

Baillif N., *La Perse millénaire*, Arthaud, Paris, 1958.

Beckwith M., *Hawaiian Mythology*, University of Hawaii Press, Honolulu, 1970.

Beckwith M., *The Kumulipo: a Hawaiian creation chant*, University of Chicago Press, Chicago, 1951.

Bessmertny A., *L'Atlantide*, Payot, Paris, 1951.

Bibby G., *Des cavernes à l'Europe des Vikings*, collection « D'un monde à l'autre », Plon, Paris, 1958.

Bibby G., *Le millénaire retrouvé : De l'an 2000 à l'an 1000 avant J.-C.*, collection « D'un monde à l'autre », Plon, Paris, 1961.

Bisschop (de) É., *Vers Nousantara*, Éditions de la Table ronde, 1962.

Bodrogi T., *L'art de l'Océanie*, Gründ, Paris, 1961.

Bond C. and Siegfried R., *Antarctique, océan et continent aux splendeurs sauvages*, Florilège, 1988.

Bosch-Gimpera P., *Les Indo-Européens*, Payot, Paris, 1961.

Buck P., *Vikings of the Sunrise*, Frederick A. Stokes, New York, 1938.

Buckland W., *Geology and Mineralogy considered with reference to natural theology*, Lea and Blanchard, Philadelphia, 1837.

Bushnell G. H. S., *L'art de l'Amérique précolombienne*, Larousse, Paris, 1965.

Bushnell G. H. S., *Les premiers Américains*, Sequoia-Elsevier, Brussels, 1968.

Caillot E., *Mythes, légendes et traditions des Polynésiens*, Leroux, Paris, 1914.

Camps G., *Introduction à la Préhistoire : À la recherche du paradis perdu*, Seuil, 1982.

Cartes et Figures de la Terre, Centre Georges Pompidou, CCI, Paris, 1980.

Champdor A., *Babylone*, Éditions Attinger-Albert Guillot, 1957.

Champeaux (de) G. and Sterckx D. S., *Le Monde des Symboles*, Éditions Zodiaque, St-Léger Vauban, 1966.

Charbonneaux J., *L'Art égéen*, Éditions Van Oest, Paris, 1929.

Chauviré R., *Histoire de l'Irlande*, PUF, 1949.

Childe G., *Le mouvement de l'Histoire*, Arthaud, Paris, 1961.

Chuvin P., *La mythologie grecque*, Fayard, 1992.

The Complete Greek Drama (eds W. J. Oates and E. O'Neill Jr), Random House, New York, 1938.

Contenau G., *La civilisation phénicienne*, Payot, Paris, 1949.

Contenau G., *Le déluge babylonien*, Payot, Paris, l952.

Contenau G., *Les civilisations anciennes du Proche-Orient*, PUF, Paris, 1960.

Corey I. P., *Ancient Fragments*, William Pickering, London, 1832.

Creel H. G., *La naissance de la Chine*, Payot, Paris, 1937.

Cuvier G., *Revolutionary Upheavals on the Surface of the Globe and on the changes which they have produced in the animal kingdom* (trans. I. C. Johnston), based on 3rd French edition 1825, http://www.mala.bc.ca/~johnstoi/cuvier/cuvier.htm.

Daly R. A., *Our Mobile Earth*, Scribners, New York, 1926.

Dana J. D., *Manual of Geology: Treating of the Principles of the Science with Special References to American Geological History*, Philadelphia, 1863.

Dante Alighieri, *Purgatorio* (trans. A. Mandelbaum), Bantam Books, Toronto / New York, 1982.

Darwin C., *Journal of Researches into the Natural History and Geology of the countries visited during the voyage round the world of H.M.S. Beagle*, 11th edition, John Murray, London, 1913.

Dumézil G., *Les dieux souverains indo-européens*, Gallimard, Paris, 1977.

Durant W., *Histoire de la civilisation*, Payot, Paris, 1947.

Effenterre (van) H., *La seconde fin du monde*, Éditions des Hespérides, 1974.

Ellis W., *Journal of William Ellis*, Tuttle Cy, Rutland, 1979.

Erman G. A., *Travels in Siberia*, Longman, London, 1848.

Euripides, *Iphigenia in Tauris* (trans. M. J. Cropp), Aris & Phillips Ltd, Warminster, 2000.

Euripides (trans. D. Kovacs), Harvard University Press, Cambridge (Mass), 1995.

Evola J., *Révolte contre le monde moderne*, Bibliothèque de l'Âge d'homme, 1982.

Favier J., *Les Grandes Découvertes : d'Alexandre à Magellan*, Fayard, Paris, 1991.

Fouchet M.-P., *Nubie*, La Guilde du Livre, 1965.

Frankfort (de) H., *Kingship and the Gods: A study of Ancient Near Eastern Religion as the Integration of Society and Nature*, The University Press of Chicago, Chicago, 1948.

Gabriel-Leroux J., *Les premières civilisations de la Méditerranée*, 10th edition, PUF, 1983.

Galanopoulos A. G. and Bacon E., *L'Atlantide, la vérité derrière la légende*, Albin Michel, Paris, 1969.

Garelli P. and Leibovici M., *La Naissance du monde*, Collection «Sources orientales», Éditions du Seuil, 1959.

Geikie A., *Text Book of Geology*, 3rd edition, Macmillan & Co., London, 1893.

Girard R., *Esotericism of the Popol-Vuh* (trans. B. A Moffett), Theosophical University Press, 1987.

Graeve (de) M. C., *The ships of the ancient Near East*, Leuven, 1981.

Granet M., *La Civilisation chinoise*, Albin Michel, Paris, 1948.

Granet M., *La Pensée chinoise*, Albin Michel, Paris, 1950.

Hapgood C., *Earth's Shifting Crust*, Museum Press Ltd, London, 1959.

Hapgood C., *Maps of the Ancient Sea Kings, Evidence of Advanced Civilization in the Ice Age*, Chitton Books, Philadelphia / New York, 1966.

Henry T., 'Ancient Tahiti', *Bishop Museum Bulletin*, 48, Honolulu, 1928.

Herman Z., *Peuples, Mers, Navires*, Éditions des Arts et Métiers Graphiques, Paris, 1964.

Herrmann P., *L'homme à la découverte du monde*, Plon, Paris, 1961.

Heyerdahl T., *American Indians in the Pacific*, Allen & Unwin, London, 1952.

Hibben F. C., *The lost Americans*, Crowell, New York, 1946.

Hibben F. C., *Evidence of early man in Alaska*, American Antiquity, 1940.

Homer, *Odyssey* (trans. A. T. Murray), William Heinemann Ltd, London, 1919.

The Homeric Hymns and Homerica (trans. H. G. Evelyn-White), William Heinemann Ltd, London, 1914.

Honoré P., *L'Énigme du dieu blanc précolombien*, Plon, Paris, 1962.

Hrozny B., *Histoire de l'Asie antérieure*, Payot, Paris, 1947.

Hugot H.-J., *Le Sahara avant le désert*, Éditions des Hespérides, 1974.

Huntington E., *Climate Pulsations*, Hylluingskrift, 1935.

The Hymns of Orpheus (trans. T. Taylor), Philosophical Research Soc., 1987.

The Hymns of the Rig Veda (trans. R. T. H. Griffith), E. J. Lazarus & Co., Benares, 1896

Iselin H., *Légendes des cités perdues*, Éditions Lanore, 1955.

Izett J., *Maori Lore: The traditions of the Maori People*, Government Printer, Wellington, 1904.

Jeannel R., *Au seuil de l'Antarctique*, PUF, 1941.

Jéquier G., *Histoire de la civilisation égyptienne*, Payot, Paris, l913.

King L. W., *The Seven Tablets of Creation*, Luzac, London, 1902.

Kirkinen H. and Sihva H., *Le Kalevala, épopée finlandaise et universelle*, Publication orientaliste de France, 1985.

Klindt-Jensen O., *Le Danemark*, collection «Mondes anciens», Arthaud, Paris, 1960.

Kolpaktchy G., *Livre des morts des anciens Égyptiens*, Dervy, Paris, 1991.

Kramer S. N., *History begins at Sumer*, Thames and Hudson, London, 1958.

Kühn H., *L'Ascension de l'Humanité*, Buchet / Chastel, 1958.

Kühn H., *L'Éveil de l'Humanité*, Buchet / Chastel, 1956.

La Bruyère R., *Contes et légendes de l'océan Pacifique*, Éditions Pierre Roger, Paris, 1930.

La dérive des continents (eds D. H. and M. P Tarling), Doin, 1980.

Lapparent (de) A., *Traité de géologie*, Masson, 1906.

Lavachery H., *Île de Pâques*, Éditions Bernard Grasset, 1935.

Laval P. H., *Mangareva*, Librairie Geuthner, 1938.

Le Danois E., *Le Rythme des climats dans l'histoire de la terre et de l'humanité*, Payot, Paris, l950.

Lefebvre G., *Romans et Contes égyptiens de l'époque pharaonique*, Librairie d'Amérique et d'Orient, Adrien Maisonneuve, 1988.

Lenormant Fr., *Histoire ancienne de l'Orient*, A. Lévy, 1882.

Lenthéric C., *Les villes mortes du golfe du Lyon*, Plon, Paris, 1876.

Lhote H., *Les chars rupestres sahariens*, Éditions des Hespérides, 1982.

Lhote H., *Search for the Tassili Frescoes, the story of the prehistoric rock-paintings of the Sahara* (trans. A. Houghton Brodrick), Hutchinson of London, l973.

Lissner I., *Ainsi vivaient nos ancêtres*, Buchet / Chastel, 1957.

Lorius C., *Glaces de l'Antarctique*, Éditions Odile Jacob, 1991.

Loverdo (de) C., *Les dieux aux épées de bronze*, Julliard, 1966.

Lydekker R., 'Mammoth Ivory', *Smithsonian Institution Annual Report 1899*, Government Printing Office, Washington D.C., 1901.

Lyell C., *Principles of geology*, 11th edition, John Murray, London, 1872.

Ma, Ying Ting H., *Research on the Past Climate and Continental Drift*, World Book Co., Taipei, 1958.

Macmillan Brown J., *Peoples and problems of the Pacific*, Fisher & Unwin, London, 1931.

Malaurie J., *Ultima Thule*, Éditions Bordas, Paris, 1990.

Maringer J., *L'homme préhistorique et ses dieux*, Arthaud, Paris, 1958.

Martial R., *Vie et constance des races*, Éditions Mercure de France, 1939.

McCready G., *Common-Sense Geology*, Pacific Press, California, 1946.

Meeks D. and Favard-Meeks C., *Daily Life of the Egyptian Gods*, John Murray, London, 1997.

Métraux A., *L'île de Pâques*, Gallimard, 1941.

Miller K., *Continents in Collision*, Time-Life, Alexandria (Va.), 1983.

Morgan (de) J., *La Préhistoire orientale*, Librairie Geuthner, 1926.

Mouly R. P., *L'île de Pâques, île de mystère et d'héroïsme*, Lemiale, Bruges, 1949.

Muck O. H., *L'Atlantide, légendes et réalité*, Plon, Paris, 1976.

Mythologie de la Méditerranée au Gange, Larousse, Paris, 1963.

Mythologie grecque et romaine, Larousse, Paris, 1985.

Mythologies des montagnes, des forêts et des îles (ed. P. Grimal), Larousse, Paris, 1963.

Oosterwyck-Gastuche (van) C., *Le radiocarbone, face au Linceul de Turin*, F. X. de Guibert, 1999.

Ovid, *Metamorphoses* (trans. Brookes More), Cornhill Publishing Co., Boston, 1922.

Pauthier G., *Livres sacrés de l'Orient*, Firmin Didot, 1840.

Périot M., *Les brachycéphales*, Marcel Leconte, 1954.

Pichon J.-C., *L'homme et les dieux*, Robert Laffont, 1965.

Plato in Twelve Volumes (trans. W. R. M. Lamb), Loeb Classical Library, Harvard University Press, Cambridge (Mass.), 1969.

Plutarch, *On the face which appears on the Orb of the Moon* (trans. A. O. Prickard), Warren and Son Ltd, London, 1911.

Poignant R., *Mythologie océanienne*, Odège, 1967.

Pomerol C., *La dérive des continents*, Doin, 1980.

Posnansky A., *Tiahuanacu: The Cradle of American Man*, J. Augustin, New York, 1945.

Powell G. E., *Les Celtes*, Arthaud, Paris, 1961.

Ramnoux C., *La nuit et les enfants de la nuit*, Flammarion, 1959.

Reppe X., *Aurore sur l'Antarctique*, Nouvelles éditions latines, 1957.

Rivet P., *Les origines de l'Homme américain*, Gallimard, Paris, 1957.

Rivet P., *Sumérien et Océanien*, Collection linguistique, Société de linguistique de Paris, 1929.

Romer F. E., *Pomponius Mela's Description of the World*, University of Michigan Press, Ann Arbor, 1998.

Sacred Books of the East, vol. 4, *Vendidad* (trans. J. Darmesteter), Oxford University Press, Oxford, 1880.

Salet G., *Hasard et certitude : le transformisme devant la biologie actuelle*, Éditions Scientifiques Saint-Edme, Paris, 1972.

Schaeffer C., *Stratigraphie comparée et chronologie de l'Asie occidentale*, Oxford University Press, Oxford, 1948.

Segalen V., *Les Immémoriaux*, Plon, Paris, 1956.

Seneca's Tragedies, vol. 2 (trans. F. J. Miller), Loeb Classical Library, William Heinemann Ltd, 1917.

Sertima (van) I., *They Came Before Columbus: The African Presence in Ancient America*, Random House, New York, 1976.

Smith S. P., *Hawaiki: The Original Home of the Maori, with a sketch of Polynesian history*, 3rd edition, Whitcombe & Tombs, Wellington, 1910.

Snorri Sturluson, *L'Edda : Récits de mythologie nordique* (trans. F. X. Dillman), collection « L'aube des peuples », Gallimard, 1991.

Snorri Sturluson, *The younger Edda, also called Snorre's Edda of the prose Edda* (ed. Rasmus B. Anderson), Scott, Foresman & Co., Chicago, 1897.

Suggs R. C., *The Island Civilizations of Polynesia*, New American Library, New York, 1960.

Summers R., *Zimbabwe, mystère rhodésien*, Éditions Planète, 1971.

Taquet P., *L'Empreinte des dinosaures*, Éditions Odile Jacob, 1994.

Temple R., *He Who Saw Everything: a verse version of the Epic of Gilgamesh*, Rider, London, 1991.

Tilak L. B. G., *The Arctic Home in the Vedas – being also a new key to the interpretation of many Vedic texts and legends*, Poona, Bombay, 1903.

Velikovsky I., *Earth in Upheaval*, Victor Gollancz Ltd / Sidgwick & Jackson Ltd, London, 1956.

Velikovsky I., *Worlds in Collision*, Abacus, London, 1972.

Velikowsky I., *Peoples of the Sea, Ramses II and his time, Oedipus and Akhnaton*, Abacus, 1977-8.

Vernet M., *La Grande Illusion de Teilhard de Chardin*, Éditions Gedalge, Paris, 1964.

Vernus P. and Yoyotte J., *Dictionnaire des pharaons*, Éditions Noêsis, 1998.

Victor P.-E., *Pôle Sud*, Hachette, 1958.

Villaret B., *Arts anciens du Pérou*, Éditions du Pacifique, 1978.

Villaret B., *Île de Pâques, nombril du monde*, Arthaud, Paris, 1970.

Villaret B., *Le Mexique aux 100 000 pyramides*, Berger-Levrault, 1963.

Warren W. F., *The Cradle of the Human Race at the North Pole, A Study of the Prehistoric World*, Houghton Mifflin Publishing Co., Boston, 1886.

Wendt H., *À la découverte des peuples de la terre*, Arthaud, Paris, 1962.

Westphal M. and Pfaff H., *Paléomagnétisme et magnétisme des roches*, Doin, 1986.

Wilhelm R., *Histoire de la civilisation chinoise*, Payot, Paris, 1931.

Wolff W., *Naissance du Monde*, La Baconnière-Neuchatel, 1956.

p. 2: Figure 1 © Periplus Publishing London Ltd – source: Robert Argod

p. 4: Figure 2 © Musée de Tahiti et des îles Te Fare Iamanaha / Collection Société des Études Océaniennes, photo: Mr Bosmel; Figure 3 © Photo RMN – H. Lewandowski, Louvre

P. 17: Figure 4 © Periplus Publishing London Ltd

p. 18: Figure 5 © The British Museum

p. 27: Figure 6 © Bishop Museum

p. 28: Figure 7 © Bishop Museum

p. 33: Figure 8 © Periplus Publishing London Ltd – source: Robert Argod

p. 42: Figure 9 © The British Museum

p. 57: Figure 10 © Periplus Publishing London Ltd – source: Robert Argod

p. 63: Figure 11 © Periplus Publishing London Ltd – source: Robert Argod

p. 74: Figure 12 © Photo RMN – Gérard Blot, Louvre

pp. 78–9: Figure 13 © The Bridgeman Art Library

p. 84: Figure 14 © Mimmo Jodice / Corbis

p. 105: Figure 15 © Photo RMN – Louvre

p. 106: Figure 16 © akg-images, London / Erich Lessing

p. 108: Figure 17 © The British Museum

p. 126: Figure 18 © The Bridgeman Art Library

p. 136: Figure 19 © Periplus Publishing London Ltd – source: Robert Argod

p. 138: Figure 20 © Periplus Publishing London Ltd – source: Robert Argod

p. 152: Figure 21 © The British Museum

p. 153: Figure 22 © Stiftsbibliothek St Gallen (MS no 237)

p. 155: Figure 23 © Bibliothèque nationale de France

pp. 156–7: Figure 24 © Bibliothèque nationale de France

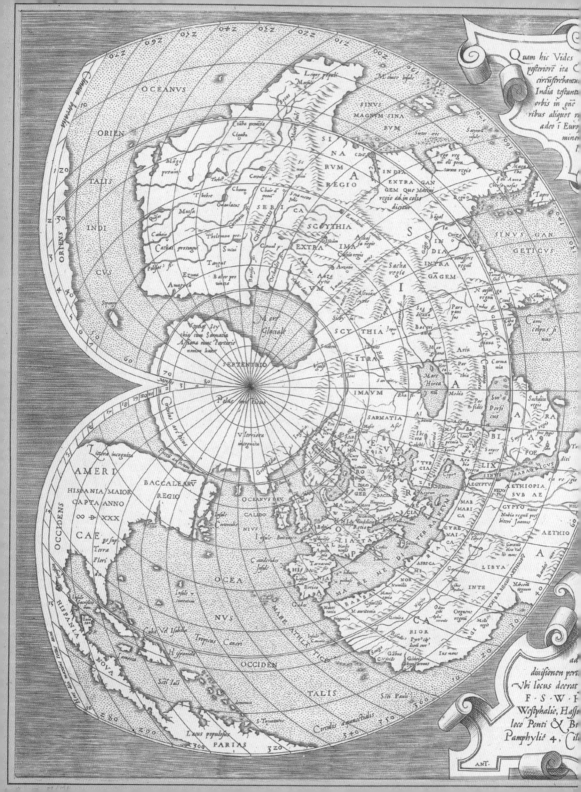